Ritual, Play,
and Performance

RITUAL, PLAY, AND PERFORMANCE
Readings in
The Social Sciences/Theatre

**EDITED BY RICHARD SCHECHNER
AND MADY SCHUMAN**

A Continuum Book
THE SEABURY PRESS · NEW YORK

1976

The Seabury Press
815 Second Avenue
New York, New York 10017

Printed in the United States of America

Library of Congress Cataloging in Publication Data
Main entry under title:

Ritual, play, and performance.

(A Continuum book)
Bibliography: p. 223
1. Theater and society. 2. Rites and ceremonies.
3. Human behavior. I. Schechner, Richard, 1934–
II. Schuman, Mady, 1950–
PN2049.R5   301.5'7   76-6910
ISBN 0–8164–9285–9

To my parents
    Sheridan Schechner
    Selma Sophia Schwarz Schechner
Who fed me a tradition I respect
                                —R. S.

To my parents
    Jack Schuman
    Rita Zwecker Schuman
Their selfless encouragement
    makes all things possible
                                —M. S.

CONTENTS

LIST OF FIGURES AND ILLUSTRATIONS

ACKNOWLEDGMENTS

The editors thank John Houchin for his hard work in helping us plan this book and gather the basic materials for it. We also are very grateful to the students of the Performance Theory seminars at New York University School of the Arts: the anthology took shape in many of those classes where this material was researched.

We are indebted to Muriel Symmons and Nancy Daniels for their ability to conquer research problems while we were preparing the manuscript.

Finally, thanks to Theodore Hoffman, Michael Kirby, Brooks McNamara, David Oppenheim, and Joan MacIntosh for being the kind of colleagues who encourage new work.

Richard Schechner
Mady Schuman

INTRODUCTION: THE FAN AND THE WEB

Richard Schechner

Victor Turner speaks of a "fan of referents" opening out from a core paradigm. The paradigm in this book is performance. The fan is ritualization, making art, play, performances in everyday life, the eruption and resolution of crises, shamanism, and the rites, ceremonies, and performances that regulate, express, remember, and carry on relationships—not only among individuals, but between groups. I perceive this fan from a special perspective, that of a director of "environmental theatre."[1] I know that I'm a local, like everyone else, and where I am puts a special distortion on what I see. This distortion is manifest in the selections Ms. Schuman and I made for our book.

The fan can be restated as a complex system: a network or web. Not everything in this web could be put into our book, but I want to touch on what I feel is the full scope of "performance theory." The web consists of: (1) shamanism, and hunting rites and practices in their prehistoric phases, (2) shamanism and hunting rites in their historic phases, (3) origins of theatre in Eurasia, (4) origins of modern European theatre in the middle ages, (5) contemporary experiments in environmental theatre, New Dance,[2] and music, (6) psychotherapies that emphasize dialog, acting through, and body work, (7) ethological studies of play and ritual, especially in primates, (8) performance in everyday life, (9) play and crisis behavior in people, especially children and adolescents. It isn't accidental that I put my own work in the center (5): this position is totally arbitrary. An ethologist would put himself at the center of another web which included items that don't figure in my scheme—genetics and evolutionary theory, for example. Also, I mix historical, speculative, and artistic "events" as if they all exist on the same plane. My method is like that of the Aborigines who credit events dreamed with the same authenticity as events experienced while awake.

The web is not uniform. Connections among the first four items can be demonstrated historically, and may be linked to performances in Africa, the New World, and elsewhere. Connections among the last four items reveal the "deep

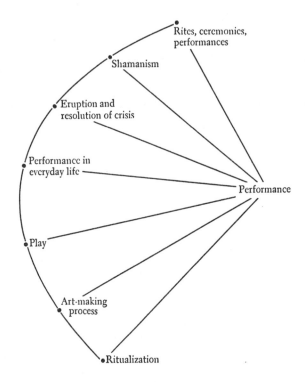

The Fan

structures" of theatre—so that items six through nine actually underlie the first five. These deep structures include preparations for performance both on the part of the performers (training, rehearsal, preparatory ceremonies) and spectators (going to the theatre, settling in, waiting) and what happens after a performance. These "cooling-off" procedures are less studied but very important. They include spreading the news of the performance, evaluating it, putting the space to rest, returning the performers to ordinary life. Also, the patterns of drama deal universally with crisis, schism, conflict, and the resolution of these disruptions. The themes of drama center on sexuality, rebellion, generational conflict, and the rites of passage (changing status). The techniques center on transformation: how people can turn into other people or other beings in order to show a there-and-then story in the theatre, a here-and-now place.

Theatre is doing something "make believe" or "in play." Events are tried out that might otherwise only be imagined. At the same time, the things enacted in theatre are hedged with conventions; these make the theatre safe, and in safe precincts actions may be carried to extremes that would be blocked in ordinary life. Also, an experimental control is possible in theatre. Of course I take a wide

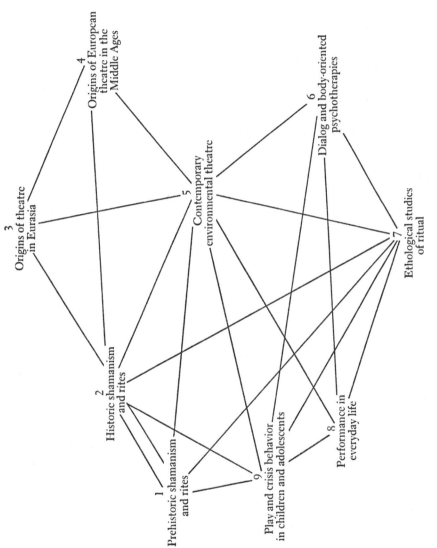

The Web

view of what theatre is: I include scientific experiments, especially those where analogic models and simulations are used; children's games, especially pretending games; rites of passage, especially puberty and initiation rites.

NOTES

1. See Schechner 1973; Grotowski 1968; Sainer 1975; McNamara, et al., 1975.
2. See *The Drama Review,* Volume 16, Number 3 (1972), 115–151; Volume 16, Number 2 (1973), 3–104.

PART ONE

ETHOLOGY

INTRODUCTORY NOTE

Ethologists say that behavior is like physiology—it evolves; thus comparison among the behaviors of different species is a fruitful science. Furthermore, some ethologists believe strongly in "cultural ritual," patterns of behavior which evolve within societies. Cultural rituals have also been observed in animals. All this indicates that the relationships between genetics (what used to be called "instinct") and environment (or learning) is very complex and not fixed. In fact, the most recent studies, such as Edward O. Wilson's *Sociobiology*, locate the evolutionary process in the relationships among species. In this way, evolutionary theory approaches communications theory.

The danger of ethology, as of evolutionary theory in general, is teleology: thinking that because there is a system, or rather systematic rules governing how organisms develop, there is also a ground plan, schedule, and goal to life. But as Jean-Paul Sartre said in *Being and Nothingness,* a life becomes a destiny only after it has been lived. So the necessary hindsight of science, looking back on what was and comparing it to what is, reveals a system and an apparent inevitability in the development of species. But actually the "tree of life" has many virtual branches—paths of development that did not occur; and as organisms develop consciousness, new alternatives rise to visibility. A great debate occurs around the question of whether or not the human species can actualize alternatives to extinction. In this way human behavior is an outcome, or temporary end-point, of animal behavior, but is not therefore restricted by it: the process of living creates environments as well as responds to them, and genetics, for better or worse, is not beyond adjustment.

There is nothing bad, and much good, in relating humanity's finest achievements in art—especially performance—to animal behavior. The process of making art—the actions of rehearsals and preparations—are variations on animal activities ethologists call "ritualization." These activities thicken—get more complicated, dense, symbolic, contradictory, and multivocal—along a continuum of

3

expanding consciousness. The human achievement, shared perhaps by a few primates and aquatic mammals but not elaborated by them, is the ability to make decisions, and create actions, even whole "worlds," based on virtual as well as actual alternatives. An experiment fitted to test a hypothesis is nothing but this. As Alexander Alland says, the "as if," "might," "could," and "maybe" are distinctly human modes. They are also theatrical modes, for theatre is the art of actualizing alternatives, if only temporarily, for fun.

1

THE ROOTS OF ART

Alexander Alland, Jr.

I begin with a disclaimer. While I propose to investigate the role of natural selection in producing (or making possible) what we call artistic behavior, I do not believe it necessary or correct to assume that art *qua* art has any direct adaptive function in the Darwinian sense of that term. Art may be adaptive or functional in some circumstances (many could be cited) but it need not be adaptive to come into being or to exist. It must be noted immediately that the fact that artistic behavior may be psychologically rewarding for some individuals does not imply that it confers a selective advantage. It must be remembered that selection is linked to reproductive success, something that would be difficult to correlate with artistic activity. I must insist, therefore, upon a separation between those factors in our evolutionary past that make art possible, and art itself as it is practiced in any human society. To put it another way, the development of the capacity for artistic behavior is a biological question while the development of art in the context of society is a socio-historical question.

My initial argument will be that artistic behavior is an evolutionary by-product of four separate adaptive responses. I shall further argue that each of these responses has its own set of selective advantages for the species *Homo sapiens*. Their intersection in human behavior results in a capacity for artistic activity. While all of these biological factors continue to play a role in art, their manifestation in a particular context will depend upon cultural historical factors, and in particular individual (artist or spectator) psychological factors.

The adaptive responses to be considered here are: (1) exploratory behavior and

Alexander Alland, Jr. is professor of anthropology at Columbia University. He is the author of *Evolution and Human Behavior* and *The Roots of Creativity*. This essay appears for the first time, courtesy of Professor Alland. It will be included in his forthcoming book.

play (found in all mammalian species as well as among other species in other phyletic lines); (2) a sense of rhythm and balance which may be referred to generally as form; (3) fine grain perceptual discrimination of visual and auditory patterns as well as high memory capacity and long term memory storage; (4) transformation-representation which includes such linguistic processes as meta-phorization, metonymy, connotation, and denotation in the general process of symbolization within the domain of semiology. Transformation-representation is a process exclusive (at least as fully formed) to the human species.

Before examining these adaptations I should like to discuss some other more general features of the human organism that contribute to the patterning we see in the various arts. None of these can be implicated directly in selection for creativity. They are, like the organs of speech, qualities and traits that were selected as adaptations for specific functions such as physical manipulation, bipedalism, high intelligence, etc.

The hand is a highly specialized organ. Bipedalism has freed the human hand to carry and manipulate objects with a finesse seen only in some of our primate cousins. The hand itself is a prehensile organ with an opposable thumb. This complex articulation, in combination with rich nerve endings in the fingers, allows us to grasp objects with ease. The hand is capable of both a power grip, with which things are firmly held, and a precision grip which can be used to manipulate small objects with great care. It is this precision grip that allows for the production of the fine detail seen in some painting and sculpture. Another development important to our overall adaptation is well tuned eye-hand coordination. The human nervous system is patterned so that what the hand does can be monitored by the eye in great detail. Through complex feedbacks controlled by special brain centers, the hand operates on the basis of instructions formed from visual patterns.

A primitive characteristic of all mammals is a flexible limb structure. Low manipulability in the limbs, as is found in elephants, for example, is a departure from the original mammalian pattern. The columnar legs of elephants are special-izations for the support of great body mass. Cats, on the other hand, have retained flexibility in both upper and lower limbs. My own pet cat often sleeps with his paws up over his eyes when the room is brightly lit. He is also able to use his paws to scoop food out of a dish and carry it to his mouth. He does this only when his food is placed in a deep narrow container against which his whiskers rub when he pushes his face down into it.

Humans have retained limb flexibility in the upper extremities. We have full rotation of the arms and may easily turn our hands over as the radius rotates over the ulna. Flexibility in the lower limbs has been sacrificed somewhat with the development of bipedal locomotion, and of course, we have lost the use of the primitive primate hands now used as our feet. Still, with proper exercise, a good deal of flexibility is also available in our legs, as this is manifested in dancers and acrobats.

There is evidence that our ability to see color and judge distance are part of our early primate heritage. Humans, like birds, are quite color conscious. Other mammals are either color blind or are only sensitive to a small range of what is, to us, the visible spectrum. The first primates were small insect-eating animals that had to perceive accurately both the distance and the color of their prey as they stalked it in an environment rich in vegetation. Three dimensional color vision continued to be advantageous for tree dwelling primates, the next stage in the development of our evolutionary line. Stereoscopic vision has an obvious value for animals who move rapidly through an arboreal environment, jumping, leaping, and swinging from limb to limb. Poor judgment of distance can lead to instant disaster. This visual acuity, which has implications for the kind of art we produce, evolved with the growth and complexification of the visual centers in the brain.

On the negative side, the olfactory centers of the brain, so highly refined in such ground-dwelling animals as members of the dog and cat families, are much attenuated in humans. This is why ethologists have, until recently, almost totally ignored chemical signaling among animals, concentrating instead on visual signals. Scents are, however, very important, even to some primates, particularly those living in the dense forests of South and Central America. In these environments visual signals are not as effective a means of social communication as chemical stimulants. Evidence for communication through odors has recently come from laboratory experiments in which captive animals are exposed to sample secretions from conspecifics. Even though humans are apparently insensitive to the subtle differences between male and female smells, and between sexually receptive and unreceptive animals, carefully monitored behavioral studies reveal that such odors are important in some primate species.

This is not to say that scents have no part to play in human behavior. Our own culture has both positive and negative associations for particular odors. Food preparation involves both taste and odor, and the perfume industry could not exist if smell had no part to play in culture. Still, our sense of smell is much less powerful than that of many other species and our ability to recall particular smells when they are absent is quite limited. It would be surprising if smell became a central concern of artists for it occupies only a small place in our symbolism.

Let me now turn to the central topic: those major evolutionary developments which contribute directly, if accidentally, to artistic behavior.

The first factor, or factors, although I choose to link them (exploratory behavior and play), are of undoubted selective advantage for a species equipped with high learning capacity. Exploration coupled with a high capacity for learning allows an organism to catalog its environmental field, while play provides a controlled experience for environmental manipulation. Play is, of course, a widespread characteristic of mammals in general and primates in particular. Irven DeVore, in his film on baboon behavior, illustrates baboon play. The young play-fight silently under the careful eyes of adults who stand ready to intervene should any of the players emit a cry of pain.

Omar Kayam Moore,[1] a sociologist, has suggested that different types of games allow individuals to learn physical, social, and intellectual skills in the context of a guarded, unthreatening environment. In addition, Moore sees the game situation as one in which rewards for good playing are self generated. He calls this "autotelic." Moore has tested this theory by teaching children as young as three years of age to touch type on electric machines, and through the typing process, to learn to read. In his early experiments Moore sat his subjects before an electric typewriter which had been prepared by painting the keys with a range of colors. The child's finger nails were color coded to match the keys. The machine was turned on. Eventually the child would touch a key, and a letter struck. If the key was hit with the appropriate finger the machine was left on; if not it was turned off momentarily, so that when the child touched another key there would be no response. After a predetermined period the machine would be turned on again, and another attempt could be made. The experimenter did nothing besides turn the machine on and off. No effort was made to encourage or discourage the child. After the keyboard had been mastered the experimenter would utter a sound appropriate to the letter struck by the key touched by the child. In a short time subjects began to write on the typewriter and to transfer this ability to the reading of texts. The teaching process was eventually automated and the necessary presence of an experimenter eliminated. Under these conditions children were perfectly content to play with the machines and, through play activity, learn to read and write. Rewards were built into the system; the process was completely "autotelic."

A further extension of game playing coupled to programmed learning (another form of autotelic experience) can be seen in a series of games developed at Yale University in cooperation with Moore. The most complicated of these is called "WFF 'N PROOF." It is designed to teach propositional logic through a series of progressively more complicated games that, in this case, involve two or more players.

Roberts, et al.[2] have tested the proposition that the geographic distribution of games of skill, strategy, and chance correlates with cultural factors. Games of skill are found in highest frequency in cultures which depend upon physical prowess for survival; games of strategy correlate with complex social structures because they provide models for social behavior; and games of chance tend to occur in association with benevolent or, at least neutral supernatural powers. The assumption here is that people will not bother to gamble when their religious systems tell them that chance events are most likely to lead to personal loss.

Moore has included art in his discussion of games, suggesting that artistic creation is play activity in which elements of the environment are explored and manipulated with no end other than the play itself. In this way play and exploratory behavior are intimately connected. Long ago the anthropologist Alfred Kroeber noted that many technological innovations had their origins in art and play. The only example of the wheel in the new world is found in toys. Archeologists working in Mexico discovered small toy wagons with clay wheels.

Michel Beaujour, a critic, has classified poetry as a game, or gamelike. To justify his position he points out that (1) no one is forced to be a poet: free choice is involved, which is another way of saying that the activity is autotelic; (2) there are game rules involving poetic structure. He defines poetry as the exploration of linguistic form within the context of specific rules "some of which are more binding than others."[3] In addition he points out that games are played to win. For him winning involves a triumph over another player and/or over an obstacle. Here I think Beaujour is guilty of tripping over his own metaphor. For some games are indeed played to win, but not all, and not all playing involves games. The satisfaction an artist gets when he has finished a piece does not necessarily derive from winning a game. In fact, even speaking in general, the successful playing of a game may mean something other than winning; that is to say, satisfaction can be purely aesthetic. If winning played so important a role, then clever cheating would probably occur more frequently (as indeed it does in professional sports).

In addition, in my opinion, Beaujour mislocates his players. He sees the poet on one side and language in combination with the subconscious on the other. The player plays against language. I think it would be more correct to say that the player plays *with* language in the sense that language is the tool with which he plays his game. He plays the game first with (or against) himself and, ultimately (if he is successful), with his audience. When an audience observes or listens to an artistic product it enters with the artist into one kind of communication game. This is the essence of the social aspect of art. The funny thing about art, however, is that it can "get away" from its creator. Once a piece of art is finished and enters the public domain, its interpretation becomes variable, depending upon the cultural and psychological characteristics of its audience. In this sense art is autonomous.

While Moore and the anthropologists cited above tend to see art as play in the context of a behavioristic framework, the views of Beaujour and other critics are more compatible with psychoanalysis. Freud himself saw creative behavior as a continuation of and substitution for the play of childhood. In his essay *The Relation of the Poet to Day-Dreaming* Freud said the following.

> Every child at play behaves like an imaginative writer, in that he creates a world of his own or, more truly, he rearranges the things of his world and orders it in a new way that pleases him better. . . .
>
> Now the writer does the same as the child at play; he creates a world of phantasy which he takes very seriously; that is, he invests it with a great deal of affect, while separating it sharply from reality.[4]
>
> . . . when a man of literary talent presents his plays, or relates what we take to be his personal day-dreams, we experience great pleasure arising probably from many sources. How the writer accomplishes this is his innermost secret. . . . The writer softens the egotistical character of the day-dream by changes and disguises, and he bribes us by the offer of a purely formal, that is aesthetic, pleasure in the presentation of his phantasies.[5]

Lest the reader think me ethnocentric because I stress a game element in art (a feature particularly manifest in modern Western art) let me reiterate my position concerning the biological underpinnings of art versus any particular artistic tradition. As I see it, the game element is one biological property that makes art possible in the human species. It is the cultural tradition that determines a particular art form and its stability through time. The game element in art appears in culture, but the degree to which it is manifested varies along an art historical dimension. Egyptian art, for example, changed very little during the many centuries of dynastic rule. Oriental art has shown much less formal change than Western art in the same time periods. How much freedom an art tradition allows is linked to such cultural factors as the purpose for which works of art are produced (icons, for example, tend to remain very stable), the role of the individual artist in society, and the set of formal rules that surround artistic production. No matter how rigid a tradition is, however, scholars can often separate the work of one artist from the work of another when the sample is big enough. In many cases the same scholars can agree about the degree of formal and aesthetic mastery in particular works. All schools of art appear, therefore, to allow some room for play (individual variation and creativity). Such creativity is expressed by individual artists in different ways and with differential aesthetic success. In those cultures in which unsigned works are the rule, individual style becomes the mark of particular artists.

Even ordinary game playing involves different degrees of freedom. Game rules, just as aesthetic rules, are defined by cultural factors. Chess, for example, has been quite stable for several hundred years although the *art* of playing chess has developed with the individual inputs of a long series of talented chess players.

In Eastern New Guinea, particularly the Sepik River area and the Papuan Gulf region, a casual look at artistic production (masks, house decorations and shields) suggests that one major formal principle involves bilateral symmetry along the vertical axis. A close look at objects in museum collections and from photographs taken in the field reveals that in almost all cases the symmetry is significantly broken. The asymmetrical patterns are so clearly a part of each individual work that it is difficult to imagine that they could occur merely by chance. It is more likely that symmetry is a conventional rule that is meant to be broken by individual artists. If we knew more about individual creation in these areas we might be able to develop a means for determining just how particular artists develop separate styles in the context of an overall cultural rule that sets limits on the outer boundaries of permissible variation. In this and other cases we would then know more about the rules of the artistic game and the allowable means available for individual strategies within the context of these games.

In my opinion the major difference between modern Western art and other traditional art forms lies not in the degree of freedom available to the artist, but rather in the locus of the game. Until the advent of modern art, both crafts-skill and the game centered primarily on the object or performance itself. In modern art the boundaries of the game extend outward to include a whole set of notions about art and its metaphysical relation to other aspects of culture. How the artist plays his or her game is just as important as the material object that is the final outcome of the artistic process. This is why it is so difficult to judge some modern art by traditional standards of craftsmanship.

Desmond Morris[6] and others (Schiller,[7] Smith[8]) working with various primates have demonstrated that these animals can be stimulated to mark paper with pencil or paint. Interestingly, such activity appears to some degree to be ordered. Apes produce fan-like patterns, and after some time and experience with a medium, their "compositions" become more and more complex, involving elaborations of the basic design. There is also some evidence (limited to only a few subjects) that color balance improves with practice. More significant, however, if the experiments are correct, is the reaction of primates to a surface marked with squares placed on different parts of an empty painting surface. When such a square is centered the animal will tend to draw within it, maintaining the centrality of the design. When the square is placed on the upper left hand side of the surface the animal will tend to limit its design to the lower right hand corner. Placing the square in different corners will elicit responses which suggest concern for design balance, and, equally interesting, design balance which involves inversion and opposition.

These rather startling results reported by Morris have been partially questioned by Smith. In a series of more controlled experiments Smith concluded the following.

> While tendencies to mark figures and to fill in blank spaces existed in all three chimpanzees, only inconclusive evidence of a genuine balancing response, and no evidence of completion of an incomplete stimulus array, emerged. . . . While it seems reasonable to suggest that tendencies in motor behavior could produce systematically similar marking patterns, it seems very unlikely that these *alone* could produce such phenomena as those we are considering here. That certain visual arrangements are more acceptable to the optic apparatus is a more interesting claim. If and when balance and closure are proven to be influential in chimpanzee drawings, then any explanation of this would seem to require some such concept as the gestalt one of "good figure." . . . Bleakney, on the basis of Morris's work, has suggested that balancing results from a desire for symmetry which in turn results from the fact that our earliest visual impressions are of symmetrical objects such as faces and hands, and also from an innate tendency to relate present and past experience.[9]

It must be emphasized that Smith is rather skeptical of these conclusions and warns that the hypothesis of "good figure" need not imply an aesthetic response. I am in full agreement with this conclusion and must make it clear here that I am in no way suggesting that painting apes are artists. As far as I am concerned art is a cultural phenomenon involving the three aspects of behavior (play-environmental exploration, pattern recognition, and balance-order) we see in ape paintings, plus a fourth: transformation-representation, to be discussed below.

It seems to me that ordering of this type, although in the experiments noted it occurs in a highly artificial situation, is a manifestation of conceptual organization which enables an animal to pattern its environment. In addition it may be linked to certain neuro-motor patterns which favor ordered rhythm.

In his book *The Naked Ape* Morris suggests that music, dance, and plastic art might be manifestations of an exploratory drive, and he derives an interesting series of rules that he believes govern such behavior: (1) investigate the unfamiliar until it becomes familiar; (2) impose rhythmic repetition on the familiar; (3) vary this repetition in as many ways as possible; (4) select the most satisfying of these variations and develop them at the expense of others; (5) combine and recombine these variations with one another; (6) do this all for its own sake, as an end in itself.

If these notions are correct, there may well be a link between exploratory behavior and play, on the one hand, and response to form, on the other. The imposition of order and a preference for certain shapes are two separate ways of coding environmental information. Such coding allows for accurate memory storage and easy retrieval, as well as the rapid discovery of disturbances in remembered patterns.

There is some evidence, although it is much more scattered than the evidence concerning play and exploratory behavior, that some mammals other than primates may be acutely aware of spatial relations and the arrangement of units in their environment. Domesticated wolves and coyotes reared as pets in the home become agitated when even small objects are dislocated from their habitual positions. This concern for order goes beyond environmental exploration to a coding of familiar surroundings. The agitation generated by changed conditions of the field tends to restimulate environmental exploration and sets the animal on guard against potential danger; thus the adaptive nature of the behavior is obvious.

It must be noted that there is a difference between sensitivity to form and change in form, on the one hand, and "good form," on the other. The evolutionary significance of the former is obvious, but is more obscure for the latter. Response to "good form" may be an artifact of inborn neuro-motor patterns and development, but I think that it is more than this.

Humans are, of course, equipped with a highly developed capacity for pattern recognition and discrimination. Such a capacity allows for the storage and coding of a great deal of useful information, including subtle differences in facial patterns which allow unambiguous social discriminations within and among groups. The complex nature of human social interactions are facilitated by this ability. Its operation, however, depends also upon long term memory storage of complex data, another feature of the human biogram. Such pattern recognition and discrimination, as well as stored memories, can be transferred to artistic behavior and the development of artistic tradition.

There is evidence that pattern recognition, particularly for faces, begins early in infancy and is the result of innate coding. Two studies of figure and shape preference in newborns shed some light on other aspects of this perceptual mode.

Maurice Hershenson, Harry Munsinger, and William Kessen reported in a 1965 issue of *Science* that "newborn humans presented with pairs of shapes, each shape differing in number of turns (angles) prefer shapes with ten turns to shapes with five turns or twenty turns, as inferred from photographic recordings of eye fixation."[10]

The preference for patterns of intermediate complexity was questioned by Maurice Hershenson in the *Journal of Comparative and Physiological Psychology.* The stimuli in this complexity experiment were checkerboard patterns varying from the least complex (two bright, two dark, squares) through medium complexity (sixteen squares) to most complex (144 squares).

> The least complex pattern was preferred over the most complex (P = .01). Comparisons of the medium stimulus with the least and the most complex were not significant. However, the number of Ss [subjects] who showed significant complexity preference regardless of direction was significant (P = .01). The pattern of complexity preference suggests a monotonic relationship between preference and complexity since the intermediate stimulus fell approximately half way between the two stimuli."[11]

The use of angles and turns versus squares in these two experiments suggests the possibility that differences in the forms of the stimuli were responsible for the conflicting results. Angles and turns may be close to those forms keyed to stimulate facial pattern recognition in newborns. If this were the case, then high response to intermediate complexity in the first experiment but not in the second would, it seems to me, be the expected result.

Charles D. Laughlin, Jr., and Eugene G. D'Aquili note in their recent book *Biogenetic Structuralism,* that, in most animals, sensory associations are

> always made between elements within the same sensory modality and form the basis of animal recognition of an object. Except in chimpanzees, there are no anatomical pathways allowing direct association between sensory modalities. . . . Man has a . . . distinct area comprising an overlap of the visual, auditory, and somaesthetic association areas where *direct* cross-modal association is possible. . . . Consequently not only is a given percept "recognized" by the associations of that sense modality but also cross-modal transfer permits all the stored associations of the other . . . sensory modalities to that percept. We can consider the analogy of several distinct computers, each programmed with different information about similar objects, being connected to each other and the information of each being made available to all. The possible permutations of associations would be staggering.[12]

This anatomical and physiological factor is taken as the basis of conceptualization.

> Cross-modal transfer permits the construction of classes of objects where formerly insufficient information was available in any one sensory storage system to serve as the basis of classification. We now have an adaptive mechanism that is capable of generating classes of objects or, in more traditional language, concepts. The implication of this mechanism in the genesis of language is far reaching. It opens up the

possibility for a referential system of communication independent of the immediate environment in which the communicators find themselves. . . . It provides the basis for a system of communication using arbitrary symbols for classes of objects.[13]

This and other evolutionary developments in brain anatomy, particularly the differentiation of speech areas, allowed full language to emerge as a main feature of human behavior.

Human language, as opposed to other forms of communication in lower animals, depends upon the ability to apply arbitrary symbols to objects and concepts, and to manipulate these symbols in the context of a grammar to produce thought patterns that can be independent of temporal and environmental elements. That is to say, humans can think backward to past events, or forward to possible future events. Humans are capable of thinking about and communicating ideas that are reflections of an inner conceptual space. Speech can communicate about the real world and about an imaginary world. The meaning of symbols may vary along the dimensions of denotation and connotation, and new combinations of conceptual order may be created and destroyed in the speech-thinking process.

Metaphoric word-image associations are enriched by the type of neural connections noted by Laughlin and D'Aquili. Such interpenetration of sensory modes allows for cross-modal metaphoric associations. Metaphoric associations as well as other forms of transformation-representation are enhanced by the right hemisphere of the brain that is known to be associated with musical and visual imagery. (The left hemisphere controls normal speech function.) Damage to the left hemisphere of the brain causes severe speech malfunction. Damage to the right hemisphere produces particular changes in the ability to handle linguistic images. In his book *The Shattered Mind*, Howard Gardner notes that while individuals with right brain damage have no difficulty in understanding the denotations of particular utterances and words, they lack the ability to appreciate the connotative or metaphorical sense of an utterance.

> For example, asked what is meant by the proverb *Too many cooks spoil the broth,* a right hemisphere patient may offer the superficially acceptable response, "What you're cooking won't be good if you have too many people cooking it." Further probing, however, may reveal that he is unable to go beyond this very literal, "concrete" interpretation and to acknowledge that the proverb needn't pertain to food or cooks at all.[14]

On the other hand, it is a curious fact that right brain patients who cannot unravel the meaning of metaphorical statements will tend to talk in puns and jokes. Gardner says, for example, if such a patient is asked what hospital he is in he might reply, "Mount Cyanide Hospital." Here the patient is able to produce a pun through the connection of sound-word concepts. The difference between metaphorization and pun formation may be the concrete nature of the linguistic material manipulated in the pun as opposed to the rather abstract connections and associations that must be made in metaphor construction. Gardner notes that right brain patients resemble a kind of language machine, a talking computer that decodes literally what is said, and gives the most immediate (but not necessarily the implicitly called for) response, a rote rejoinder insensitive to the ideas behind the questions, the intentions or implications of the questioner.[15]

I should like to suggest that cross-modal neural connections combined with the interaction between right and left hemispheres underlie the capacity for language as well as art. These brain patterns provide the common basis for transformation-representation and the kind of semiotic function we see in language and the arts.

Humans, because they have real language (as opposed to even the cleverest ape communication), are capable of extending and limiting meaning in surprising and creative ways. There is no such thing as permanently closed symbolism in human speech. Metaphorization, a form of transformation-representation, as Arthur Koestler[16] has pointed out, constitutes the basis of jokes, scientific discoveries, and art, for it is the potential connection between previously unrelated signs that is realized in all three domains. What Koestler does not realize is that the connectability of signs in art and jokes is completely open. This is in fact one major difference between these two aspects of metaphorization and scientific discovery which must be related to what is possible in the empirical sense. Koestler suggests that there must be a previously existing common dimension which is activated when two signs are related.

André Breton knew better. He used to play a game with his friends called "one in the other." In this game the active player goes out of the room and decides upon an image. The other players choose a second image. When the active player returns he is informed of the group choice and must then relate the two images in a short narrative, converting one into the other through the creation of complex metaphor.

Caillois, noting Breton's thesis, agrees with Koestler that the game has limits.

> We must not neglect the importance of the element of surprise in the image: the shock and pleasure provoked by stating an unperceived relationship which suddenly becomes apparent. This comparison, however, must be successful, it must be *workable.* At bottom André Breton's thesis is that absolutely everything in this domain may be ratified by imagination. The image's value would thus be a function of its absolute novelty, of the unheard of, disturbing, and literally-unimaginable quality of the comparison. This is a complete contradiction. On the contrary, it is essential that the image remain imaginable.[17]

It seems to me that what Caillois fails to realize is that it is the intervention of the artist that makes *any* image realizable. Whether it is interesting enough to be aesthetically satisfying in every case is another matter. There are poor, good, and excellent metaphors in the infinite realm of all possible metaphors. The excellence of metaphor will depend upon two factors: (1) its goodness of fit in an aesthetic structure, and (2) cultural criteria that touch upon art but that are not necessarily within the domain of art.

According to Caillois, Breton's game included the following identifications: a terrier as a flowerpot, a lock of hair as an evening gown, a sorcerer's wand as a butterfly, a leer as a partridge, a shooting gallery as a church proctor, Mme. Sabatier as an elephant's tusk, a pair of sheets as a path, a child being born as an hourglass, a rainbow as the Rue de la Paix, a glowworm as the assassination of the Duc de Guise, an amazon as a coffee container, a candle as Nicolas Flamel making a pilgrimage to Saint-Jacques-de-Compostelle.

We have no difficulty, I think, in picking out which of these images are easy and which are hard to convert in the process of metaphorization, but the ease and difficulty involved as well as the way in which such images are made to work will depend upon the syntax and semantics of a particular language and upon structural configurations buried within the culture at large. This latter aspect of metaphor construction is part of the transformation-representation aspect of artistic production. Its existence in art comes from its existence in language.

As I have stated above, it is my opinion that any image is realizable. What is limited or determined in the formation of "good" transformations is the pathway employed to make the connection. In structural terms the pathway is limited by transformation rules as well as rules of relationship which exist among elements of a system, in this case a semiological system.

If we accept the above argument, then, art may now be defined as play with form, the end of which is to produce some aesthetically successful transformation-representation. Art is a kind of autotelic communication game. This, of course, immediately raises a new question, for what do I mean by aesthetically successful? I mean that the work engenders an emotional response in the creator and hopefully, from his or her point of view, in some communicant as well. That is to say, art as a part of semiology should involve a successful transaction, in this case a communication between the producer of the "signal" and some audience. I agree with Langer that what is communicated in these transactions is the subjective aspect of experience. Art communicates experience that has no linguistic signs in spoken language.

This aspect of artistic communication applies to literary as well as other arts, because even the verbal arts communicate on a level separate from ordinary discourse. Most aestheticians admit that there is such a thing as an "aesthetic" emotion, although some also attempt to tie artistic appreciation to more specific, namable emotions. I have already expressed my disagreement with this approach. If the capacity to produce art and to "enjoy" art, even sad art, is part of our biological heritage, then there should be a specific artistic emotion which we experience when we confront a work of art which is successful for us, and which is not reducible to any other emotion. The roots of this emotion, as I have attempted to show, lie in selection for the behaviors discussed thus far.

When we look at or hear a work of art that we like, we engage ourselves in a game which the artist has set in motion. We begin the game when our attention is arrested and we feel emotionally aroused. Because art is capable of arresting attention in this way, and because it shares certain features with other communication systems, it can carry an additional semantic load. The additional load that art may carry can include specific emotional messages and/or messages which communicate specific didactic information of a sacred or secular nature. The first thing art does is bind our attention. Afterwards we may attempt to analyze it. If it has structure we will tend to think that it must also have a specific intellectual content as well. But what makes art special is the original *nonintellectual* impact that it has on an observer. If this is what Langer meant by presentational symbolism then I agree with her.

In my opinion the seductive aspect of art is biological in origin, and is the essence of art. Its force upon a particular individual through the medium of a specific work is, however, constrained by that individual's perceptual capacities, personality, and cultural background. What I am saying here is that art is rooted in biology and that it obeys the biological rule that both nature *and* nurture contribute to the realization of its potential in both artists and public.

Let me put the argument another way. Art, for biological reasons (which have their roots in four separate aspects of mammalian evolution), is capable of arresting attention because it produces an emotional impact which we may properly call aesthetic. What happens after this is purely a cultural question.

NOTES

1. Moore 1960.
2. Roberts, et al. 1962.
3. Beaujour 1968:59.
4. Freud 1959 (1908):174.
5. Freud 1959:182–83.
6. Morris 1962.
7. Schiller 1951.
8. Smith 1973.
9. Smith 1973:412–413. Bleakney 1970.
10. Hershenson, Munsinger, and Kessen 1965: 630–631.
11. Hershenson 1964:270–276.
12. Laughlin and D'Aquili 1974:52–53.
13. Laughlin and D'Aquili 1974:57.
14. Gardner 1975:295.
15. Gardner 1974:196.
16. Koestler 1964.
17. Caillois 1968:156.

2

HABIT, RITUAL, AND MAGIC

Konrad Lorenz

Redirection of the attack is evolution's most ingenious expedient for guiding aggression into harmless channels, and it is not the only one, for rarely do the great constructors, selection and mutation, rely on a *single* method. It is in the nature of their blind trial and error, or to be more exact, trial and success, that they often hit upon *several* possible ways of dealing with the same problem, and use them all to make its solution doubly and triply sure. This applies particularly to the various physiological mechanisms of behavior whose function it is to prevent the injuring and killing of members of the same species. As a prerequisite for the understanding of these mechanisms it is necessary for us to familiarize ourselves with a still mysterious, phylogenetic phenomenon laying down inviolable laws which the social behavior of many higher animals obeys much in the same way as the behavior of civilized man obeys his most sacred customs.

Shortly before the First World War when my teacher and friend, Sir Julian Huxley, was engaged in his pioneer studies on the courtship behavior of the Great Crested Grebe, he discovered the remarkable fact that certain movement patterns lose, in the course of phylogeny, their original specific function and become purely "symbolic" ceremonies. He called this process ritualization and used this term without quotation marks; in other words, he equated the cultural processes leading to the development of human rites with the phylogenetic processes giving rise to such remarkable "ceremonies" in animals.[1] From a purely functional point of view this equation is justified, even bearing in mind the difference between the cultural and phylogenetic processes. I shall try to show how the astonishing analogies between the

Konrad Lorenz is Director of the Max Planck Institute for the Physiology of Behavior. He is a Nobel Laureate for 1973 in Physiology and Medicine. His books include *King Solomon's Ring* and *On Aggression.*

phylogenetic and cultural rites find their explanation in the similarity of their functions.

A good example of how a rite originates phylogenetically, how it acquires a meaning, and how this becomes altered in the course of further development, can be found by studying a certain ceremony of females of the duck species. This ceremony is called "inciting." As in many birds with a similar family life, the females of this species are smaller but no less aggressive than the males. Thus in quarrels between two couples it often happens that the duck, impelled by anger, advances too near the enemy couple, then gets "frightened by her own courage," turns around, and hurries back to her own strong, protective drake. Beside him, she gathers new courage and begins to threaten the neighbors again, without however leaving the safe proximity of her mate.

In its original form, this succession of behavior patterns is variable according to the varying force of the conflicting drives by which the duck is impelled. The successive dominance of aggression, fear, protection-seeking, and renewed aggressiveness can clearly be read in the expression movements and, above all, in the different positions of the duck. In our European Common Shelduck for example, the whole process, with the exception of a certain head movement coupled with a special vocal utterance, contains no ritually fixed component parts. The duck runs, as every bird of this species does when attacking, with long, lowered neck toward her opponent and immediately afterward with raised head back to her mate. She often takes refuge behind the drake, describing a semicircle around him so that finally, when she starts threatening again, she is standing beside him, with her head pointing straight forward toward the enemy couple. But if she is not in a particularly frightened mood when fleeing, she merely runs to her drake and stops in front of him. Now her breast faces the drake, so if she wants to threaten her enemy she must stretch her head and neck backward over her shoulder. If she happens to stand sideways before or behind the drake, she stretches her neck at right angles to her body axis. Thus the angle between the long axis of her body and her outstretched neck depends entirely upon her position in relation to that of her drake and that of the enemy; she shows no special preference for any of these positions [or] movement patterns.

In the nearly related East European-Asiatic Ruddy Sheldrake, the motor pattern of "inciting" is a small step further ritualized. In this species the duck may "still," on some occasions, stand beside her drake, threatening forward, or she may run around him, describing every kind of angle between the long axis of her body and the threatening direction of her neck; but in the majority of cases she stands with her breast to the drake, threatening backward over her shoulder. I once saw the female of an isolated couple of this species carrying out the movements of inciting without any eliciting object, and she threatened backward over her shoulder just as though she could see the nonexistent enemy in this direction.

In surface-feeding ducks, including our Mallard, the ancestor of the domestic duck, threatening backward over the shoulder has become the only possible, obligatory motor co-ordination. Before beginning to incite, the duck always stands with her breast as close as possible to the drake, or if he is moving she runs or swims closely after him. The head movement, directed backward over the shoulder, still contains the original orientation responses which produce, in the Ruddy Sheldrake, a motor pattern identical in its phenotype, that is, in its outer appearance, but composed of independently variable elements. This is best seen when the duck begins to perform the movement in a mild state of excitation and gradually works herself into a fury. If the enemy is standing directly in front of her, she may first threaten directly forward, but in direct proportion to her rising excitement, an irresistible force seems to pull her head backward over her shoulder. Yet an orientation reaction is still at work, striving to direct her threatening toward the enemy; this can literally be read in her eyes, which remain resolutely fixed on the object of her anger, although the new, ritually fixed movement is pulling her head in another direction. If she could speak, she would say, "I want to threaten that odious, strange drake but my head is being pulled in another direction." The existence of two conflicting directional tendencies can be demonstrated objectively: if the enemy bird is standing in front of the duck the deflection of her head backward over the shoulder is least, and it increases in direct proportion to the size of the angle between the long axis of the duck and the position of the enemy. If he is standing directly behind her, that is at an angle of 180°, she almost touches her tail with her beak.

This conflict behavior observed in most female dabbling ducks has only one explanation, which must be correct however remarkable it may at first seem; in addition to those factors which originally produced the movements described, and which are easy to understand, there has evolved, in the course of phylogeny, a further, new one. In the Common Shelduck, the flight toward the drake and the attack on the enemy suffice to explain the behavior of the duck; in the Mallard, the same impulses are obviously still at work, but the behavior pattern determined by them is superseded by an independent new motor co-ordination. Analysis of the whole process is made extremely difficult by the fact that the new fixed motor pattern, which has arisen by "ritualization," is a hereditarily fixed copy of a behavior pattern originally induced by several other motives. The original behavior differs from case to case according to the varying force of each separate, independently variable impulse; the newly arisen, fixed motor co-ordination represents only one stereotyped average case. This has now become "schematized" in a manner strongly reminiscent of symbols in human cultural history. In the Mallard, the original variability of the positions in which drake and enemy may be situated is schematically programmed so that the drake must stand in front of the duck and the enemy behind her. The retreat toward the drake, originally motivated by escape drive, and the aggressive advance on the enemy are welded into one fixed, ceremonial to-and-fro movement whose rhythmical repetition increases its effectiveness as a signal. The newly arisen fixed motor pattern does not suddenly become preponderant but exists first beside the unritualized model over which it predominates only slightly. In the Ruddy Shelduck, for example, the motor co-ordinations forcing the head backward over the shoulder are seen only when the ceremony is performed *in vacuo* like the fly-catching of [a] starling, that is, in the absence of the enemy at which, through dominance of the original orientation mechanisms, the threatening movements would otherwise be aimed.

The above example of inciting in the Mallard is typical of most cases of phylogenetic ritualization: a new instinctive motor pattern arises whose form copies that of a behavior pattern which is variable and which is caused by several independent motivations.

For those interested in the laws of heredity and phylogenetics it may here be said that the process described above is the exact opposite of the so-called phenocopy. We speak of this when through extrinsic individually acting influences, an appearance, a phenotype, is produced which is identical with one that, in other cases, is determined by hereditary factors. In ritualization, a newly arisen hereditary disposition copies forms of behavior formerly caused phenotypically by the concurrence of very different environmental influences. We might well speak of a genocopy.

The example of inciting may further serve to illustrate the peculiarity of rite formation. In diving ducks, the inciting of the females is ritualized in a somewhat different and more complicated way: in the Crested Pochard, not only the enemy-threatening movement but also the protection-seeking movement is ritualized, that is established by a fixed motor pattern which has evolved *ad hoc*. The female Crested Pochard alternates rhythmically between a backward thrusting of her head over her shoulder and a pronounced turning of the head toward her drake, each time moving her chin up and down, a set of movements corresponding to a mimically exaggerated fleeing movement.

In the White-eye, the female advances threateningly some distance toward the enemy and then swims quickly back to her drake, making repeated chin-lifting movements which are here scarcely distinguishable from the movements of taking off. In the Golden-eye, inciting is almost entirely independent of the presence of a member of her species representing the enemy. The duck swims behind her drake and performs, in rhythmic regularity, extensive neck and head movements, alternately to the right backward and to the left backward. These would hardly be recognized as threatening movements if the phylogenetic intermediate steps were not known.

Just as the form of these movements, in the course of their progressive ritualization, has become different from those of the nonritualized prototype, so also has their meaning. The inciting of the Common Shelduck is "still" exactly like the ordinary threatening of the species and its effect on the drake is in no way different from that which, in species lacking a special inciting ceremony, the threatening of one member of a group has on another: the latter may be infected by the anger of the companion and join in the attack. In the somewhat stronger and more aggressive Ruddy Sheldrake and particularly in the Egyptian Goose, this originally mildly stimulating effect of inciting is many times stronger. In these birds, inciting really deserves its name, for the males react like fierce dogs which only await their master's signal to release their fury. In these species, the function of inciting is intimately connected with that of territorial defense. Heinroth found that the males could agree in a communal enclosure if all the females were removed.

In dabbling and in diving ducks, it is relatively seldom that the drake responds to the inciting of his duck by attacking the "enemy"; in this case the quotation marks are merited. In an unpaired Mallard, for example, inciting simply implies an invitation to pair, though *not* to mate: the precopulatory ceremony looks quite different and is called pumping. Inciting is the invitation to permanent pair formation. If the drake is inclined to accept the proposal, he lifts his chin, turns his head slightly away from the duck, and says very quickly, "Rabrab, rabrab," or, especially when he is in the water, he answers with a certain likewise ritualized ceremony: drinking and sham preening. Both these ceremonies mean that the drake Mallard is answering, "I will!" The utterance "Rabrab" contains an element of aggression; the turning away of the head with lifted chin is a typical gesture of appeasement. If he is very excited, the drake may actually make a small demonstration attack on another drake which chances to be standing near. In the second ceremony, drinking and sham preening, this never happens. Inciting on the one hand, and drinking and sham preening on the other, mutually elicit each other, and the couple can persist in them for a long time. Though drinking and sham preening have arisen from a gesture of embarrassment in whose original form aggression was present, this is no longer contained in the ritualized movement seen in dabbling ducks. In these birds, the ceremony acts as a pure appeasement gesture. In Crested Pochards and other diving ducks, I have never known the inciting of the duck to rouse the drake to serious attack.

Thus while the message of inciting in Ruddy Shelduck and Egyptian Geese could be expressed in the words "Drive him off, thrash him!," in diving ducks it simply means, "I love you." In several groups, midway between these two extremes, as for example in the Gadwall and the Widgeon, an intermediate meaning may be found: "You are my hero. I rely on you." Naturally the signal function of these symbols fluctuates even within the same species according to the situation, but the gradual phylogenetic change of meaning of the symbol has undoubtedly progressed in the direction indicated.

Many more examples of analogous processes could be given: for instance, in cichlids an ordinary swimming movement has become a means of summoning the young and, in a special case, a warning signal to the young; in the domestic fowl, the eating sound has become the enticement call of the cock and has given rise to sound expressions of sharply defined sexual meaning.

In insects, there is a certain differentiated series of ritual behavior patterns which I will discuss in more detail, not only because it illustrates even better than the above examples the parallels between the phylogenetic origin of such a ceremony and the cultural development of symbols, but also because in this unique case the "symbol" is not only a behavior pattern but it takes on a physical form which literally becomes an idol.

In several species of so-called Empid Flies (in German very appropriately called *Tanzfliegen*—Dancing Flies), closely related to the fly-eating Asalid Flies, a rite has developed as pretty as it is expedient. In this rite the male presents the female, immediately before copulation, with a slaughtered insect of suitable size. While she is engaged in eating it, he can mate her without fear of being eaten by her himself, a risk apparently threatening the suitors of fly-eating flies, particularly as the male is smaller than the female. Without any doubt, this menace exerted the selection pressure that has caused the evolution of this remarkable behavior. However, the ceremony has also been preserved in a species, the Hyperborean Empis, in which the female no longer eats flies except at her marriage feast. In a North American species, the male spins a pretty white balloon that attracts the female visually; it contains a few small insects which she eats during copulation. Similar conditions can be observed in the Southern Empid, Hilara maura, whose males spin little waving veils in which food is sometimes, but not always, interwoven. But in Hilara sartor, the Tailor Fly, found in Alpine regions and deserving more than all its relations the name of dancing fly, the males no longer catch flies but spin a lovely little veil, spanned during flight between the middle and hind legs, to which optical stimulus the female reacts. In the revised edition of Brehm's *Tierleben,* Heymons describes the collective courtship dance of these flies: "Hundreds of these little veil-carriers whirl through the air in their courtship dance, their tiny veils, about 2 mm. in size, glistening like opals in the sun."

In discussing the inciting ceremony of female ducks, I have tried to show how the origin of a new hereditary co-ordination plays an essential part in the formation of a new rite, and how in this way an autonomous and essentially fixed sequence of movements, a new instinctive motor pattern, arises. The example of the dancing flies is perhaps relevant to show us the other, equally important side of ritualization, namely the newly arising reaction with which the member of the species to whom the message is addressed answers it. In those dancing fly species in which the females are presented with a purely symbolic veil or balloon without edible contents, they obviously react to this idol just as well as or better than their ancestors did to the material gift of edible prey. And so there arises not only an instinctive movement which was not there before and which has a definite signal function in the one member of the species, the "actor," but also an innate understanding of it by the other, the "reactor." What appears to us, on superficial examination, as one ceremony, often consists of a whole number of behavior elements eliciting each other mutually.

The newly arisen motor co-ordination of the ritualized behavior pattern bears the character of an independent instinctive movement; the eliciting situation, too, which in such cases is largely determined by the answering behavior of the addressee, acquires all the properties of the drive-relieving end situation, aspired to for its own sake. In other words, the chain of actions that originally served other objective and subjective ends, becomes an end in itself as soon as it has become an autonomic rite. It would be misleading to call the ritualized movement pattern of inciting in the Mallard, or even in most diving ducks, the "expression" of love, or of affinity to the mate. The independent instinctive movement is not a by-product, not an "epiphenomenon" of the bond holding the two animals together, it is itself the bond. The constant repetition of these ceremonies which hold the pair together gives a good measure of the strength of the autonomous drive which sets them in motion. If a bird loses its mate, it loses the only object on which it can discharge this drive, and the way it seeks the lost partner bears all the characteristics of so-called appetitive behavior, that is the purposeful struggle to reach that relieving end situation wherein a dammed instinct can be assuaged.

What I have here tried to show is the inestimably important fact that by the process of phylogenetic ritualization a new and completely autonomous instinct may evolve which is, in principle, just as independent as any of the so-called "great" drives such as hunger, sex, fear, or aggression, and which—like these— has its seat in the great parliament of instincts. This again is important for our theme, because it is particularly the drives that have arisen by ritualization which are so often called upon, in this parliament, to oppose aggression, to divert it into harmless channels, and to inhibit those of its actions that are injurious to the survival of the species. . . .

Those other rites, which evolve in the course of human civilization, are not hereditarily fixed but are transmitted by tradition and must be learned afresh by every individual. In spite of this difference, the parallel goes so far that it is quite justifiable to omit the quotation marks, as Huxley did. At the same time the functional analogies show what different causal mechanisms the great constructors use to achieve almost identical effects.

Among animals, symbols are not transmitted by tradition from generation to generation, and it is here, if one wishes, that one may draw the border line between "the animal" and man. In animals, individually acquired experience is sometimes transmitted by teaching and learning, from elder to younger individuals, though such true tradition is only seen in those forms whose high capacity for learning is combined with a higher development of their social life. True tradition has been demonstrated in jackdaws, greylag geese, and rats. But knowledge thus transmitted is limited to very simple things, such as pathfinding, recognition of certain foods and of enemies of the species, and—in rats—knowledge of the danger of poisons. However, no means of communication, no learned rituals are ever handed down by tradition in animals. In other words, animals have no culture.

One indispensable element which simple animal traditions have in common with the highest cultural traditions of man is habit. Indubitably it is habit which, in its tenacious hold on the already acquired, plays a similar part in culture as heredity does in the phylogenetic origin of rites. Once an unforgettable experience brought home to me how similar the basic function of habit can be in such dissimilar processes as the simple formation of path habits in a goose and the cultural development of sacred rites in Man. At the time, I was making observations on a young greylag goose which I had reared from the egg and which had transferred to me, by that remarkable process called imprinting, all the behavior patterns that she would normally have shown to her parents. In her earliest childhood, Martina had acquired a fixed habit: when she was about a week old I decided to let her walk upstairs to my bedroom instead of carrying her up, as until then had been my custom. Greylag geese resent being touched, and it frightens them, so it is better to spare them this indignity if possible. In our house in Altenberg the bottom part of the staircase, viewed from the front door, stands out into the middle of the right-hand side of the hall. It ascends by a right-angled turn to the left, leading up to the gallery on the first floor. Opposite the front door is a very large window. As Martina, following obediently at my heels, walked into the hall, the unaccustomed situation suddenly filled her with terror and she strove, as frightened birds always do, toward the light. She ran from the door straight toward the window, passing me where I now stood on the bottom stair. At the window, she waited a few moments to calm down, then, obedient once more, she came to me on the step and followed me up to my bedroom. This procedure was repeated in the same way the next evening, except that this time her detour to the window was a little shorter and she did not remain there so long. In the following days there were further developments: her pause at the window was discontinued and she no longer gave the impression of being frightened. The detour acquired more and more the character of a habit, and it was funny to see how she ran resolutely to the window and, having arrived there, turned without pausing and ran just as resolutely back to the stairs, which she then mounted. The habitual detour to the window became shorter and shorter, the 180° turn became an acute angle, and after a year there remained of the whole path habit only a right-angled turn where the goose, instead of mounting the bottom stair at its right-hand end, nearest the door, ran along the stair to its left and mounted it at right angles.

One evening I forgot to let Martina in at the right time, and when I finally remembered her it was already dusk. I ran to the front door, and as I opened it she thrust herself hurriedly and anxiously through, ran between my legs into the hall and, contrary to her usual custom, in front of me to the stairs. Then she did something even more unusual: she deviated from her habitual path and chose the shortest way, skipping her usual right-angle turn and mounting the stairs on the right-hand side, "cutting" the turn on the stairs and starting to climb up. Upon this, something shattering happened: arrived at the fifth step, she suddenly stopped, made a long neck, in geese a sign of fear, and spread her wings as for flight. Then she uttered a warning cry and very nearly took off. Now she hesitated a moment, turned around, ran hurriedly down the five steps and set forth resolutely, like someone on a very important mission, on her original path to the window and back. This time she mounted the steps according to her former custom from the left side. On the fifth step she stopped again, looked around, shook herself and greeted, behavior mechanisms regularly seen in greylags when anxious tension has given place to relief. I hardly believed my eyes. To me there is no doubt about the interpretation of this occurrence: the habit had become a custom which the goose could not break without being stricken by fear.

This interpretation will seem odd to some people but I can testify that similar behavior is well known to people familiar with the higher animals. Margaret Altmann, who studied wapiti and moose in their natural surroundings and followed their tracks for months in the company of her old horse and older mule, made very significant observations on her two hoofed collaborators. If she had camped several times in a certain place, she could never afterward move her animals past that place without at least "symbolically" stopping and making a show of unpacking and repacking.[2]

There is an old tragicomic story of a preacher in a small town of the American West, who bought a horse without knowing that it had been ridden for years by a habitual drunkard. The reverend gentleman was forced by his horse to stop at every inn and, in a way analogous to the feigned camping of Margaret Altmann, to go in for at least a few minutes. Thus he fell into disrepute in his parish and finally, in desperation, took to drink himself. This fictitious comedy could, at least with regard to the horse's behavior, be literally true.

To the pedagogue, the psychologist, the ethnologist, and the psychiatrist, the above described behavior pattern of higher animals will seem strangely familiar. Anyone who has children of his own, or has learned how to be a tolerably useful aunt or uncle, knows from experience how tenaciously little children cling to every detail of the accustomed, and how they become quite desperate if a storyteller diverges in the very least from the text of a familiar fairy tale. And anyone capable of self-observation will concede that even in civilized adults habit, once formed, has a greater power than we generally admit. I once suddenly realized that when driving a car in Vienna I regularly used two different routes when approaching and when leaving a certain place in the city, and this was at a time when no one-way streets compelled me to do so. Rebelling against the creature of habit in myself, I tried using my customary return route for the outward journey, and vice versa. The astonishing result of this experiment was an undeniable feeling of anxiety so unpleasant that when I came to return I reverted to the habitual route.

My description will call to the mind of the ethnologist the magic and witchcraft of many primitive peoples; that these are very much alive today even in civilized people can be seen by the fact that most of us still perform undignified little "sorceries" such as "touching wood" or throwing spilled salt over our shoulder.

My examples of animal behavior will remind the psychiatrist and the psychoanalyst of the compulsive repetition of some acts, a symptom of certain types of neurosis. In a mild form, the same phenomenon can be observed in many children. I remember clearly that, as a child, I had persuaded myself that something terrible would happen if I stepped on one of the lines, instead of into the squares of the paving stones in front of the Vienna Town Hall. A. A. Milne gives an excellent impression of this same fancy of a child in his poem "Lines and Squares."

All these phenomena are related. They have a common root in a behavior mechanism whose species-preserving function is obvious: for a living being lacking insight into the relation between causes and effects it must be extremely useful to cling to a behavior pattern which has once or many times proved to achieve its aim, and to have done so without danger. If one does not know which details of the whole performance are essential for its success as well as for its safety, it is best to cling to them all with slavish exactitude. The principle, "You never know what might happen if you don't," is fully expressed in such superstitions.

Even when a human being is aware of the purely fortuitous origin of a certain habit and knows that breaking it does not portend danger, nevertheless an undeniable anxiety impels him to observe it, and gradually the ingrained behavior becomes a custom. So far, the situation is the same in animals as in man. However, a new and significant note is struck from the moment when the human being no longer acquires the habit for himself but learns it from his parents by cultural transmission. First, he no longer knows the reasons for the origin of the particular behavior prescription. The pious Jew or Moslem abhors pork without being conscious that it was insight into the danger of trichinosis which probably caused his lawmakers to impose the prohibition. Second, the revered father-figure of the lawmaker, remote in time as in mythology, undergoes an apotheosis, making all his laws seem godly and their infringement a sin.

The North American Indians have evolved an appeasement ceremony which stirred my imagination in the days when I still played Red Indians: it is the ritual of smoking the pipe of peace, the calumet of friendship. Later, when I knew more about the phylogenetic origin of innate rites, about their aggression-inhibiting action, and above all, about the amazing analogies between the phylogenetic and the cultural origin of symbols, I suddenly visualized the scene that must have taken place when, for the first time, two enemy Indians became friends by smoking a pipe together.

Spotted Wolf and Piebald Eagle, chiefs of neighboring tribes, both old and experienced and rather tired of war, have agreed to make an unusual experiment: they want to settle the question of hunting rights on the island in Little Beaver River, which separates the hunting grounds of their tribes, by peaceful talks instead of by war. This attempt is, [in] the beginning, rather embarrassing, because the wish to negotiate might be misinterpreted as cowardice. Thus when they finally meet, in the absence of their followers, they are both very embarrassed, but as neither dares to admit it, either to himself or to the other, they approach each other in a particularly proud, provocative attitude, staring fixedly at each other and sitting down with the utmost dignity. And then for a long time nothing happens. Anyone who has ever bought a piece of land from an Austrian or a Bavarian farmer knows that whichever one first mentions the matter in hand has already half lost the bargain; and probably the same thing applies to Red Indians. Who knows how long the two chiefs sat face to face?

If you have to sit without moving so much as a face muscle, so as not to betray inner tension, if you are longing to do something but prevented by strong opposing motives from doing it, if in other words you are in a conflict situation, it is often a relief to do a third, neutral thing which has nothing to do with the two conflicting motives and which, moreover, shows apparent indifference to them. The ethologist calls this a displacement activity; colloquially it is called a gesture of embarrassment. All the smokers I know exhibit the same behavior in cases of inward conflict: they put their hand in their pocket, take out their cigarettes or pipe, and light it. Why should the people who invented tobacco-smoking, and from whom we first learned it, do otherwise?

And so Spotted Wolf, or perhaps Piebald Eagle, lighted his pipe, at that time not yet the pipe of peace, and the other chief did the same. Who does not know it, the heavenly, tension-relieving catharsis of smoking? Both chiefs became calmer, more self-assured, and their relaxation led to complete success of the negotiations. Perhaps at the next meeting one of the chiefs lighted his pipe at once, perhaps at the third encounter one had forgotten his pipe and the other —now more tolerant—shared his with him. But perhaps a whole series of count-less repetitions of the ceremony was necessary before it gradually became com-mon knowledge that a pipe-smoking Indian is more ready to negotiate than a nonsmoking one. Perhaps it may have taken centuries before the symbol of pipe-smoking unequivocally meant peace. But it is quite certain that in the course of generations the original gesture of embarrassment developed into a fixed ritual which became law for every Indian and prohibited aggression after pipe-smoking. Fundamentally this is the same inviolable inhibition as that which prevented Margaret Altmann's horse from passing the camping site and Martina from missing her customary detour to the window.

However, we would be neglecting an essential side of the matter if we only stressed the inhibiting function of the culturally evolved ritual. Though governed and sanctified by the superindividual, tradition-bound, and cultural superego, the ritual has retained, unaltered, the nature of a habit which is precious to us and to which we cling more fondly than to any habit formed only in the course of an individual life. And herein lies the deep significance of the movement patterns and pageantry of cultural ceremonies. The austere iconoclast regards the pomp of the ritual as an unessential superficiality which even diverts the mind from a deeper absorption in the spirit of the thing symbolized. I believe that he is entirely wrong. If we take pleasure in all the pomp and ceremony of an old custom, such as decorating the Christmas tree and lighting its candles, this presupposes that we love the traditionally transmitted. Our fidelity to the symbol implies fidelity to everything it signifies, and this depends on the warmth of our affection for the old custom. It is this feeling of affection that reveals to us the value of our cultural heritage. The independent existence of any culture, the creation of a superindividual society which outlives the single being, in other words all that represents true humanity is based on this autonomy of the rite making it an independent motive of human action.

The formation of traditional rites must have begun with the first dawning of human culture, just as at a much lower level, phylogenetic rite formation was a prerequisite for the origin of social organization in higher animals. In the following brief description of these two processes I should stress their analogous nature, which is explained by their common functions.

In both cases, a behavior pattern by means of which a species in the one case, a cultured society in the other, deals with certain environmental conditions, acquires an entirely new function, that of communication. The primary function may still be performed, but it often recedes more and more into the background and may disappear completely so that a typical change of function is achieved. Out of communication two new equally important functions may arise, both of which still contain some measure of communicative effects. The first of these is the channeling of aggression into innocuous outlets, the second is the formation of a bond between two or more individuals.

In both cases, the selection pressure of the new function has wrought analogous changes on the form of the primal, nonritualized behavior. It quite obviously lessens the chance of ambiguity in the communication that a long series of independently variable patterns should be welded into one obligatory sequence. The same aim is served by strict regulation of the speed and amplitude of the motor patterns. Desmond Morris has drawn attention to this phenomenon which he has termed the typical intensity of movements serving as signals.[3] The display of animals during threat and courtship furnishes an abundance of examples, and so does the culturally developed ceremonial of man. The deans of the university walk into the hall with a "measured step"; pitch, rhythm, and loudness of the Catholic priest's chanting during mass are all strictly regulated by liturgic prescription. The unambiguity of the communication is also increased by its frequent repetition. Rhythmical repetition of the same movement is so characteristic of very many rituals, both instinctive and cultural, that it is hardly necessary to describe examples. The communicative effect of the ritualized movements is further increased, in both cases, by exaggerating all those elements which, in the unritualized prototype, produce visual or auditory stimulation while those of its parts that are originally effective in some other, mechanical way are greatly reduced or completely eliminated.

This "mimic exaggeration" results in a ceremony which is, indeed, closely akin to a symbol and which produces that theatrical effect that first struck Sir Julian Huxley as he watched his Great Crested Grebes. A riot of form and color, developed in the service of that particular effect, accompanies both phyletic and cultural rituals. The beautiful forms and colors of a Siamese Fighting Fish's fins, the plumage of a Bird of Paradise, the Peacock's tail, and the amazing colors on both ends of a Mandrill have one and all evolved to enhance some particular ritualized movements. There is hardly a doubt that all human art primarily developed in the service of rituals and that the autonomy of "art for art's sake" was achieved only by another, secondary step of cultural progress.

The direct cause of all these changes which make the instinctive and the cultural ceremonies so similar to each other, indubitably is to be sought in the selection pressure exerted by the limitations of the "receiving set" which must respond correctly and selectively to the signal emanating from the "sender," if the system of communication is to function properly. For obvious reasons, it is the easier to construct a receiver selectively responding to a signal, the more simple and, at the same time, unmistakable the signal is. Of course, sender and receiver also exert a selection pressure on each other's development and may become very highly differentiated in adaptation to each other. Many instinctive rituals, many cultural ceremonies, indeed all the words of all human languages owe their present form to this process of convention between the sender and the receiver in which both are partners in a communicative system developing in time. In such cases, it is often quite impossible to trace back, to an "unritualized model," the origin of a ritual, because its form is changed to a degree that renders it unrecognizable. However, if, in some other living species, or in some still surviving other cultures, some intermediate steps on the same line of development are accessible to study, comparative investigation may still succeed in tracing back the path along which the present form of some bizarre and complicated ceremony has come into being. This, indeed, is one of the tasks that make comparative studies so fascinating.

Both in phylogenetic and in cultural ritualization the newly evolved behavior patterns achieve a very peculiar kind of autonomy. Both instinctive and cultural rituals become independent motivations of behavior by creating new ends or goals toward which the organism strives for their own sake. It is in their character of independent motivating factors that rituals transcend their original function of communication and become able to perform their equally important secondary tasks of controlling aggression and of forming a bond between certain individuals. . . .

In cultural ritualization, the two steps of development leading from communication to the control of aggression and, from this, to the formation of a bond, are strikingly analogous to those that take place in the evolution of instinctive rituals. . . . The triple function of suppressing fighting within the group, of holding the group together, and of setting it off, as an independent entity, against other, similar units, is performed by culturally developed ritual in so strictly analogous a manner as to merit deep consideration.

Any human group which exceeds in size that which can be held together by personal love and friendship, depends for its existence on these three functions of culturally ritualized behavior patterns. Human social behavior is permeated by cultural ritualization to a degree which we do not realize for the very reason of its omnipresence. Indeed, in order to give examples of human behavior which, with certainty, can be described as nonritualized, we have to resort to patterns which are not supposed to be performed in public at all, like uninhibited yawning and stretching, picking one's nose or scratching in unmentionable places. Everything that is called manners is, of course, strictly determined by cultural ritualization. "Good" manners are by definition those characteristic of one's own group, and we conform to their requirements constantly; they have become "second nature" to us. We do not, as a rule, realize either their function of inhibiting aggression or that of forming a bond. Yet it is they that effect what sociologists call "group cohesion."

The function of manners in permanently producing an effect of mutual conciliation between the members of a group can easily be demonstrated by observing what happens in their absence. I do not mean the effect produced by an active, gross breach of manners, but by the mere absence of all the little polite looks and gestures by which one person, for example on entering a room, takes cognizance of another's presence. If a person considers him- or herself offended by members of his group and enters the room occupied by them without these little rituals, just as if they were not there, this behavior elicits anger and hostility just as overt aggressive behavior does; indeed, such intentional suppression of the normal appeasing rituals is equivalent to overt aggressive behavior.

Aggression elicited by any deviation from a group's characteristic manners and mannerisms forces all its members into a strictly uniform observance of these norms of social behavior. The nonconformist is discriminated against as an "outsider" and, in primitive groups, for which school classes or small military units serve as good examples, he is mobbed in the most cruel manner. Any university teacher who has children and has held positions in different parts of a country, has had occasion to observe the amazing speed with which a child acquires the local dialect spoken in the region where it has to go to school. It has to, in order not to be mobbed by its school-fellows, while at home it retains the dialect of the family group. Characteristically, it is very difficult to prevail on such a child to speak, in the family circle, the "foreign language" learned at school, for instance in reciting a poem. I believe that the clandestine membership of another than the family group is felt to be treacherous by young children.

Culturally developed social norms and rites are characteristics of smaller and larger human groups much in the same manner as inherited properties evolved in phylogeny are characteristics of subspecies, species, genera, and greater taxonomic units. Their history can be reconstructed by much the same methods of comparative study. Their divergence in historical development erects barriers between cultural units in a similar way as divergent evolution does between species; Erik Erikson has therefore aptly called this process pseudo-speciation.

Though immeasurably faster than phylogenetic speciation, cultural pseudo-speciation does need time. Its slight beginnings, the development of mannerisms in a group and discrimination against outsiders not initiated to them, may be seen in any group of children, but to give stability and the character of inviolability to the social norms and rites of a group, its continued existence over the period of at least a few generations seems to be necessary. For this reason, the smallest cultural pseudo-subspecies I can think of is the school, and it is surprising how old schools preserve their pseudo-subspecific characters throughout the years. The "old school tie," though often an object of ridicule nowadays, is something very real. When I meet a man who speaks in the rather snobbish nasal accent of the old Schotten-Gymnasium in Vienna, I cannot help being rather attracted to him; also I am curiously inclined to trust him just as I myself would probably be more meticulously fair in my social behavior to a man of my old school group than to an outsider.

The important function of polite manners can be studied to great advantage in the social interaction between different cultures and subcultures. A considerable proportion of the mannerisms enjoined by good manners are culturally ritualized exaggerations of submissive gestures most of which probably have their roots in phylogenetically ritualized motor patterns conveying the same meaning. Local traditions of good manners, in different subcultures, demand that a quantitatively different emphasis be put on these expression movements. A good example is furnished by the attitude of polite listening which consists in stretching the neck forward and simultaneously tilting the head sideways, thus emphatically "lending an ear" to the person who is speaking. The motor pattern conveys readiness to listen attentively and even to obey. In the polite manners of some Asiatic cultures it has obviously undergone strong mimic exaggeration; in Austrians, particularly in well-bred ladies, it is one of the commonest gestures of politeness; in other Central European countries it appears to be less emphasized. In some parts of northern Germany it is reduced to a minimum, if not absent. In these subcultures it is considered correct and polite for the listener to hold the head high and look the speaker straight in the face, exactly as a soldier is supposed to do when listening to orders. When I came from Vienna to Königsberg, two cities in which the difference of the motor pattern under discussion was particularly great, it took me some little time to get used to the polite listening gesture of East Prussian ladies. Expecting a tilt of the chin, however small, from a lady to whom I was speaking, I could not help feeling that I had said something shocking when she sat rigidly upright looking me in the face.

Of course the meaning of any conciliatory gesture of this kind is determined exclusively by the convention agreed upon by the sender and the receiver of one system of communication. Between cultures in which this convention is different, misunderstandings are unavoidable. By East Prussian standards a polite Japanese performing the "ear-tending" movement would be considered to be cringing in abject slavish fear, while by Japanese standards an East Prussian listening politely would evoke the impression of uncompromising hostility.

Even very slight differences in conventions of this kind may create misinterpretation of culturally ritualized expression movements. Latin peoples are very often considered as "unreliable" by Anglo-Saxons and Germans, simply because, on a basis of their own convention, they expect more social good will than actually lies behind the more pronounced "effusive" motor patterns of conciliation and friendliness of the French or the Italians. The general unpopularity of North Germans and particularly Prussians in Latin countries is, at least partly, due to this type of misunderstanding. In polite American society I have often suspected that I must give the impression of being rather rude, because I find it difficult to smile quite as much as is demanded by American good manners.

Indubitably, little misunderstandings of this kind contribute considerably to inter-group hate. The man who, in the manner described, has misinterpreted the social signals of a member of another pseudo-subspecies, feels that he has been intentionally cheated or wronged. Even the mere inability to understand the expression movements and rituals of a strange culture creates distrust and fear in a manner very easily leading to overt aggression.

From the little peculiarities of speech and manner which cause the smallest possible subcultural groups to stick together, an uninterrupted gradation leads up to the most elaborated, consciously performed, and consciously symbolical social norms and rites which unite the largest social units of humanity in one nation, one culture, one religion, or one political ideology. Studying this system by the comparative method, in other words, investigating the laws of pseudo-speciation, would be perfectly possible, though more complicated than the study of speciation, because of the frequent overlapping of group concepts, as for instance of the national and the religious units.

I have already said that an emotional appreciation of values gives motivational power to every ritualized norm of social behavior. Erik Erikson[4] has recently shown that the conditioning to the distinction of good and bad begins in early babyhood and continues all through the ontogeny of a human being. In principle, there is no difference between the rigidity with which we adhere to our early toilet training and our fidelity to the national or political norms and rites to which we become object-fixated in later life. The rigidity of the transmitted rite and the tenacity with which we cling to it are essential to its indispensable function. At the same time, like the corresponding function of even more rigid instinctive patterns of social behavior, they need supervision by our rational, responsible morality.

It is perfectly right and legitimate that we should consider as "good" the manners which our parents have taught us, that we should hold sacred social norms and rites handed down to us by the tradition of our culture. What we must guard against, with all the power of rational responsibility, is our natural inclination to regard the social rites and norms of other cultures as inferior. The dark side of pseudo-speciation is that it makes us consider the members of pseudo-species other than our own as not human, as many primitive tribes are demonstrably doing, in whose language the word for their own particular tribe is synonymous with "Man." From their viewpoint it is not, strictly speaking, cannibalism if they eat fallen warriors of an enemy tribe. The moral of the natural history of pseudo-speciation is that we must learn to tolerate other cultures, to shed entirely our own cultural and national arrogance, and to realize that the social norms and rites of other cultures, to which their members keep faith as we do to our own, have the same right to be respected and to be regarded as sacred. Without the tolerance born of this realization, it is all too easy for one man to see the personification of all evil in the god of his neighbor, and the very inviolability of rites and social norms which constitutes their most important property can lead to the most terrible of all wars, to religious war—which is exactly what is threatening us today.

Here, as so often when discussing human behavior from the viewpoint of natural science, I am in danger of being misunderstood. I did indeed say that man's fidelity to all his traditional customs is caused by creature habit and by animal fear at their infraction. I did indeed emphasize the fact that all human rituals have originated in a natural way, largely analogous to the evolution of social instincts in animals and man. I have even stressed the other fact that everything which man by tradition venerates and reveres, does not represent an absolute ethical value, but is sacred only within the frame of reference of one particular culture. However, all this does not in any sense derogate from the unfaltering tenacity with which a good man clings to the handed-down customs of his culture. His fidelity might seem to be worthy of a better cause, but there *are* few better causes! If social norms and customs did not develop their peculiar autonomous life and power, if they were not raised to sacred ends in themselves, there would be no trustworthy communication, no faith, and no law. Oaths cannot bind, nor agreements count, if the partners to them do not have in common a basis of ritualized behavior standards at whose infraction they are overcome by the same magic fear as seized my little greylag on the staircase in Altenberg.

—translated by Marjorie Kenwilson

NOTES

1. Huxley 1914:491–562.   3. Morris 1962.
2. Altmann 1951:351–354.   4. Erikson 1963.

3

THE CHEST-BEATING SEQUENCE OF THE MOUNTAIN GORILLA

George Schaller

One hundred years ago Du Chaillu[1] first described a male gorilla "beating his chest in rage." Almost every hunter, traveler, and scientist who since that time has encountered gorillas in the wild mentions this striking display, in which the animal rises on its hind legs and beats a rapid tattoo on the chest with its hands. But it is a curious fact that none of these observers noted that the chest beat is merely the climax of a complex series of actions. Although other apes and man share some of the basic movements of the display, several of its distinct manifestations appear to be species-specific and lend themselves well to an ethological analysis. Before this can be attempted, however, each part of the display and the numerous variations, as well as the stimuli which release them, the functions, and the ontogeny will be discussed.

INDIVIDUAL ACTS IN THE CHEST-BEATING SEQUENCE. The chest-beating display consists of nine more or less distinct acts. These are given individually or in several combinations of two or more, although there is a definite tendency for some to precede others and for several to be united in a series. The whole sequence is given infrequently and then only by silverbacked males. The complete series of events occurs typically as follows:

1. Hooting. The display begins as the animal emits a series of soft, clear hoots, which start slowly but grow faster and faster until the individual sounds merge into one another at or near the climax of the display.

2. "Symbolic feeding." The hooting is sometimes interrupted at one point as the animal plucks a leaf from nearby vegetation and places it between the lips.

George Schaller is research zoological coordinator at the Center for Field Biology and Conservation, New York Zoological Society (Bronx Zoo). He is author of several studies of the mountain gorilla.

3. Rising. Just before the climax the gorilla rises onto its hind legs and stands bipedally.

4. Throwing. As the animal rises, it often grabs a handful of vegetation and throws it into the air.

5. Chest beating. The chest beat occurs at the climax of the display, and usually consists of a rapid, alternate slapping of the chest.

6. Leg kicking. While beating its chest, the gorilla may kick one leg into the air.

7. Running. Immediately after the climax and sometimes during the latter part of it, the gorilla runs sideways for several feet.

8. Slapping and tearing. While running or immediately afterwards, the animal slaps the vegetation and tears off branches by hand.

9. Ground thumping. The final gesture in the sequence is a single loud thump of the ground with the palm of the hand.

This impressive display may require as long as thirty seconds to complete, although all but the first two acts follow each other in one continuous, violent motion which is usually finished in five seconds or less. . . .

COMBINATIONS OF INDIVIDUAL ACTS IN THE SEQUENCE. With the exception of the leg kick, all acts in the full chest-beating sequence occurred also by themselves, although many of them, such as the bipedal posture, running, and slapping could not always be classed as displays under such conditions. By far the most frequently heard and seen display is the chest beat followed by slapping, throwing, running, ground thumping, hooting, and "symbolic feeding" in approximately that order.

Numerous combinations of the nine acts exist, with some tending to precede or follow one another more frequently than others. The bipedal posture and the chest beat are seen during almost every encounter with gorillas, preceded sometimes either by "symbolic feeding" or by hooting. The latter two are readily interchanged as the first act in the sequence. Chest beating is often followed by slapping or ground thumping. Other frequent combinations are: hooting followed by ground thumping; rising and chest beating followed by running; "symbolic feeding" and running followed by chest beating and slapping; throwing followed by ground thumping; hooting and thumping followed by rising and chest beating. Hooting and "symbolic feeding" never occurred after the climax of the display.

The frequency with which gorillas exhibit the various combinations of the display depends on their sex, on the intensity of the display, and on individual variation. I have only seen silverbacked males give the complete sequence of nine acts, and even with them I have observed it only about a dozen times. Silverbacked males also tend to average more individual acts in each display than the other members of the group. . . .

SITUATIONS ELICITING CHEST-BEATING DISPLAYS. Six situations were observed to elicit all or part of the chest-beating display.

1. *The presence of man.* The most intense, prolonged, and diverse displays are exhibited by gorillas unhabituated to the presence of man. Detection of man is usually visual, but at times also auditory or olfactory. All members of the group, except the younger infants, display, but the silverbacked males do so with greater frequency and intensity than the others.

2. *The presence of another gorilla group or a lone male.* If one group hears the distant hooting, ground thumping, or chest beating of another group, it either ignores the sounds or responds by displaying. Frequently the silverbacked males are the only members of the group to react at such times. Individual differences in the readiness to respond are readily observable. One peripheral silverbacked male in group IV, for example, beat his chest several times during the night whenever a lone male displayed uphill, but the other three silverbacked males in the group did not react.

When seeing each other, two groups commonly display by beating the chest, thumping the ground, and slapping the vegetation. Most displays are given by the males, although some chest beating occurs also in females and juveniles.

3. *In response to an undetermined disturbance.* Gorillas which note fleeting glimpses of moving objects such as a partially hidden observer, become uneasy until they have determined the nature of the disturbance. The whole group sometimes approaches, with several animals beating their chests, throwing herbs, thumping the ground, and slapping the vegetation.

4. *Displays by another member of the group.* Chest beating and other displays are contagious in that such behavior in one animal sometimes induces another to act likewise. This is especially prominent among males. Females, blackbacked males, and juveniles frequently display simultaneously and in unison with the silverbacked male.

5. *Play.* Playing infants rise to beat their chests, they slap at vegetation, and they sometimes place a leaf between the lips.

6. *Without apparent outside stimulus.* Gorillas occasionally start seemingly spontaneous movements of the fingers and hands in the pattern of the chest-beating display while sitting or lying quietly.

FUNCTIONS AND CAUSATION OF THE CHEST-BEATING DISPLAY. The hooting, the bipedal stance, the vegetation held in the mouth and thrown about, the kicking, the running and breaking of vegetation—all are actions which serve to make the animal conspicuous. It seems to be advertising its presence or "showing off." Human response tendencies and those of other gorillas suggest that the display serves to repel intruders by intimidation.

The displays also appear to have secondary communicatory value both within the group and between groups. Group members become alert if the dominant male beats his chest without obvious reason, and they become aware that another group or a lone male is in the vicinity upon hearing displays in the distance.

Yet intimidation and communication alone do not explain the causes of display in several other situations. Why, for example, does it occur prominently in play, and why do gorillas beat their chests when there is nothing obvious to intimidate or communicate? Yerkes "gathered the impression that chest-beating indicates impatience or other mild dissatisfaction, sometimes lonesomeness or slight irritation, and that it may be done to attract attention or to startle or intimidate the observer."[2]

The most general emotional term which encompasses all the diverse manifestations of the display is excitement. Gorillas are excited in the presence of man, at the visual or auditory proximity of another group, and during play. When displaying, the animals find release for the tension which has accumulated in their system in an excitable situation. Thus, the primary causation of the chest-beating sequence appears to be the build-up of tension (excitement) above a certain threshold. After the display, the level of excitement temporarily drops below the threshold, and the animals behave calmly until a new accumulation of tension erupts in display. . . .

COMPARISON WITH DISPLAYS IN OTHER APES AND MAN. Various aspects of the chest-beating display sequence are present in the gibbon, orang-utan, chimpanzee, and man, although the specificity is sometimes lacking. For example, wild gibbons in Sarawak hooted several times before the climax, which was marked by sounds of very high pitch, bipedal running, and a final rapid swinging through the trees. The similarity to hooting, rising, and running in gorillas is obvious. Orang-utans broke off and threw branches when excited.[3] Chimpanzees in Uganda shook branches and beat the edge of the nest with both hands in response to my presence. A large aggregation of chimpanzees in the Budongo Forest in Uganda hooted at first slowly, then increased the tempo and loudness of the vocalization until at the climax they screamed, slapped branches, and beat the hollow buttresses of ironwood trees *(Cynometra)* with their hands to produce a loud drumming sound. In zoological gardens I have observed chimpanzees throw objects, slap floors, walls, and themselves, and stamp their feet. Emlen saw a chimpanzee beat its chest in the zoo at Elisabethville, Congo. Chimpanzees, therefore, exhibit most of the displays noted in gorillas.

Man behaves remarkably like a chimpanzee or a gorilla in conflicting situations. Sporting events are ideal locations for watching the behavior of man when he is generally excited and emotionally off guard. A spectator at a sporting event perceives actions which excite him. Yet he cannot participate in them directly, nor does he want to cease observing them. The tension thus produced finds release in chanting, clapping of hands, stamping of feet, jumping up and down, and the throwing of objects. This behavior is sometimes guided into a pattern by the efforts of cheerleaders who, by repeating similar sounds over and over again, channel the displays into a violent but synchronized climax. The intermittent nature of such behavior, the transfer of excitement from one individual to the next, and other similarities with the displays of gorillas are readily apparent.

Other situations in the daily life of man likewise show similarities to the behavior of displaying gorillas. Dictators know well the usefulness of repeated slogans and cheers to excite a crowd, and native peoples chant and beat the same simple tune on a drum over and over again to produce the desired climax. Marital squabbles and similar human interactions, where neither person cares to attack or retreat, may end with objects being thrown, doors being slammed, furniture being kicked—all means of reducing tension.

NOTES

1. Du Chaillu 1861.
2. Yerkes 1927.
3. Schaller 1961.

4

THE RAIN DANCE

Jane van Lawick-Goodall

At about noon the first heavy drops of rain began to fall. The chimpanzees climbed out of the tree and one after the other plodded up the steep grassy slope toward the open ridge at the top. There were seven adult males in the group, including Goliath and David Graybeard, several females, and a few youngsters. As they reached the ridge the chimpanzees paused. At that moment the storm broke. The rain was torrential, and the sudden clap of thunder, right overhead, made me jump. As if this were a signal, one of the big males stood upright and as he swayed and swaggered rhythmically from foot to foot I could just hear the rising crescendo of his pant-hoots above the beating of the rain. Then he charged to, flat-out down the slope toward the trees he had just left. He ran some thirty yards, and then, swinging round the trunk of a small tree to break his headlong rush, leaped into the low branches and sat motionless.

Almost at once two other males charged after him. One broke off a low branch from a tree as he ran and brandished it in the air before hurling it ahead of him. The other, as he reached the end of his run, stood upright and rhythmically swayed the branches of a tree back and forth before seizing a huge branch and dragging it farther down the slope. A fourth male, as he too charged, leaped into a tree and, almost without breaking his speed, tore off a large branch, leaped with it to the ground, and continued down the slope. As the last two males called and charged down, so the one who had started the whole performance climbed from his tree and began plodding up the slope again. The others, who had also climbed into trees near the bottom of the slope, followed suit. When they reached the ridge, they started charging down all over again, one after the other, with equal vigor.

Jane van Lawick-Goodall is scientific director of the Gombe Stream Research Center in Tanzania, and a member of the psychiatry department of Stanford University. Her writings include *In the Shadow of Man*.

The females and youngsters had climbed into trees near the top of the rise as soon as the displays had begun, and there they remained watching throughout the whole performance. As the males charged down and plodded back up, so the rain fell harder, jagged forks or brilliant flares of lightning lit the leaden sky, and the crashing of the thunder seemed to shake the very mountains.

My enthusiasm was not merely scientific as I watched, enthralled, from my grandstand seat on the opposite side of the narrow ravine, sheltering under a plastic sheet. In fact it was raining and blowing far too hard for me to get at my notebook or use my binoculars. I could only watch, and marvel at the magnificence of those splendid creatures. With a display of strength and vigor such as this, primitive man himself might have challenged the elements.

Twenty minutes from the start of the performance the last of the males plodded back up the slope for the last time. The females and youngsters climbed down from their trees and the whole group moved over the crest of the ridge. One male paused, and with his hand on a tree trunk, looked back—the actor taking his final curtain. Then he too vanished over the ridge.

I continued to sit there, staring almost in disbelief at the white scars on the tree trunks and the discarded branches on the grass—all that remained, in that rain-lashed landscape, to prove that the wild "rain dance" had taken place at all. I should have been even more amazed had I known then that I would only see such a display twice more in the next ten years. Often, it is true, male chimpanzees react to the start of heavy rain by performing a rain dance, but this is usually an individual affair.

PART TWO

PLAY

INTRODUCTORY NOTE

Some works that perhaps should have been included in this section were not: Roger Caillois's *Man, Play, and Games;* Iona and Peter Opie's *Children's Games in Street and Playground;* Caroline Loizos's "Play Behaviour in Higher Primates," and the extensive literature on games and gaming both from behavioristic and mathematical points of view. We excluded these fine works because we wanted to emphasize a certain quality of play which clusters around a difficult problem: what is the play-mood, the play-world? Play and art have long been treated as the dimmest shadows in Plato's cave—as "representations," "imitations," "expressions," and "versions" of some more authentic reality. But playing is a primary and irreducible way of living. Building a hedge of known rules guiding behavior around certain experiences, so that they may be pursued "to the end," their permutations worked out elegantly and consciously, and for/with fun, is recognizable not only in play but also in scientific experimentation and model-building. In fact, by understanding play, people will find the links between scientific and artistic process.

5

NATURE AND SIGNIFICANCE OF PLAY AS A CULTURAL PHENOMENON

Johan Huizinga

Play is older than culture, for culture, however inadequately defined, always presupposes human society, and animals have not waited for man to teach them their playing. We can safely assert, even, that human civilization has added no essential feature to the general idea of play. Animals play just like men. We have only to watch young dogs to see that all the essentials of human play are present in their merry gambols. They invite one another to play by a certain ceremoniousness of attitude and gesture. They keep to the rule that you shall not bite, or not bite hard, your brother's ear. They pretend to get terribly angry. And—what is most important—in all these doings they plainly experience tremendous fun and enjoyment. Such rompings of young dogs are only one of the simpler forms of animal play. There are other, much more highly developed forms: regular contests and beautiful performances before an admiring public.

Here we have at once a very important point: even in its simplest forms on the animal level, play is more than a mere physiological phenomenon or a psychological reflex. It goes beyond the confines of purely physical or purely biological activity. It is a *significant* function—that is to say, there is some sense to it. In play there is something "at play" which transcends the immediate needs of life and imparts meaning to the action. All play means something. If we call the active principle that makes up the essence of play, "instinct", we explain nothing; if we call it "mind" or "will" we say too much. However we may regard it, the very fact that play has a meaning implies a nonmaterialistic quality in the nature of the thing itself.

Psychology and physiology deal with the observation, description, and explana-

Johan Huizinga (1872–1945) was professor of Hindu studies at Amsterdam University, and later professor of Dutch history at Gröningen and professor of medieval studies at the University of Leiden. His work includes *The Waning of the Middle Ages, Erasmus,* and *Homo Ludens.*

tion of the play of animals, children, and grown-ups. They try to determine the nature and significance of play and to assign it its place in the scheme of life. The high importance of this place and the necessity, or at least the utility, of play as a function are generally taken for granted and form the starting-point of all such scientific researches. The numerous attempts to define the biological function of play show a striking variation. By some the origin and fundamentals of play have been described as a discharge of superabundant vital energy, by others as the satisfaction of some "imitative instinct," or again as simply a "need" for relaxation. According to one theory play constitutes a training of the young creature for the serious work that life will demand later on. According to another it serves as an exercise in restraint needful to the individual. Some find the principle of play in an innate urge to exercise a certain faculty, or in the desire to dominate or compete. Yet others regard it as an "abreaction"—an outlet for harmful impulses, as the necessary restorer of energy wasted by one-sided activity, as "wish-fulfilment," as a fiction designed to keep up the feeling of personal value, etc.

All these hypotheses have one thing in common: they all start from the assumption that play must serve something which is *not* play, that it must have some kind of biological purpose. They all enquire into the why and the wherefore of play. The various answers they give tend rather to overlap than to exclude one another. It would be perfectly possible to accept nearly all the explanations without getting into any real confusion of thought—and without coming much nearer to a real understanding of the play-concept. They are all only partial solutions of the problem. If any of them were really decisive it ought either to exclude all the others or comprehend them in a higher unity. Most of them only deal incidentally with the question of what play is *in itself* and what it means for the player. They attack play direct with the quantitative methods of experimental science without first paying attention to its profoundly aesthetic quality. As a rule they leave the primary quality of play as such, virtually untouched. To each and every one of the above "explanations" it might well be objected: "So far so good, but what actually is the *fun* of playing? Why does the baby crow with pleasure? Why does the gambler lose himself in his passion? Why is a huge crowd roused to frenzy by a football match?" This intensity of, and absorption in, play finds no explanation in biological analysis. Yet in this intensity, this absorption, this power of maddening, lies the very essence, the primordial quality of play. Nature, so our reasoning mind tells us, could just as easily have given her children all those useful functions of discharging superabundant energy, of relaxing after exertion, of training for the demands of life, of compensating for unfulfilled longings, etc., in the form of purely mechanical exercises and reactions. But no, she gave us play, with its tension, its mirth, and its fun.

Now this last-named element, the *fun* of playing, resists all analysis, all logical interpretation. As a concept, it cannot be reduced to any other mental category. No other modern language known to me has the exact equivalent of the English "fun." The Dutch "aardigkeit" perhaps comes nearest to it (derived from "aard" which means the same as "Art" and "Wesen"[1] in German, and thus evidence, perhaps, that the matter cannot be reduced further). We may note in passing that "fun" in its current usage is of rather recent origin. French, oddly enough, has no corresponding term at all; German half makes up for it by "Spass" and "Witz" together. Nevertheless it is precisely this fun-element that characterizes the essence of play. Here we have to do with an absolutely primary category of life, familiar to everybody at a glance right down to the animal level. We may well call play a "totality" in the modern sense of the word, and it is as a totality that we must try to understand and evaluate it.

Since the reality of play extends beyond the sphere of human life it cannot have its foundations in any rational nexus, because this would limit it to mankind. The incidence of play is not associated with any particular stage of civilization or view of the universe. Any thinking person can see at a glance that play is a thing on its own, even if his language possesses no general concept to express it. Play cannot be denied. You can deny, if you like, nearly all abstractions: justice, beauty, truth, goodness, mind, God. You can deny seriousness, but not play.

But in acknowledging play you acknowledge mind, for whatever else play is, it is not matter. Even in the animal world it bursts the bounds of the physically existent. From the point of view of a world wholly determined by the operation of blind forces, play would be altogether superfluous. Play only becomes possible, thinkable and understandable when an influx of *mind* breaks down the absolute determinism of the cosmos. The very existence of play continually confirms the supra-logical nature of the human situation. Animals play, so they must be more than merely mechanical things. We play and know that we play, so we must be more than merely rational beings, for play is irrational.

In tackling the problem of play as a function of culture proper and not as it appears in the life of the animal or the child, we begin where biology and psychology leave off. In culture we find play as a given magnitude existing before culture itself existed, accompanying it and pervading it from the earliest beginnings right up to the phase of civilization we are now living in. We find play present everywhere as a well-defined quality of action which is different from "ordinary" life. We can disregard the question of how far science has succeeded in reducing this quality to quantitative factors. In our opinion it has not. At all events it is precisely this quality, itself so characteristic of the form of life we call "play," which matters. Play as a special form of activity, as a "significant form," as a social function—that is our subject. We shall not look for the natural impulses and habits conditioning play in general, but shall consider play in its manifold concrete forms as itself a social construction. We shall try to take play as the player himself takes it: in its primary significance. If we find that play is based on the manipulation of certain images, on a certain "imagination" of reality (i.e. its conversion into images), then our main concern will be to grasp the value and significance of these images and their "imagination." We shall observe their action in play itself and thus try to understand play as a cultural factor in life.

The great archetypal activities of human society are all permeated with play from the start. Take language, for instance—that first and supreme instrument which man shapes in order to communicate, to teach, to command. Language allows him to distinguish, to establish, to state things; in short, to name them and by naming them to raise them into the domain of the spirit. In the making of speech and language the spirit is continually "sparking" between matter and mind, as it were, playing with this wondrous nominative faculty. Behind every abstract expression there lie the boldest of metaphors, and every metaphor is a play upon words. Thus in giving expression to life man creates a second, poetic world alongside the world of nature.

Or take myth. This, too, is a transformation or an "imagination" of the outer world, only here the process is more elaborate and ornate than is the case with individual words. In myth, primitive man seeks to account for the world of phenomena by grounding it in the Divine. In all the wild imaginings of mythology a fanciful spirit is playing on the border-line between jest and earnest. Or finally, let us take ritual. Primitive society performs its sacred rites, its sacrifices, consecrations and mysteries, all of which serve to guarantee the well-being of the world, in a spirit of pure play truly understood.

Now in myth and ritual the great instinctive forces of civilized life have their origin: law and order, commerce and profit, craft and art, poetry, wisdom and science. All are rooted in the primaeval soil of play.

The object of the present essay is to demonstrate that it is more than a rhetorical comparison to view culture *sub specie ludi.* The thought is not at all new. There was a time when it was generally accepted, though in a limited sense quite different from the one intended here: in the 17th century, the age of world theatre. Drama, in a glittering succession of figures ranging from Shakespeare and Calderon to Racine, then dominated the literature of the West. It was the fashion to liken the world to a stage on which every man plays his part. Does this mean that the play-element in civilization was openly acknowledged? Not at all. On closer examination this fashionable comparison of life to a stage proves to be little more than an echo of the Neo-platonism that was then in vogue, with a markedly moralistic accent. It was a variation on the ancient theme of the vanity of all things. The fact that play and culture are actually interwoven with one another was neither observed nor expressed, whereas for us the whole point is to show that genuine, pure play is one of the main bases of civilisation.

To our way of thinking, play is the direct opposite of seriousness. At first sight this opposition seems as irreducible to other categories as the play-concept itself. Examined more closely, however, the contrast between play and seriousness proves to be neither conclusive nor fixed. We can say: play is non-seriousness. But apart from the fact that this proposition tells us nothing about the positive qualities of play, it is extraordinarily easy to refute. As soon as we proceed from "play is non-seriousness" to "play is not serious," the contrast leaves us in the lurch—for some play can be very serious indeed. Moreover we can immediately name several other fundamental categories that likewise come under the heading "non-seriousness" yet have no correspondence whatever with "play." Laughter, for instance, is in a sense the opposite of seriousness without being absolutely bound up with play. Children's games, football, and chess are played in profound seriousness; the players have not the slightest inclination to laugh. It is worth noting that the purely physiological act of laughing is exclusive to man, whilst the significant function of play is common to both men and animals. The Aristotelian *animal ridens* characterizes man as distinct from the animal almost more absolutely than *homo sapiens*.

What is true of laughter is true also of the comic. The comic comes under the category of non-seriousness and has certain affinities with laughter—it provokes to laughter. But its relation to play is subsidiary. In itself play is not comical either for player or public. The play of young animals or small children may sometimes be ludicrous, but the sight of grown dogs chasing one another hardly moves us to laughter. When we call a farce or a comedy "comic," it is not so much on account of the play-acting as such as on account of the situation or the thoughts expressed. The mimic and laughter-provoking art of the clown is comic as well as ludicrous, but it can scarcely be termed genuine play.

The category of the comic is closely connected with *folly* in the highest and lowest sense of that word. Play, however, is not foolish. It lies outside the antithesis of wisdom and folly. The later Middle Ages tended to express the two cardinal moods of life—play and seriousness—somewhat imperfectly by opposing *folie* to *sense*, until Erasmus in his *Laus Stultitiae* showed the inadequacy of the contrast.

All the terms in this loosely connected group of ideas—play, laughter, folly, wit, jest, joke, the comic, etc.—share the characteristic which we had to attribute to play, namely, that of resisting any attempt to reduce it to other terms. Their rationale and their mutual relationships must lie in a very deep layer of our mental being.

The more we try to mark off the form we call "play" from other forms apparently related to it, the more the absolute independence of the play-concept stands out. And the segregation of play from the domain of the great categorical antitheses does not stop there. Play lies outside the antithesis of wisdom and folly, and equally outside those of truth and falsehood, good and evil. Although it is a non-material activity it has no moral function. The valuations of vice and virtue do not apply here.

If, therefore, play cannot be directly referred to the categories of truth or goodness, can it be included perhaps in the realm of the aesthetic? Here our judgement wavers. For although the attribute of beauty does not attach to play as such, play nevertheless tends to assume marked elements of beauty. Mirth and grace adhere at the outset to the more primitive forms of play. In play the beauty of the human body in motion reaches its zenith. In its more developed forms it is saturated with rhythm and harmony, the noblest gifts of aesthetic perception known to man. Many and close are the links that connect play with beauty. All the same, we cannot say that beauty is inherent in play as such; so we must leave it at that: play is a function of the living, but is not susceptible of exact definition either logically, biologically, or aesthetically. The play-concept must always remain distinct from all the other forms of thought in which we express the structure of mental and social life. Hence we shall have to confine ourselves to describing the main characteristics of play.

Since our theme is the relation of play to culture we need not enter into all the possible forms of play but can restrict ourselves to its social manifestations. These we might call the higher forms of play. They are generally much easier to describe than the more primitive play of infants and young animals, because they are more distinct and articulate in form and their features more various and conspicuous, whereas in interpreting primitive play we immediately come up against that irreducible quality of pure playfulness which is not, in our opinion, amenable to further analysis. We shall have to speak of contests and races, of performances and exhibitions, of dancing and music, pageants, masquerades and tournaments. Some of the characteristics we shall enumerate are proper to play in general, others to social play in particular.

First and foremost, then, all play is a voluntary activity. Play to order is no longer play: it could at best be but a forcible imitation of it. By this quality of freedom alone, play marks itself off from the course of the natural process. It is something added thereto and spread out over it like a flowering, an ornament, a garment. Obviously, freedom must be understood here in the wider sense that leaves untouched the philosophical problem of determinism. It may be objected that this freedom does not exist for the animal and the child; they *must* play because their instinct drives them to it and because it serves to develop their bodily faculties and their powers of selection. The term "instinct," however, introduces an unknown quantity, and to presuppose the utility of play from the start is to be guilty of a *petitio principii*. Child and animal play because they enjoy playing, and therein precisely lies their freedom.

Be that as it may, for the adult and responsible human being play is a function which he could equally well leave alone. Play is superfluous. The need for it is only urgent to the extent that the enjoyment of it makes it a need. Play can be deferred or suspended at any time. It is never imposed by physical necessity or moral duty. It is never a task. It is done at leisure, during "free time." Only when play is a recognized cultural function—a rite, a ceremony—is it bound up with notions of obligation and duty.

Here, then, we have the first main characteristic of play: that it is free, is in fact freedom. A second characteristic is closely connected with this, namely, that play is not "ordinary" or "real" life. It is rather a stepping out of "real" life into a temporary sphere of activity with a disposition all of its own. Every child knows perfectly well that he is "only pretending," or that it was "only for fun." How deep-seated this awareness is in the child's soul is strikingly illustrated by the following story, told to me by the father of the boy in question. He found his four-year-old son sitting at the front of a row of chairs, playing "trains." As he hugged him the boy said: "Don't kiss the engine, Daddy, or the carriages won't think it's real." This "only pretending" quality of play betrays a consciousness of the inferiority of play compared with "seriousness," a feeling that seems to be something as primary as play itself. Nevertheless, as we have already pointed out, the consciousness of play being "only a pretend" does not by any means prevent it from proceeding with the utmost seriousness, with an absorption, a devotion that passes into rapture and, temporarily at least, completely abolishes that troublesome "only" feeling. Any game can at any time wholly run away with the players. The contrast between play and seriousness is always fluid. The inferiority of play is continually being offset by the corresponding superiority of its serious- ness. Play turns to seriousness and seriousness to play. Play may rise to heights of beauty and sublimity that leave seriousness far beneath. Tricky questions such as these will come up for discussion when we start examining the relationship between play and ritual.

As regards its formal characteristics, all students lay stress on the *disinterested- ness* of play. Not being "ordinary" life, it stands outside the immediate satisfac- tion of wants and appetites, indeed it interrupts the appetitive process. It interpo- lates itself as a temporary activity satisfying in itself and ending there. Such at least is the way in which play presents itself to us in the first instance: as an intermezzo, an *interlude* in our daily lives. As a regularly recurring relaxation, however, it becomes the accompaniment, the complement, in fact an integral part of life in general. It adorns life, amplifies it and is to that extent a necessity both for the individual—as a life function—and for society by reason of the meaning it contains, its significance, its expressive value, its spiritual and social associations, in short, as a culture function. The expression of it satisfies all kinds of communal ideals. It thus has its place in a sphere superior to the strictly biological processes of nutrition, reproduction and self-preservation. This asser- tion is apparently contradicted by the fact that play, or rather sexual display, is predominant in animal life precisely at the mating-season. But would it be too absurd to assign a place *outside* the purely physiological, to the singing, cooing and strutting of birds just as we do to human play? In all its higher forms the latter at any rate always belongs to the sphere of festival and ritual—the sacred sphere.

Now, does the fact that play is a necessity, that it subserves culture, or indeed that it actually becomes culture, detract from its disinterested character? No, for the purposes it serves are external to immediate material interests or the individ- ual satisfaction of biological needs. As a sacred activity play naturally contributes to the well-being of the group, but in quite another way and by other means than the acquisition of the necessities of life.

Play is distinct from "ordinary" life both as to locality and duration. This is the third main characteristic of play: its secludedness, its limitedness. It is "played out" within certain limits of time and place. It contains its own course and meaning.

Play begins, and then at a certain moment it is "over." It plays itself to an end. While it is in progress all is movement, change, alternation, succession, association, separation. But immediately connected with its limitation as to time there is a further curious feature of play: it at once assumes fixed form as a cultural phenomenon. Once played, it endures as a new-found creation of the mind, a treasure to be retained by the memory. It is transmitted, it becomes tradition. It can be repeated at any time, whether it be "child's play" or a game of chess, or at fixed intervals like a mystery. In this faculty of repetition lies one of the most essential qualities of play. It holds good not only of play as a whole but also of its inner structure. In nearly all the higher forms of play the elements of repetition and alternation (as in the *refrain*), are like the warp and woof of a fabric.

More striking even than the limitation as to time is the limitation as to space. All play moves and has its being within a playground marked off beforehand either materially or ideally, deliberately or as a matter of course. Just as there is no formal difference between play and ritual, so the "consecrated spot" cannot be formally distinguished from the play-ground. The arena, the card-table, the magic circle, the temple, the stage, the screen, the tennis court, the court of justice, etc., are all in form and function play-grounds, i.e. forbidden spots, isolated, hedged round, hallowed, within which special rules obtain. All are temporary worlds within the ordinary world, dedicated to the performance of an act apart.

Inside the play-ground an absolute and peculiar order reigns. Here we come across another, very positive feature of play: it creates order, *is* order. Into an imperfect world and into the confusion of life it brings a temporary, a limited perfection. Play demands order absolute and supreme. The least deviation from it "spoils the game," robs it of its character and makes it worthless. The profound affinity between play and order is perhaps the reason why play, as we noted in passing, seems to lie to such a large extent in the field of aesthetics. Play has a tendency to be beautiful. It may be that this aesthetic factor is identical with the impulse to create orderly form, which animates play in all its aspects. The words we use to denote the elements of play belong for the most part to aesthetics, terms with which we try to describe the effects of beauty: tension, poise, balance, contrast, variation, solution, resolution, etc. Play casts a spell over us; it is "enchanting," "captivating." It is invested with the noblest qualities we are capable of perceiving in things: rhythm and harmony.

The element of tension in play to which we have just referred plays a particularly important part. Tension means uncertainty, chanciness; a striving to decide the issue and so end it. The player wants something to "go," to "come off"; he wants to "succeed" by his own exertions. Baby reaching for a toy, pussy patting a bobbin, a little girl playing ball—all want to achieve something difficult, to succeed, to end a tension. Play is "tense," as we say. It is this element of tension and solution that governs all solitary games of skill and application such as puzzles, jig-saws, mosaic-making, patience, target-shooting, and the more play bears the character of competition the more fervent it will be. In gambling and athletics it is at its height. Though play as such is outside the range of good and bad, the element of tension imparts to it a certain ethical value in so far as it means a testing of the player's prowess: his courage, tenacity, resources and, last but not least, his spiritual powers—his "fairness"; because, despite his ardent desire to win, he must still stick to the rules of the game.

These rules in their turn are a very important factor in the play-concept. All play has its rules. They determine what "holds" in the temporary world circumscribed by play. The rules of a game are absolutely binding and allow no doubt. Paul Valéry once in passing gave expression to a very cogent thought when he said: "No scepticism is possible where the rules of a game are concerned, for the principle underlying them is an unshakable truth. . . ." Indeed, as soon as the rules are transgressed the whole play-world collapses. The game is over. The umpire's whistle breaks the spell and sets "real" life going again.

The player who trespasses against the rules or ignores them is a "spoil-sport." The spoil-sport is not the same as the false player, the cheat; for the latter pretends to be playing the game and, on the face of it, still acknowledges the magic circle. It is curious to note how much more lenient society is to the cheat than to the spoil-sport. This is because the spoil-sport shatters the play-world itself. By withdrawing from the game he reveals the relativity and fragility of the play-world in which he had temporarily shut himself with others. He robs play of its *illusion*—a pregnant word which means literally "in-play" (from *inlusio, illudere* or *inludere*). Therefore he must be cast out, for he threatens the existence of the play-community. The figure of the spoil-sport is most apparent in boy's games. The little community does not enquire whether the spoil-sport is guilty of defection because he dares not enter into the game or because he is not allowed to. Rather, it does not recognize "not being allowed" and calls it "not daring." For it, the problem of obedience and conscience is no more than fear of punishment. The spoil-sport breaks the magic world, therefore he is a coward and must be ejected. In the world of high seriousness, too, the cheat and the hypocrite have always had an easier time of it than the spoil-sports, here called apostates, heretics, innovators, prophets, conscientious objectors, etc. It sometimes happens, however, that the spoil-sports in their turn make a new community with rules of its own. The outlaw, the revolutionary, the cabbalist or member of a secret society, indeed heretics of all kinds are of a highly associative if not sociable disposition, and a certain element of play is prominent in all their doings.

A play-community generally tends to become permanent even after the game is over. Of course, not every game of marbles or every bridge-party leads to the founding of a club. But the feeling of being "apart together" in an exceptional situation, of sharing something important, of mutually withdrawing from the rest of the world and rejecting the usual norms, retains its magic beyond the duration of the individual game. The club pertains to play as the hat to the head. It would be rash to explain all the associations which the anthropologist calls "phratria" —e.g. clans, brotherhoods, etc.—simply as play-communities; nevertheless it has been shown again and again how difficult it is to draw the line between, on the one hand, permanent social groupings—particularly in archaic cultures with their extremely important, solemn, indeed sacred customs—and the sphere of play on the other.

The exceptional and special position of play is most tellingly illustrated by the fact that it loves to surround itself with an air of secrecy. Even in early childhood the charm of play is enhanced by making a "secret" out of it. This is for *us*, not for the "others." What the "others" do "outside" is no concern of ours at the moment. Inside the circle of the game the laws and customs of ordinary life no longer count. We are different and do things differently. This temporary abolition of the ordinary world is fully acknowledged in child-life, but it is no less evident in the great ceremonial games of savage societies. During the great feast of initiation when the youths are accepted into the male community, it is not the neophytes only that are exempt from the ordinary laws and regulations: there is a truce to all feuds in the tribe. All retaliatory acts and vendettas are suspended. This temporary suspension of normal social life on account of the sacred play-season has numerous traces in the more advanced civilizations as well. Everything that pertains to saturnalia and carnival customs belongs to it. Even with us a bygone age of robuster private habits than ours, more marked class-privileges and a more complaisant police recognized the orgies of young men of rank under the name of a "rag." The saturnalian licence of young men still survives, in fact, in the ragging at English universities, which the *Oxford English Dictionary* defines as "an extensive display of noisy and disorderly conduct carried out in defiance of authority and discipline."

The "differentness" and secrecy of play are most vividly expressed in "dressing up." Here the "extra-ordinary" nature of play reaches perfection. The disguised or masked individual "plays" another part, another being. He *is* another being. The terrors of childhood, open-hearted gaiety, mystic fantasy and sacred awe are all inextricably entangled in this strange business of masks and disguises.

Summing up the formal characteristics of play we might call it a free activity standing quite consciously outside "ordinary" life as being "not serious," but at the same time absorbing the player intensely and utterly. It is an activity connected with no material interest, and no profit can be gained by it. It proceeds within its own proper boundaries of time and space according to fixed rules and in an orderly manner. It promotes the formation of social groupings which tend to surround themselves with secrecy and to stress their difference from the common world by disguise or other means.

The function of play in the higher forms which concern us here can largely be derived from the two basic aspects under which we meet it: as a contest *for* something or a representation *of* something. These two functions can unite in such a way that the game "represents" a contest, or else becomes a contest for the best representation of something.

Representation means display, and this may simply consist in the exhibition of something naturally given, before an audience. The peacock and the turkey merely display their gorgeous plumage to the females, but the essential feature of it lies in the parading of something out of the ordinary and calculated to arouse admiration. If the bird accompanies this exhibition with dance-steps we have a performance, a *stepping out of* common reality into a higher order. We are ignorant of the bird's sensations while so engaged. We know, however, that in child-life performances of this kind are full of imagination. The child is *making an image* of something different, something more beautiful, or more sublime, or more dangerous than what he usually *is*. One is a Prince, or one is Daddy or a wicked witch or a tiger. The child is quite literally "beside himself" with delight, transported beyond himself to such an extent that he almost believes he actually is such and such a thing, without, however, wholly losing consciousness of "ordinary reality." His representation is not so much a sham-reality as a realization in appearance: "imagination" in the original sense of the word.

Passing now from children's games to the sacred performances in archaic culture we find that there is more of a mental element "at play" in the latter, though it is excessively difficult to define. The sacred performance is more than an actualization in appearance only, a sham reality; it is also more than a symbolical actualization—it is a mystical one. In it, something invisible and inactual takes beautiful, actual, holy form. The participants in the rite are convinced that the action actualizes and effects a definite beatification, brings about an order of things higher than that in which they customarily live. All the same this "actualization by representation" still retains the formal characteristics of play in every respect. It is played or performed within a playground that is literally "staked out," and played moreover as a feast, i.e. in mirth and freedom. A sacred space, a temporarily real world of its own, has been expressly hedged off for it. But with the end of the play its effect is not lost; rather it continues to shed its radiance on the ordinary world outside, a wholesome influence working security, order and prosperity for the whole community until the sacred play-season comes round again.

Examples can be taken from all over the world. According to ancient Chinese lore the purpose of music and the dance is to keep the world in its right course and to force Nature into benevolence towards man. The year's prosperity will depend on the right performance of sacred contests at the seasonal feasts. If these gatherings do not take place the crops will not ripen.

The rite is a *dromenon*, which means "something acted," an act, action. That which is enacted, or the stuff of the action, is a *drama*, which again means act, action represented on a stage. Such action may occur as a performance or a contest. The rite, or "ritual act" represents a cosmic happening, an event in the natural process. The word "represents," however, does not cover the exact meaning of the act, at least not in its looser, modern connotation; for here "representation" is really *identification*, the mystic repetition or *re-presentation* of the event. The rite produces the effect which is then not so much *shown figuratively* as *actually reproduced* in the action. The function of the rite, therefore, is far from being merely imitative; it causes the worshippers to participate in the sacred happening itself. As the Greeks would say, "it is *methectic* rather than *mimetic.* "[2] It is "a helping-out of the action."[3]

Anthropology is not primarily interested in how psychology will assess the mental attitude displayed in these phenomena. The psychologist may seek to settle the matter by calling such performances an *identification compensatrice*, a kind of substitute, "a representative act undertaken in view of the impossibility of staging real, purposive action."[4] Are the performers mocking, or are they mocked? The business of the anthropologist is to understand the significance of these "imaginations" in the mind of the peoples who practise and believe in them.

We touch here on the very core of comparative religion: the nature and essence of ritual and mystery. The whole of the ancient Vedic sacrificial rites rests on the idea that the ceremony—be it sacrifice, contest or performance—by representing a certain desired cosmic event, compels the gods to effect that event in reality. We could well say, by "playing" it. Leaving the religious issues aside we shall only concern ourselves here with the play-element in archaic ritual.

Ritual is thus in the main a matter of shows, representations, dramatic performances, imaginative actualizations of a vicarious nature. At the great seasonal festivals the community celebrates the grand happenings in the life of nature by staging sacred performances, which represent the change of seasons, the rising and setting of the constellations, the growth and ripening of crops, birth, life and death in man and beast. As Leo Frobenius puts it, archaic man *plays* the order of nature as imprinted on his consciousness.[5] In the remote past, so Frobenius thinks, man first assimilated the phenomena of vegetation and animal life and then conceived an idea of time and space, of months and seasons, of the course of the sun and moon. And now he plays this great processional order of existence in a sacred play, in and through which he actualizes anew, or "recreates," the events represented, and thus helps to maintain the cosmic order. Frobenius draws even more far-reaching conclusions from this "playing at nature." He deems it the starting-point of all social order and social institutions, too. Through this ritual play, savage society acquires its rude forms of government. The king is the sun, his kingship the image of the sun's course. All his life the king plays "sun" and in the end he suffers the fate of the sun: he must be killed in ritual forms by his own people.

We can leave aside the question of how far this explanation of ritual regicide and the whole underlying conception can be taken as "proved." The question that interests us here is: what are we to think of this concrete projection of primitive nature-consciousness? What are we to make of a mental process that begins with an unexpressed experience of cosmic phenomena and ends in an imaginative rendering of them in play?

Frobenius is right to discard the facile hypothesis which contents itself with hypothecating an innate "play instinct." The term "instinct," he says, is "a makeshift, an admission of helplessness before the problem of reality."[6] Equally explicitly and for even better reasons he rejects as a vestige of obsolete thinking the tendency to explain every advance in culture in terms of a "special purpose," a "why" and a "wherefore" thrust down the throat of the culture-creating community. "Tyranny of causality at its worst," "antiquated utilitarianism" he calls such a point of view.[7]

The conception Frobenius has of the mental process in question is roughly as follows. In archaic man the experience of life and nature, still unexpressed, takes the form of a "seizure"—being seized on, thrilled, enraptured. "The creative faculty in a people as in the child or every creative person, springs from this state of being seized." "Man is seized by the revelation of fate." "The reality of the natural rhythm of genesis and extinction has seized hold of his consciousness, and this, inevitably and by reflex action, leads him to represent his emotion in an act." So that according to him we are dealing with a necessary mental process of transformation. The thrill, the "being seized" by the phenomena of life and nature is condensed by reflex action, as it were, to poetic expression and art. It is difficult to describe the process of creative imagination in words that are more to the point, though they can hardly be called a true "explanation." The mental road from aesthetic or mystical, or at any rate meta-logical, perception of cosmic order to ritual play remains as dark as before.

While repeatedly using the term "play" for these performances the great anthropologist omits, however, to state what exactly he understands by it. He would even seem to have surreptitiously re-admitted the very thing he so strongly deprecates and which does not altogether fit in with the essential quality of play: the concept of purpose. For, in Frobenius' description of it, play quite explicitly *serves* to represent a cosmic event and thus bring it about. A quasi-rationalistic element irresistibly creeps in. For Frobenius, play and representation have their *raison d'être* after all, in the expression of something else, namely, the "being seized" by a cosmic event. But the very fact that the dramatization is *played* is, apparently, of secondary importance for him. Theoretically at least, the emotion could have been communicated in some other way. In our view, on the contrary, the whole point is the *playing*. Such ritual play is essentially no different from one of the higher forms of common child-play or indeed animal-play. Now in the case of these two latter forms one could hardly suppose their origin to lie in some cosmic emotion struggling for expression. Child-play possesses the play-form in its veriest essence, and most purely.

We might, perhaps, describe the process leading from "seizure" by nature to ritual performance, in terms that would avoid the above-mentioned inadequacy without, however, claiming to lay bare the inscrutable. Archaic society, we would say, plays as the child or animal plays. Such playing contains at the outset all the elements proper to play: order, tension, movement, change, solemnity, rhythm, rapture. Only in a later phase of society is play associated with the idea of something to be expressed in and by it, namely, what we would call "life" or "nature." Then, what was wordless play assumes poetic form. In the form and function of play, itself an independent entity which is senseless and irrational, man's consciousness that he is embedded in a sacred order of things finds its first, highest, and holiest expression. Gradually the significance of a sacred act permeates the playing. Ritual grafts itself upon it; but the primary thing is and remains play.

We are hovering over spheres of thought barely accessible either to psychology or to philosophy. Such questions as these plumb the depths of our consciousness. Ritual is seriousness at its highest and holiest. Can it nevertheless be play? We began by saying that all play, both of children and of grown-ups, can be performed in the most perfect seriousness. Does this go so far as to imply that play is still bound up with the sacred emotion of the sacramental act? Our conclusions are to some extent impeded by the rigidity of our accepted ideas. We are accustomed to think of play and seriousness as an absolute antithesis. It would seem, however, that this does not go to the heart of the matter.

Let us consider for a moment the following argument. The child plays in complete—we can well say, in sacred—earnest. But it plays and knows that it plays. The sportsman, too, plays with all the fervour of a man enraptured, but he still knows that he is playing. The actor on the stage is wholly absorbed in his playing, but is all the time conscious of "the play." The same holds good of the violinist, though he may soar to realms beyond this world. The play-character, therefore, may attach to the sublimest forms of action. Can we now extend the line to ritual and say that the priest performing the rites of sacrifice is only playing? At first sight it seems preposterous, for if you grant it for one religion you must grant it for all. Hence our ideas of ritual, magic, liturgy, sacrament and mystery would all fall within the play-concept. In dealing with abstractions we must always guard against overstraining their significance. We would merely be playing with words were we to stretch the play-concept unduly. But, all things considered, I do not think we are falling into that error when we characterize ritual as play. The ritual act has all the formal and essential characteristics of play which we enumerated above, particularly in so far as it transports the participants to another world. This identity of ritual and play was unreservedly recognized by Plato as a given fact. He had no hesitation in comprising the *sacra* in the category of play. "I say that a man must be serious with the serious," he says (*Laws*, vii, 803). "God alone is worthy of supreme seriousness, but man is made God's plaything, and that is the best part of him. Therefore every man and woman should live life accordingly, and play the noblest games and be of another mind from what they are at present. . . . For they deem war a serious thing, though in war there is neither play nor culture worthy the name (οὔτ' οὖν παιδιὰ . . . οὔτ' αὖ παιδεία), which are the things *we* deem most serious. Hence all must live in peace as well as they possibly can. What, then, is the right way of living? Life must be lived as play, playing certain games, making sacrifices, singing and dancing, and then a man will be able to propitiate the gods, and defend himself against his enemies, and win in the contest."[8]

The close connections between mystery and play have been touched on most tellingly by Romano Guardini in his book *The Spirit of the Liturgy* (Ecclesia Orans I, Freiburg, 1922), particularly the chapter entitled "Die Liturgie als Spiel."[9] He does not actually cite Plato, but comes as near the above quotation as may be. He ascribes to liturgy more than one of the features we held to be characteristic of play, amongst others the fact that, in its highest examples, liturgy is "zwecklos aber doch sinnvoll"—"pointless but significant."

The Platonic identification of play and holiness does not defile the latter by calling it play, rather it exalts the concept of play to the highest regions of the spirit. We said at the beginning that play was anterior to culture; in a certain sense it is also superior to it or at least detached from it. In play we may move below the level of the serious, as the child does; but we can also move above it —in the realm of the beautiful and the sacred.

From this point of view we can now define the relationship between ritual and play more closely. We are no longer astonished at the substantial similarity of the two forms, and the question as to how far every ritual act falls within the category of play continues to hold our attention.

We found that one of the most important characteristics of play was its spatial separation from ordinary life. A closed space is marked out for it, either materially or ideally, hedged off from the everyday surroundings. Inside this space the play proceeds, inside it the rules obtain. Now, the marking out of some sacred spot is also the primary characteristic of every sacred act. This requirement of isolation for ritual, including magic and law, is much more than merely spatial and temporal. Nearly all rites of consecration and initiation entail a certain artificial seclusion for the performers and those to be initiated. Whenever it is a question of taking a vow or being received into an Order or confraternity, or of oaths and secret societies, in one way or another there is always such a delimitation of room for play. The magician, the augur, the sacrificer begins his work by circumscribing his sacred space. Sacrament and mystery presuppose a hallowed spot.

Formally speaking, there is no distinction whatever between marking out a space for a sacred purpose and marking it out for purposes of sheer play. The turf, the tennis-court, the chess-board and pavement-hopscotch cannot formally be distinguished from the temple or the magic circle. The striking similarity between sacrificial rites all over the earth shows that such customs must be rooted in a very fundamental, an aboriginal layer of the human mind. As a rule people reduce this over-all congruity of cultural forms to some "reasonable," "logical" cause by explaining the need for isolation and seclusion as an anxiety to protect the consecrated individual from noxious influences—because, in his consecrated state, he is particularly exposed to the malign workings of ghosts, besides being himself a danger to his surroundings. Such an explanation puts intellection and utilitarian purpose at the beginning of the cultural process: the very thing Frobenius warned against. Even if we do not fall back here on the antiquated notion of a priestcraft inventing religion, we are still introducing a rationalistic element better avoided. If, on the other hand, we accept the essential and original identity of play and ritual we simply recognize the hallowed spot as a play-ground, and the misleading question of the "why and the wherefore" does not arise at all.

If ritual proves to be formally indistinguishable from play the question remains whether this resemblance goes further than the purely formal. It is surprising that anthropology and comparative religion have paid so little attention to the problem of how far such sacred activities as proceed within the forms of play also proceed in the attitude and mood of play. Even Frobenius has not, to my knowledge, asked this question.

Needless to say, the mental attitude in which a community performs and experiences its sacred rites is one of high and holy earnest. But let it be emphasized again that genuine and spontaneous play can also be profoundly serious. The player can abandon himself body and soul to the game, and the consciousness of its being "merely" a game can be thrust into the background. The joy inextricably bound up with playing can turn not only into tension, but into elation. Frivolity and ecstasy are the twin poles between which play moves.

The play-mood is *labile* in its very nature. At any moment "ordinary life" may reassert its rights either by an impact from without, which interrupts the game, or by an offence against the rules, or else from within, by a collapse of the play spirit, a sobering, a disenchantment.

What, then, is the attitude and mood prevailing at holy festivals? The sacred act is "celebrated" on a "holiday"—i.e. it forms part of a general feast on the occasion of a holy day. When the people foregather at the sanctuary they gather together for collective rejoicing. Consecrations, sacrifices, sacred dances and contests, performances, mysteries—all are comprehended within the act of celebrating a festival. The rites may be bloody, the probations of the young men awaiting initiation may be cruel, the masks may be terrifying, but the whole thing has a festal nature. Ordinary life is at a standstill. Banquets, junketings and all kinds of wanton revels are going on all the time the feast lasts. Whether we think of the Ancient Greek festivities or of the African religions to-day we can hardly draw any sharp line between the festival mood in general and the holy frenzy surrounding the central mystery.

Almost simultaneously with the appearance of the Dutch edition of this book the Hungarian scholar Karl Kerényi published a treatise on the nature of the festival which has the closest ties with our theme.[10] According to Kerényi, the festival too has that character of primacy and absolute independence which we predicated of play. "Among the psychic realities," he says, "the feast is a thing in itself, not to be confused with anything else in the world." Just as we thought the play-concept somewhat negligently treated by the anthropologist, so in his view is the feast. "The phenomenon of the feast appears to have been completely passed over by the ethnologist." "For all science is concerned it might not exist at all." Neither might play, we would like to add.

In the very nature of things the relationship between feast and play is very close. Both proclaim a standstill to ordinary life. In both mirth and joy dominate, though not necessarily—for the feast too can be serious; both are limited as to time and place; both combine strict rules with genuine freedom. In short, feast and play have their main characteristics in common. The two seem most intimately related in dancing. According to Kerényi, the Cora Indians inhabiting the Pacific coast of Mexico call their sacred feast of the young corn-cobs and the corn-roasting the "play" of their highest god.

Kerényi's ideas about the feast as an autonomous culture-concept amplify and corroborate those on which this book is built. For all that, however, the establishment of a close connection between the spirit of play and ritual does not explain everything. Genuine play possesses besides its formal characteristics and its joyful mood, at least one further very essential feature, namely, the consciousness, however latent, of "only pretending." The question remains how far such a consciousness is compatible with the ritual act performed in devotion.

If we confine ourselves to the sacred rites in archaic culture it is not impossible to adumbrate the degree of seriousness with which they are performed. As far as I know, ethnologists and anthropologists concur in the opinion that the mental attitude in which the great religious feasts of savages are celebrated and witnessed is not one of complete illusion. There is an underlying consciousness of things "not being real." A vivid picture of this attitude is given by Ad. E. Jensen in his book on the circumcision and puberty ceremonies in savage society.[11] The men seem to have no fear of the ghosts that are hovering about everywhere during the feast and appear to everyone at its height. This is small wonder, seeing that these same men have had the staging of the whole ceremony: they have carved and decorated the masks, wear them themselves and after use conceal them from the women. They make the noises heralding the appearance of the ghosts, they trace their footprints in the sand, they blow the flutes that represent the voices of the ancestors, and brandish the bull-roarers. In short, says Jensen, "their position is much like that of parents playing Santa Claus for their children: they know of the mask, but hide it from them." The men tell the women gruesome tales about the goings-on in the sacred bush. The attitude of the neophytes alternates between ecstasy, feigned madness, flesh-creeping and boyish swagger. Nor, in the last resort, are the women wholly duped. They know perfectly well who is hiding behind this mask or that. All the same they get fearfully excited when a mask comes up to them with minatory gestures, and fly shrieking in all directions. These expressions of terror, says Jensen, are in part quite genuine and spontaneous, and in part only acting up to a part imposed by tradition. It is "the done thing." The women are, as it were, the chorus to the play and they know that they must not be "spoil-sports."

In all this it is impossible to fix accurately the lower limit where holy earnest reduces itself to mere "fun." With us, a father of somewhat childish disposition might get seriously angry if his children caught him in the act of preparing Christmas presents. A Kwakiutl father in British Columbia killed his daughter who surprised him whilst carving things for a tribal ceremony.[12] The unstable nature of religious feeling among the Loango negroes is described by Pechuel-

Loesche in terms similar to those used by Jensen. Their belief in the sanctities is a sort of half-belief, and goes with scoffing and pretended indifference. The really important thing is the *mood,* he concludes by saying.[13] R. R. Marrett, in his chapter on "Primitive Credulity" in *The Threshold of Religion,*[14] develops the idea that a certain element of "make-believe" is operative in all primitive religions. Whether one is sorcerer or sorcerized one is always knower and dupe at once. But one chooses to be the dupe. "The savage is a good actor who can be quite absorbed in his role, like a child at play; and, also like a child, a good spectator who can be frightened to death by the roaring of something he knows perfectly well to be no 'real' lion." The native, says Malinowski, feels and fears his belief rather than formulates it clearly to himself.[15] He uses certain terms and expressions, and these we must collect as documents of belief just as they are, without working them up into a consistent theory. The behaviour of those to whom the savage community attributes "supernatural" powers can often be best expressed by "acting up to the part."[16]

Despite this partial consciousness of things "not being real" in magic and supernatural phenomena generally, these authorities still warn against drawing the inference that the whole system of beliefs and practices is only a fraud invented by a group of "unbelievers" with a view to dominating the credulous. It is true that such an interpretation is given not only by many travellers but sometimes even by the traditions of the natives themselves. Yet it cannot be the right one. "The origin of any sacred act can only lie in the credulity of all, and the spurious maintaining of it in the interests of a special group can only be the final phase of a long line of development." As I see it, psychoanalysis tends to fall back on this antiquated interpretation of circumcision and puberty practices, so rightly rejected by Jensen.

From the foregoing it is quite clear, to my mind at least, that where savage ritual is concerned we never lose sight of the play-concept for a single moment. To describe the phenomena we have to use the term "play" over and over again. What is more, the unity and indivisibility of belief and unbelief, the indissoluble connection between sacred earnest and "make-believe" or "fun," are best understood in the concept of play itself. Jensen, though admitting the similarity of the child's world to that of the savage, still tries to distinguish in principle between the mentality of the two. The child, he says, when confronted with the figure of Santa Claus, has to do with a "ready-made concept," in which he "finds his way" with a lucidity and endowment of his own. But "the creative attitude of the savage with regard to the ceremonies here in question is quite another thing. He has to do not with ready-made concepts but with his natural surroundings, which themselves demand interpretation; he grasps their mysterious daemonism and tries to give it in representative form."[17] Here we recognize the views of Frobenius, who was Jensen's teacher. Still, two objections occur. Firstly, when calling the process in the savage mind "quite another thing" from that in the child-mind, he is speaking of the *originators* of the ritual on the one hand and of the child of *to-day* on the other. But we know nothing of these originators.

All we can study is a ritualistic community which receives its religious imagery as traditional material just as "ready-made" as the child does, and responds to it similarly. Secondly, even if we ignore this, the process of "interpreting" the natural surroundings, of "grasping" them and "representing" them in a ritual image remains altogether inaccessible to our observation. It is only by fanciful metaphors that Frobenius and Jensen force an approach to it. The most we can say of the function that is operative in the process of image-making or imagination is that it is a poetic function; and we define it best of all by calling it a function of play—the *ludic* function, in fact.

So that the apparently quite simple question of what play really is, leads us deep into the problem of the nature and origin of religious concepts. As we all know, one of the most important basic ideas with which every student of comparative religion has to acquaint himself is the following. When a certain form of religion accepts a sacred identity between two things of a different order, say a human being and an animal, this relationship is not adequately expressed by calling it a "symbolical correspondence" as *we* conceive this. The identity, the essential oneness of the two goes far deeper than the correspondence between a substance and its symbolic image. It is a mystic unity. The one has *become* the other. In his magic dance the savage *is* a kangaroo. We must always be on our guard against the deficiencies and differences of our means of expression. In order to form any idea at all of the mental habits of the savage we are forced to give them in our terminology. Whether we will or not we are always transposing the savage's ideas of religion into the strictly logical modes of our own thought. We express the relationship between him and the animal he "identifies" himself with, as a "being" for him but a "playing" for us. He has taken on the "essence" of the kangaroo, says the savage; he is playing the kangaroo, say we. The savage, however, knows nothing of the conceptual distinctions between "being" and "playing"; he knows nothing of "identity," "image," or "symbol." Hence it remains an open question whether we do not come nearest to the mental attitude of the savage performing a ritual act, by adhering to this primary, universally understandable term "play." In play as we conceive it the distinction between belief and make-believe breaks down. The concept of play merges quite naturally with that of holiness. Any Prelude of Bach, any line of tragedy proves it. By considering the whole sphere of so-called primitive culture as a play-sphere we pave the way to a more direct and more general understanding of its peculiarities than any meticulous psychological or sociological analysis would allow.

Primitive, or let us say, archaic ritual is thus sacred play, indispensable for the well-being of the community, fecund of cosmic insight and social development but always play in the sense Plato gave to it—an action accomplishing itself outside and above the necessities and seriousness of everyday life. In this sphere of sacred play the child and the poet are at home with the savage. His aesthetic sensibility has brought the modern man closer to this sphere than the "enlightened" man of the 18th century ever was. Think of the peculiar charm that the mask as an *objet d'art* has for the modern mind. People nowadays try to feel the essence of savage life. This kind of exoticism may sometimes be a little affected, but it goes a good deal deeper than the 18th century *engouement* for Turks, "Chinamen," and Indians. Modern man is very sensitive to the far-off and the strange. Nothing helps him so much in his understanding of savage society as his feeling for masks and disguise. While ethnology has demonstrated their enormous social importance, they arouse in the educated layman and art-lover an immediate aesthetic emotion compounded of beauty, fright, and mystery. Even for the cultured adult of to-day the mask still retains something of its terrifying power, although no religious emotions are attached to it. The sight of the masked figure, as a purely aesthetic experience, carries us beyond "ordinary life" into a world where something other than daylight reigns; it carries us back to the world of the savage, the child and the poet, which is the world of play.

Even if we can legitimately reduce our ideas on the significance of primitive ritual to an irreducible play-concept, one extremely troublesome question still remains. What if we now ascend from the lower religions to the higher? From the rude and outlandish ritual of the African, American or Australian aborigines our vision shifts to Vedic sacrificial lore, already, in the hymns of the *Rig-Veda,* pregnant with the wisdom of the Upanishads, or to the profoundly mystical identifications of god, man, and beast in Egyptian religion, or to the Orphic and Eleusinian mysteries. In form and practice all these are closely allied to the so-called primitive religions, even to bizarre and bloody particulars. But the high degree of wisdom and truth we discern, or think we can discern in them, forbids us to speak of them with that air of superiority which, as a matter of fact, is equally out of place in "primitive" cultures. We must ask whether this formal similarity entitles us to extend the qualification "play" to the consciousness of the holy, the faith embodied in these higher creeds. If we accept the Platonic definition of play there is nothing preposterous or irreverent in doing so. Play consecrated to the Deity, the highest goal of man's endeavour—such was Plato's conception of religion. In following him we in no way abandon the holy mystery, or cease to rate it as the highest attainable expression of that which escapes logical understanding. The ritual act, or an important part of it, will always remain within the play category, but in this seeming subordination the recognition of its holiness is not lost.

NOTES

1. *Wesen* may be translated as nature, kind, being, essence, etc.
2. Harrison 1912:125.
3. Marrett 1912:48.
4. Buytendijk 1932:70–71.
5. Frobenius 1932.
6. Frobenius 1932:122.
7. Frobenius 1932:21.
8. Plato *Laws* vii:796.
9. Guardini 1922: see chapter entitled "Die Liturgie als Spiel."
10. Kerényi 1938:59–74.

11. Jensen 1933.
12. Boas 1897:435.
13. Pechuel-Loesche 1907:345.
14. Marrett 1912.

15. Malinowski 1922:339.
16. Malinowski 1922:240.
17. Jensen 1933:149.

6

A THEORY OF PLAY AND FANTASY

Gregory Bateson

Earlier fundamental work of Whitehead, Russell,[1] Wittgenstein,[2] Carnap,[3] Whorf,[4] etc., as well as my own attempt[5] to use this earlier thinking as an epistemological base for psychiatric theory, led to a series of generalizations:

(1) That human verbal communication can operate and always does operate at many contrasting levels of abstraction. These range in two directions from the seemingly simple denotative level ("The cat is on the mat"). One range or set of these more abstract levels includes those explicit or implicit messages where the subject of discourse is the language. We will call these metalinguistic (for example, "The verbal sound 'cat' stands for any member of such and such class of objects," or "The word, 'cat,' has no fur and cannot scratch"). The other set of levels of abstraction we will call metacommunicative (e.g., "My telling you where to find the cat was friendly," or "This is play"). In these, the subject of discourse is the relationship between the speakers.

It will be noted that the vast majority of both metalinguistic and metacommunicative messages remain implicit; and also that, especially in the psychiatric interview, there occurs a further class of implicit messages about how metacommunicative messages of friendship and hostility are to be interpreted.

(2) If we speculate about the evolution of communication, it is evident that a very important stage in this evolution occurs when the organism gradually ceases to respond quite "automatically" to the mood-signs of another and becomes able to recognize the sign as a signal: that is, to recognize that the other individual's and its own signals are only signals, which can be trusted, distrusted, falsified, denied, amplified, corrected, and so forth.

Clearly this realization that signals are signals is by no means complete even

---

Gregory Bateson is senior lecturer at Kresge College, University of California, Santa Cruz. Among his books are *Haven, Communication* (with Jurgen Reusch) and *Steps to an Ecology of Mind.*

among the human species. We all too often respond automatically to newspaper headlines as though these stimuli were direct object-indications of events in our environment instead of signals concocted and transmitted by creatures as complexly motivated as ourselves. The nonhuman mammal is automatically excited by the sexual odor of another; and rightly so, inasmuch as the secretion of that sign is an "involuntary" mood-sign; i.e., an outwardly perceptible event which is a part of the physiological process which we have called a mood. In the human species a more complex state of affairs begins to be the rule. Deodorants mask the involuntary olfactory signs, and in their place the cosmetic industry provides the individual with perfumes which are not involuntary signs but voluntary signals, recognizable as such. Many a man has been thrown off balance by a whiff of perfume, and if we are to believe the advertisers, it seems that these signals, voluntarily worn, have sometimes an automatic and autosuggestive effect even upon the voluntary wearer.

Be that as it may, this brief digression will serve to illustrate a stage of evolution —the drama precipitated when organisms, having eaten of the fruit of the Tree of Knowledge, discover that their signals are signals. Not only the characteristically human invention of language can then follow, but also all the complexities of empathy, identification, projection, and so on. And with these comes the possibility of communicating at the multiplicity of levels of abstraction mentioned above.

(3) The first definite step in the formulation of the hypothesis guiding this research occurred in January, 1952, when I went to the Fleishhacker Zoo in San Francisco to look for behavioral criteria which would indicate whether any given organism is or is not able to recognize that the signs emitted by itself and other members of the species are signals. In theory, I had thought out what such criteria might look like—that the occurrence of metacommunicative signs (or signals) in the stream of interaction between the animals would indicate that the animals have at least some awareness (conscious or unconscious) that the signs about which they metacommunicate are signals.

I knew, of course, that there was no likelihood of finding denotative messages among nonhuman mammals, but I was still not aware that the animal data would require an almost total revision of my thinking. What I encountered at the zoo was a phenomenon well known to everybody: I saw two young monkeys *playing*, i.e., engaged in an interactive sequence of which the unit actions or signals were similar to but not the same as those of combat. It was evident, even to the human observer, that the sequence as a whole was not combat, and evident to the human observer that to the participant monkeys this was "not combat."

Now, this phenomenon, play, could only occur if the participant organisms were capable of some degree of metacommunication, i.e., of exchanging signals which would carry the message "this is play."

(4) The next step was the examination of the message "This is play," and the realization that this message contains those elements which necessarily generate a paradox of the Russellian or Epimenides type—a negative statement containing

an implicit negative metastatement. Expanded, the statement "This is play" looks something like this: "These actions in which we now engage do not denote what those actions *for which they stand* would denote."

We now ask about the italicized words, *"for which they stand."* We say the word "cat" stands for any member of a certain class. That is, the phrase "stands for" is a near synonym of "denotes." If we now substitute "which they denote" for the words "for which they stand" in the expanded definition of play, the result is: "These actions, in which we now engage, do not denote what would be denoted by those actions which these actions denote." The playful nip denotes the bite, but it does not denote what would be denoted by the bite.

According to the Theory of Logical Types such a message is of course inadmissible, because the word "denote" is being used in two degrees of abstraction, and these two uses are treated as synonymous. But all that we learn from such a criticism is that it would be bad natural history to expect the mental processes and communicative habits of mammals to conform to the logician's ideal. Indeed, if human thought and communication always conformed to the ideal, Russell would not—in fact could not—have formulated the ideal.

(5) A related problem in the evolution of communication concerns the origin of what Korzybski[6] has called the map-territory relation: the fact that a message, of whatever kind, does not consist of those objects which it denotes ("The word 'cat' cannot scratch us"). Rather, language bears to the objects which it denotes a relationship comparable to that which a map bears to a territory. Denotative communication as it occurs at the human level is only possible *after* the evolution of a complex set of metalinguistic (but not verbalized)[7] rules which govern how words and sentences shall be related to objects and events. It is therefore appropriate to look for the evolution of such metalinguistic and/or metacommunicative rules at a prehuman and preverbal level.

It appears from what is said above that play is a phenomenon in which the actions of "play" are related to, or denote, other actions of "not play." We therefore meet in play with an instance of signals standing for other events, and it appears, therefore, that the evolution of play may have been an important step in the evolution of communication.

(6) *Threat* is another phenomenon which resembles play in that actions denote, but are different from, other actions. The clenched fist of threat is different from the punch, but it refers to a possible future (but at present nonexistent) punch. And threat also is commonly recognizable among nonhuman mammals. Indeed it has lately been argued that a great part of what appears to be combat among members of a single species is rather to be regarded as threat (Tinbergen,[8] Lorenz[9]).

(7) Histrionic behavior and deceit are other examples of the primitive occurrence of map-territory differentiation. And there is evidence that dramatization occurs among birds: a jackdaw may imitate her own mood-signs (Lorenz[10]), and deceit has been observed among howler monkeys (Carpenter[11]).

(8) We might expect threat, play, and histrionics to be three independent phenomena all contributing to the evolution of the discrimination between map and territory. But it seems that this would be wrong, at least so far as mammalian communication is concerned. Very brief analysis of childhood behavior shows that such combinations as histrionic play, bluff, playful threat, teasing play in response to threat, histrionic threat, and so on form together a single total complex of phenomena. And such adult phenomena as gambling and playing with risk have their roots in the combination of threat and play. It is evident also that not only threat but the reciprocal of threat—the behavior of the threatened individual—are a part of this complex. It is probable that not only histrionics but also spectatorship should be included within this field. It is also appropriate to mention self-pity.

(9) A further extension of this thinking leads us to include ritual within this general field in which the discrimination is drawn, but not completely, between denotative action and that which is to be denoted. Anthropological studies of peace-making ceremonies, to cite only one example, support this conclusion.

In the Andaman Islands, peace is concluded after each side has been given ceremonial freedom to strike the other. This example, however, also illustrates the labile nature of the frame "This is play," or "This is ritual." The discrimination between map and territory is always liable to break down, and the ritual blows of peace-making are always liable to be mistaken for the "real" blows of combat. In this event, the peace-making ceremony becomes a battle (Radcliffe-Brown[12]).

(10) But this leads us to recognition of a more complex form of play; the game which is constructed not upon the premise "This is play" but rather around the question "Is this play?" And this type of interaction also has its ritual forms, e.g., in the hazing of initiation.

(11) Paradox is doubly present in the signals which are exchanged within the context of play, fantasy, threat, etc. Not only does the playful nip not denote what would be denoted by the bite for which it stands, but, in addition, the bite itself is fictional. Not only do the playing animals not quite mean what they are saying but, also, they are usually communicating about something which does not exist. At the human level, this leads to a vast variety of complications and inversions in the fields of play, fantasy, and art. Conjurers and painters of the *trompe l'oeil* school concentrate upon acquiring a virtuosity whose only reward is reached after the viewer detects that he has been deceived and is forced to smile or marvel at the skill of the deceiver. Hollywood film-makers spend millions of dollars to increase the realism of a shadow. Other artists, perhaps more realistically, insist that art be nonrepresentational; and poker players achieve a strange addictive realism by equating the chips for which they play with dollars. They still insist, however, that the loser accept his loss as part of the game.

Finally, in the dim region where art, magic, and religion meet and overlap, human beings have evolved the "metaphor that is meant," the flag which men will die to save, and the sacrament that is felt to be more than "an outward and visible sign, given unto us." Here we can recognize an attempt to deny the difference between map and territory, and to get back to the absolute innocence of communication by means of pure mood-signs.

(12) We face then two peculiarities of play: *(a)* that the messages or signals exchanged in play are in a certain sense untrue or not meant; and *(b)* that that which is denoted by these signals is nonexistent. These two peculiarities sometimes combine strangely to reverse a conclusion reached above. It was stated (4) that the playful nip denotes the bite, but does not denote that which would be denoted by the bite. But there are other instances where an opposite phenomenon occurs. A man experiences the full intensity of subjective terror when a spear is flung at him out of the 3D screen or when he falls headlong from some peak created in his own mind in the intensity of nightmare. At the moment of terror there was no questioning of "reality," but still there was no spear in the movie house and no cliff in the bedroom. The images did not denote that which they seemed to denote, but these same images did really evoke that terror which would have been evoked by a real spear or a real precipice. By a similar trick of self-contradiction, the film-makers of Hollywood are free to offer to a puritanical public a vast range of pseudosexual fantasy which otherwise would not be tolerated. In *David and Bathsheba,* Bathsheba can be a Troilistic link between David and Uriah. And in *Hans Christian Andersen,* the hero starts out accompanied by a boy. He tries to get a woman, but when he is defeated in this attempt, he returns to the boy. In all of this, there is, of course, no homosexuality, but the choice of these symbolisms is associated in these fantasies with certain characteristic ideas, e.g., about the hopelessness of the heterosexual masculine position when faced with certain sorts of women or with certain sorts of male authority. In sum, the pseudohomosexuality of the fantasy does not stand for any real homosexuality, but does stand for and express attitudes which might accompany a real homosexuality or feed its etiological roots. The symbols do not denote homosexuality, but do denote ideas for which homosexuality is an appropriate symbol. Evidently it is necessary to re-examine the precise semantic validity of the interpretations which the psychiatrist offers to a patient, and, as preliminary to this analysis, it will be necessary to examine the nature of the frame in which these interpretations are offered.

(13) What has previously been said about play can be used as an introductory example for the discussion of frames and contexts. In sum, it is our hypothesis that the message "This is play" establishes a paradoxical frame comparable to Epimenides' paradox. This frame may be diagrammed thus:

> All statements within this
> frame are untrue.
>
> I love you.
>
> I hate you.

The first statement within this frame is a self-contradictory proposition about itself. If this first statement is true, then it must be false. If it be false, then it must be true. But this first statement carries with it all the other statements in the frame. So, if the first statement be true, then all the others must be false; and vice versa, if the first statement be untrue then all the others must be true.

(14) The logically minded will notice a *non-sequitur*. It could be urged that even if the first statement is false, there remains a logical possibility that some of the other statements in the frame are untrue. It is, however, a characteristic of unconscious or "primary-process" thinking that the thinker is unable to discriminate between "some" and "all," and unable to discriminate between "not all" and "none." It seems that the achievement of these discriminations is performed by higher or more conscious mental processes which serve in the nonpsychotic individual to correct the black-and-white thinking of the lower levels. We assume, and this seems to be an orthodox assumption, that primary process is continually operating, and that the psychological validity of the paradoxical play frame depends upon this part of the mind.

(15) But, conversely, while it is necessary to invoke the primary process as an explanatory principle in order to delete the notion of "some" from between "all" and "none," this does not mean that play is simply a primary-process phenomenon. The discrimination between "play" and "nonplay," like the discrimination between fantasy and nonfantasy, is certainly a function of secondary process, or "ego." Within the dream the dreamer is usually unaware that he is dreaming, and within "play" he must often be reminded that "This is play."

Similarly, within dream or fantasy the dreamer does not operate with the concept "untrue." He operates with all sorts of statements but with a curious inability to achieve metastatements. He cannot, unless close to waking, dream a statement referring to (i.e., framing) his dream.

It therefore follows that the play frame as here used as an explanatory principle implies a special combination of primary and secondary processes. This, however, is related to what was said earlier, when it was argued that play marks a step forward in the evolution of communication—the crucial step in the discovery of map-territory relations. In primary process, map and territory are equated; in secondary process, they can be discriminated. In play, they are both equated and discriminated. . . .

(19) This whole matter of frames and paradoxes may be illustrated in terms of animal behavior, where three types of message may be recognized or deduced: *(a)* messages of the sort which we here call mood-signs; *(b)* messages which simulate mood-signs (in play, threat, histrionics, etc.); and *(c)* messages which enable the receiver to discriminate between mood-signs and those other signs which resemble them. The message "This is play" is of this third type. It tells the receiver that certain nips and other meaningful actions are not messages of the first type.

The message "This is play" thus sets a frame of the sort which is likely to precipitate paradox: it is an attempt to discriminate between, or to draw a line between, categories of different logical types.

(20) This discussion of play and psychological frames establishes a type of

triadic constellation (or system of relationships) between messages. One instance of this constellation is analyzed in paragraph 19, but it is evident that constellations of this sort occur not only at the nonhuman level but also in the much more complex communication of human beings. A fantasy or myth may simulate a denotative narrative, and, to discriminate between these types of discourse, people use messages of the frame-setting type, and so on.

NOTES

1. Whitehead and Russell 1910–1913.
2. Wittgenstein 1922.
3. Carnap 1937.
4. Whorf 1940:229–278.
5. Ruesch and Bateson 1951.
6. Korzybski 1941.
7. The verbalization of these metalinguistic rules is a much later achievement which can only occur after the evolution of a non-verbalized meta-metalinguistics.
8. Tinbergen 1953.
9. Lorenz 1952.
10. Lorenz 1952.
11. Carpenter 1934:1–168.
12. Radcliffe-Brown 1922.

7

THE SCIENCE OF THE CONCRETE

Claude Lévi-Strauss

We have seen that there are analogies between mythical thought on the theoretical, and "bricolage" on the practical plane and that artistic creation lies mid-way between science and these two forms of activity. There are relations of the same type between games and rites.

All games are defined by a set of rules which in practice allow the playing of any number of matches. Ritual, which is also "played," is, on the other hand, like a favoured instance of a game, remembered from among the possible ones because it is the only one which results in a particular type of equilibrium between the two sides. The transposition is readily seen in the case of the Gahuku-Gama of New Guinea who have learnt football but who will play, several days running, as many matches as are necessary for both sides to reach the same score.[1] This is treating a game as a ritual.

The same can be said of the games which took place among the Fox Indians during adoption ceremonies. Their purpose was to replace a dead relative by a living one and so to allow the final departure of the soul of the deceased. The main aim of funeral rites among the Fox seems indeed to be to get rid of the dead and to prevent them from avenging on the living their bitterness and their regret that they are no longer among them. For native philosophy resolutely sides with the living: "Death is a hard thing. Sorrow is especially hard."

Death originated in the destruction by supernatural powers of the younger of two mythical brothers who are cultural heroes among all the Algonkin. But it was not yet final. It was made so by the elder brother when, in spite of his sorrow, he rejected the ghost's request to be allowed to return to his place among the

Claude Lévi-Strauss is director of studies and professor of comparative religions of non-literate peoples at the École Practique des Hautes Études in Paris. He is also professor of social anthropology at the Collège de France. His books include *The Savage Mind, The Raw and the Cooked,* and *From Honey to Ashes.*

living. Men must follow this example and be firm with the dead. The living must make them understand that they have lost nothing by dying since they regularly receive offerings of tobacco and food. In return they are expected to compensate the living for the reality of death which they recall to them and for the sorrow their demise causes them by guaranteeing them long life, clothes, and something to eat. "It is the dead who make food increase," a native informant explains. "They [the Indians] must coax them that way."[2]

Now, the adoption rites which are necessary to make the soul of the deceased finally decide to go where it will take on the role of a protecting spirit are normally accompanied by competitive sports, games of skill or chance between teams which are constituted on the basis of an *ad hoc* division into two sides, Tokan and Kicko. It is said explicitly over and over again that it is the living and the dead who are playing against each other. It is as if the living offered the dead the consolation of a last match before finally being rid of them. But, since the two teams are asymmetrical in what they stand for, the outcome is inevitably determined in advance:

> This is how it is when they play ball. When the man for whom the adoption-feast is held is a Tokana, the Tokanagi win the game. The Kickoagi cannot win. And if it is a Kicko woman for whom the adoption-feast is given, the Kickoagi win, as in turn the Tokanagi do not win.[3]

And what is in fact the case? It is clear that it is only the living who win in the great biological and social game which is constantly taking place between the living and the dead. But, as all the North American mythology confirms, to win a game is symbolically to "kill" one's opponent; this is depicted as really happening in innumerable myths. By ruling that they should always win, the dead are given the illusion that it is they who are really alive, and that their opponents, having been "killed" by them, are dead. Under the guise of playing with the dead, one plays them false and commits them. The formal structure of what might at first sight be taken for a competitive game is in fact identical with that of a typical ritual such as the Mitawit or Midewinin of these same Algonkin peoples in which the initiates get symbolically killed by the dead whose part is *played* by the initiated; they feign death in order to obtain a further lease of life. In both cases, death is brought in but only to be duped.

Games thus appear to have a *disjunctive* effect: they end in the establishment of a difference between individual players or teams where originally there was no indication of inequality. And at the end of the game they are distinguished into winners and losers. Ritual, on the other hand, is the exact inverse; it *conjoins*, for it brings about a union (one might even say communion in this context) or in any case an organic relation between two initially separate groups, one ideally merging with the person of the officiant and the other with the collectivity of the faithful. In the case of games the symmetry is therefore preordained and it is of a structural kind since it follows from the principle that the rules are the same for both sides. Asymmetry is engendered: it follows inevitably from the contingent nature of events, themselves due to intention, chance or talent. The reverse is true of ritual. There is an asymmetry which is postulated in advance between profane and sacred, faithful and officiating, dead and living, initiated and uninitiated, etc., and the "game" consists in making all the participants pass to the winning side by means of events, the nature and ordering of which is genuinely structural. Like science (though here again on both the theoretical and the practical plane) the game produces events by means of a structure; and we can therefore understand why competitive games should flourish in our industrial societies. Rites and myths, on the other hand, like "bricolage" (which these same societies only tolerate as a hobby or pastime), take to pieces and reconstruct sets of events (on a psychical, socio-historical or technical plane) and use them as so many indestructible pieces for structural patterns in which they serve alternatively as ends or means.

(translated from the French)

NOTES

1. Read 1959:429.
2. Michelson 1925:369, 407.
3. Michelson 1925:385.

PART THREE

RITUAL AND PERFORMANCE IN
EVERYDAY LIFE

INTRODUCTORY NOTE

Erving Goffman writes, "All the world is not, of course, a stage, but the crucial ways in which it isn't are not easy to specify." Why not? Because the basic actions of theatre are common human activities: kids playing the Dozens in a ghetto invent rhythmic dialog-combats like those between Beatrice and Benedict in *Much Ado About Nothing;* a parade of missiles in Red Square or a temper tantrum in the kitchen are both shows staged to secure an effect; the development of "character" by means of public competition—in school, business, or a men's house in Papua–New Guinea—is the same in ordinary life as it is in drama. And it isn't that drama "represents" or "imitates" ordinary life. Rather the basic integers of theatre and of ordinary life are the same: arrangement of space and bodies in places (kinesics); communication through formal languages of great symbolic density, including dances and musical progressions as much as speech.

The ongoing conversion of relationships into displays, and the progression of displays as a means of ordering relationships, is the connecting action between theatre and social life. The differences lie in how conscious all players are, or can be, of the conventions, the rules, that define the games—and how much these rules can change. In theatre a whole range of activity is devoted to changing the rules; that is what avant-garde or experimental theatre is licensed to do. The more closely theatre is identified with social structure—the more it is a ritual theatre —the more traditional it is, and the less easy it becomes to change the rules. In a word, society is conservative, art is radical.

In addition to the selections presented here we suggest the following: the writings of Goffman, especially *Interaction Ritual* and *Frame Analysis;* Elizabeth Burns's *Theatricality;* Stanford M. Lyman's and Marvin B. Scott's *The Drama of Social Reality;* and as much Gregory Bateson as you can lay your mind on.

8

IT DEPENDS ON THE POINT OF VIEW

Ray L. Birdwhistell

There is a large though scarcely comprehensive, literature dealing with the rules, the etiquette, the conventions of formal, interpersonal exchanges. In a sense, such studies might be regarded as describing interpersonal exchanges from above. We are concerned here with studying them from below. That is, by studying that systematic and patterned behavior by means of which men engage in communication with each other, we may be able to understand how these processes order, set limits upon, or, at times, determine the interactive process.

Concern with communication is probably as old as man himself, but the history of the scientific investigation of communicative activity begins relatively recently. Only within the past quarter of a century has there been an effort to describe communication as a systematic process. Up until that time most of the discussion centered upon the talents of men as "good" or "bad" communicators. And, as long as the communicational universe is divided into "good" speakers or listeners and "bad" speakers or listeners or, by extension, into "good" or "bad" writers or readers, the nature of communication can be neither conceptualized nor investigated. Further, if communication is seen as only the expression of the abilities or the personalities of individual men, its nature will remain hidden behind more primary misconceptions about the nature of man.

The intellectual history of Western society could be written in terms of philosophies which describe man as basically good but influenced by evil, or basically bad but influenced by good. A variation on the same theme is provided by those who see man as neutral but torn by the tug-of-war between the imp who rides the left shoulder and the angel on the right. There are those too, who, more discriminating than their fellows who generalize upon all men, distribute good and evil along racial or geographical lines. But the theme remains the same.

Ray L. Birdwhistell is professor of communication at the University of Pennsylvania. He is author of *Kinesics and Context.*

Western man is psycholinguistically dichotomous. That is, he finds it comfortable, logical, and reasonable to divide the universe into paired categories like tall and short, good and bad, black and white, and simple and complex. We should not be surprised to discover that when man began to investigate man, he should find dichotomous categories such as rational and irrational and intellectual and emotional both familiar and natural.

It has not been sufficient to describe man's *behavior* as either rational or emotional. Western man has always believed that any behavior which the observer sees has to have been the result of a behaver, a causal agent. So, he located emotion in the glandular complex somewhere below the rib case, rationality in the head. By association, "bad" became located with the emotions, "good" with mentality. To be good it was necessary to keep any of the evil from leaking out of the lower aspects of the body (the nether regions) into the upper. Parenthetically, while maintaining the same devotion to the original dichotomy, "experts" have recently advised us not to be *too* mental. They tell us that we should learn to control our emotions properly. And, while I listen respectfully to my fellows who advocate temperance in emotions, I am old enough to remember when temperance meant total abstention.

But what has this to do with communication? By and large those who have discussed communication have been concerned with the production of words and their *proper* usage. Communication has been seen as the result of mental activity which is distorted by emotional activity. Thus, the conception has been that the brain, by definition a naturally good producer of logical thoughts composed of words with precise meanings, emits these under proper stimulation. That is, good, clean, logical, rational, denotative, semantically correct utterances are emitted out of the head if the membrane between mind and body efficiently separates this area of the body from that which produces the bad, dirty, illogical, irrational, connotative, and semantically confusing adulterants. Good communication thus takes place if the unadulterated message enters the ear of the receiver and goes through a clean pipe into an aseptic brain. Of course, it is recognized that the brain may be either imperfect or out of repair. The focus upon communication and its measurement from this perspective is dominated by such an atomistic and loaded conception of man and his behavior that research or theory about communication becomes prescriptive rather than descriptive.

Communication, furthermore, in logical extension of these preconceptions, is seen as a process remarkably like that portrayed in the cartoon strips. Man A sends words, assembled grammatically by certain rules, through the air in little balloons into the ear of Man B, who runs them through his mental machinery and sends response sentences in little balloons into the ear of A and so on. It is presumed that if both A and B have properly learned their grammar, have good enough dictionaries which they studied adequately, spoke loud enough and were neither of them deaf, and did not become too emotional, communication has taken place. It is further assumed that by the study of these words, utilizing the same grammars and dictionaries, an outsider will be able to ascertain what it is that was communicated.

With such philosophies as these, scholars were hardly encouraged to look at the actual behavior of communication. The records which we are able to review about early conceptions of communication are records left by literate men. Not only were these men literate, but they were devoted to the perfection of literacy. It is scarcely surprising that they placed such a high evaluation upon reading and writing that they unconsciously conceived the spoken language to be a clumsy and imperfect derivation of the written. Such a position cannot possibly reveal that the written language is rather a special shorthand of the spoken. A majority of all discussions of communication have thus been phrased in terms of the passage of words from writer to reader, from speaker to auditor. The accompanying behavior, even when recognized as coterminous with the words, has been by and large relegated to a position of being, at best, a modifier of the messages carried by the words. More commonly, the accompanying behavior is seen to interfere with the transmission of meaning, and "good" communication depends upon the elimination or reduction of the extraneous circumlexical behavior.

Let us pause for a moment to consider this more fully. By such definitions as these preconceptions invoke, communication is that process whereby A, having information not possessed by B, passes that information or some portion of it on to B. B then, in response, informs A what he has received. Hopefully, B responds in a way that makes it possible for A to repeat or amend the message to make the original information more completely accessible to B. It requires little thought to recognize that communication is thus restricted to those situations in which we have a teacher (A) and a learner (B), A possessing and sending the knowledge, B receiving it. If we examine as communicative *only* situations like the relationships between a priest and the parishioner, a sergeant and a private, a doctor and a patient, an omnipotent parent and a totally dependent child, we are going to have a very special conception of communication. And we are likely to think of these situations in a very narrow and limited way. We shall return to this point later in our discussion.

It has been this conception which has occasioned much of the prevalent misuse of that highly useful tool, information theory. As a theory or as a model, information theory is not to be denigrated because borrowers have misused it. However, at its simplest—and, unfortunately, it has been the simplest conception of the work of the information theorists which has been borrowed by specialists from other fields—information theory sets out the following model:

In Figure 8.1, a black box, A, has only three pieces of information in it. These are □ □ and △. A has a transmission orifice (a) through which the information passes on its way to B, a black box with a reception orifice (b). All of the difficulties of encoding or decoding which intervene between A and B are described as "noise." By this theory, the information to be found in B following transmission as compared with the information emitted by A—if the noise is taken into account—can be regarded as a measure of the communication. Now,

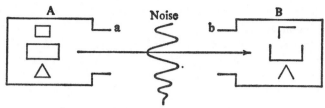

Fig. 8.1: Information theory model

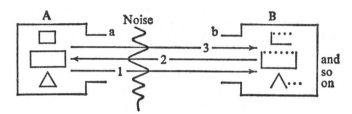

Fig. 8.2: Information theory model expanded

as far as I know, no information theorist is so naive as to fail to see that the situation is much more complicated than this and that this is hardly a model for the exhaustive examination of human behavior.

Customarily, a second diagram is designed to come closer to, although not to be taken as more than a model of, certain very limited real situations:

Figure 8.2 indicates that A and B have orifices (a) and (b) which are both senders and receivers. Thus, (1) is a stimulus message, which is followed by a response (2) from B. This message (2) is a corrective to A who sends (3). B responds to (3) by correcting the originally received message. He then transmits the shape of the correction back to A who then sends another message, and so on. This model represents a theoretical position which is elegant and attractive, particularly so since it is so easily relatable to simplistic psychological models about man. It is a fine model of certain aspects of a telegraphic system, of a telephonic or radio message system, but it is not about the structured behavior which constitutes *social* communication—or, at least, as a model it relegates to "noise" such a major proportion of all social communication as to make the model, as it stands, of little value to the communication theorist as a device for the investigation of the significant elements of human communication. Information theory has been of incalculable value in delineating fields for investigation for the student of communication analysis. It has been an efficient instrument for the location of communicational problems—it is not a tool for the solution of many of them. Its greatest utility has come from the fact that it serves to desentimentalize the message process. With such an outline of our universe of investigation, we are freed to tackle problems which had not been seen before. Moreover, information models provide excellent tools for the description of myths about unilateral transmission of knowledge. It can make especially clear those situations which are so constructed that the respondent can only inform the sender about imperfect transmission. We shall return to make use of this model later in our discussion.

One of the reasons that inappropriately borrowed models such as these—and there are many which are more popular and far less descriptive—have come into usage as ways of describing human communication is that they stand the test of naive review. That is, such models "feel right" to us. Or to say it another way, this kind of stimulus-response model is descriptive of communication in a way in which we were taught to reflect upon it. When we introspect about an interaction, a conversation, an interchange, our memory is that our discussion was a dialogue during which silence was interrupted by vocalization, followed by silence, followed by silence, followed by vocalization, and so on (see Fig. 8.3).

Our memory (or an observation which is made in terms of this preconception) tells us thus that communication is, at its simplest, a dialogue. It seems to be structured like a play, made up of more or less serial messages which are punctuated by silences in which nothing is happening. This is a folk reflection which happens to coincide with an overextended information model. Emerging social communication theory based upon behavioral research, however, maintains that this is not the case at all. We get an entirely different picture of communication if we recognize that communication is not just what happens in one channel. We cannot investigate communication by isolating and measuring one channel, the acoustic (that is, the sound-sending and sound-receiving channel). Communication, upon investigation, appears to be a system which makes use of the channels of all of the sensory modalities. By this model, communication is a continuous process utilizing the various channels and the combinations of them as appropriate to the particular situation. Figure 8.4 abstracts this model.

If we think of Channel 1 as being in Figure 8.4 the audio-acoustic (vocal) channel, Channel 2 as the kinesthetic-visual channel, Channel 3 would be the odor-producing-olfactory channel. Channel 4 would be the tactile and so on. Thus, while no single channel is in constant use, one or more channels are always in operation. Communication is the term which I apply to this continuous process.

The structured and systematic organization of the behavior of the individual channels I describe as infracommunicational. Thus, the scientific discipline of linguistics examines language in its broadest sense. Language and paralanguage is that formal behavior which utilizes the audio-acoustic channel and is an infracommunicational system. We can no more understand communication by exhaustive investigation of language and paralanguage than we can understand physiology by, say, the exhaustive investigation of the circulatory or nervous system.

Channel 2, the kinesthetic-visual channel, is utilized by communicative body motion. Kinesics is the discipline concerned with such behavior. Communicational body motion, like language and paralanguage, is organized into an infracommunicational system. I and other students of the infracommunicational systems have been studying the structures of these systems and have been trying

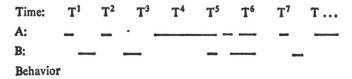

Fig. 8.3: Patterns of vocalization/silence alternation

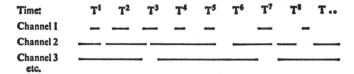

Fig. 8.4: Channels of communication

to discover how they interact or combine in the communication process. This is not the occasion to discuss the technical problems involved here. Let me say only that as experimentation proceeds, the intimate relationship between them becomes more evident. Certainly by the time one deals with phrases or sentences, their roles are inseparable. Since we have only the most preliminary knowledge about the tactile, the gustatory, or the olfactory channels, it is impossible at this time to predict their special contributions to the communicative process. It is already clear, however, that they are ultimately inseparable in the larger system.

What led to the decision to abandon the older model which maintained that communication was essentially a verbal (and lexical at that) process, modified by gestures, pushing and holding, tasting and odor emitting and receiving? As late as 1955 a leading scholar told me that he thought of communication as a picture —language being the image-figure, body motion being the frame around it. Certainly the traditional version makes good sense. It has the further virtue that it requires no new special training for the investigator. A trained philosopher or psychologist or a team of judges equipped with a good dictionary can study a verbal transcript, hold all other behavior as constant, and derive a judgment about communication. This is a perfectly useful and limited conception of *derived* human behavior. From my point of view, such a conception as: "Verbal (actually lexical) material when modified by other behavior (which is not examined, but assumed constant or trivial) equals communication," builds in an experimental error exactly as one which would describe the physiological system as endocrine or circulatory behavior with the other component systems held constant or as of trivial influence. One of the unfortunate results of this kind of thinking has been a plethora of discussion of "nonverbal communication" which is no more than an inversion of the earlier model. Experimentation using such a model has been interesting but largely noncontributory. The simplest answer is that the data of interaction, once examined, demanded a reorganization of basic theory. The old theories were just too limited to explain the observed behavior. In short, they are insufficiently productive theories.

Traditionally, as outlined above, communication has been discussed as a psychological process. The emphasis has been placed upon the individual sender or receiver. Logically, such investigations have stressed mechanisms of central concern to the psychologist. Perception, afferent-efferent nerve systems, and learning studies have dominated research from this perspective. From the point of view of the analyst of social communication, these studies are more directly relevant to the nature, state, and activity of the sensory modality and perhaps to the channel. They are of concern to him in communication research only when he seeks to understand particular distortional behaviors in particular interactional situations. For him, communication is a social, not a psychological phenomenon; psychological reductionism serves only to obscure the central issues involved in the investigation of human interaction.

Albert Scheflen has elucidated this point, in lectures, by analogy with the impossibility of understanding a baseball game by the summation of the behavior of the individual players. As he has pointed out, even if it were possible to exhaustively describe the behavior of each of the eighteen men involved, such a technique would be so inefficient as to indefinitely postpone our comprehension of the game. On the other hand, he continues, once we understand the regularities imposed by the game, it is relatively easy to measure the individual performances of the players. Such an operation will not *explain* individual variations in behavior, but it does point them up for further examination.

Research on human communication as a systematic and structured organization could not be initiated until we had some idea about the organization of society itself. So long as we conceived of communication as merely a mechanical process of action and reaction—either trial and error or the result of some kind of contract between individual men—its systematic nature remained as hidden from investigation as was that of physiology a hundred years ago. Physiological processes could not be detected so long as all research upon the body was predicated upon the proposition that the behavior of the body was to be described as the sum of the behaviors of the individual organs plus some mysterious implanted force called life. Vesalius tells how medieval anatomists, sitting high on a chair above the cadaver of a pig, pointed out to faithful students the "natural" parts of the body. His philosophical ruminations about the functions of these parts effectively prevented any but the most heretical from suggesting that this was not a particularly productive exercise. Even when grave robbers provided the anatomist with human cadavers and the anatomist himself wielded the dissecting knife, his preconceptions precluded discovery.

It is well to remember that physiology as we know it is less than a century old. The discovery of electricity led to the development of information about neural processes: the emergence of modern biochemistry laid the groundwork for endocrinology: clinical and, particularly, military medicine established a basis for the comprehension of the circulatory system. However, until the living system as a whole was examined, modern physiology with its complex considerations of homeostasis, balance, and organization of its subsystems, could not be conceived.

As long as the investigation of communication was limited to the dissection of the cadaver of speech, writing—by anatomists who used imperfectly understood Latin rules of grammar to describe its parts, and relied on introspectively derived dictionaries to determine its meanings—the communication process could not be detected, much less understood. This operation, like the researches, psychological or sociological that depend on its products, can do no more than prescriptive or deceptively elaborate but clearly inconclusive correlation studies. No statistical procedure can assemble bark, dead leaves, maple sugar, and the ashes from a burning log into a comprehensible tree.

The accumulating scientific behavioral investigations of many societies, human and animal, over the past half-century have led us to the point where we have had to recognize that for both men and animals society is a natural habitat, that both are by nature social. When growing sophistication carried us beyond either simple instinct theory or equally simple learning theory to the point where we could recognize the necessary interdependence of members of social groupings, animal or human, atomistic explanations no longer sufficed to elucidate either individual or group behavior.

This has occasioned major revolutions in theory. It has made us recognize that man did not, in his special wisdom, invent society. We have been forced to see that even the earliest complex animals were born into a social system to which they had to be adapted if they were to subsist—that these social groupings were organized so that the functions of sustaining life are complexly distributed. The individual member could not sustain life without certain special relationships with his fellows. Within the past decade the old formula of evolution (from inanimate to animate—from single-cell to multicelled animals—from sea dweller to land dweller, through the amphibians—to man—to society) has been restated. Today we know that while man *may* be the only animal to have culture, he is certainly not the first to be social.

We have had to re-turn our attention to social learning: if animals were not merely systems which responded to the genetic, the instinctual, imperative, how did they become part of the complex behavioral systems which the ethologists and comparative psychologists have described for us? We have no clear evidence yet of any animal engaging in teaching, but (if we do not allow ourselves to be misled by charming studies of bees, termites, and ants) it is clear that they learn.

The psychologist has made tremendous strides in delineating some of the mechanisms of animal learning—there are even studies that contain suggestive ideas about certain aspects of human learning—but we are here concerned with the transmission system between the members of a social grouping, rather than with its particular mechanism within the organism. Our attention has been redirected toward that process by which the member of the group makes and maintains contact with his fellows so that patterned participation is possible.

There is an increasing body of evidence that not only do animals signal relational states like anger and sexual readiness to one another (and even these in a far more complex manner than hitherto surmised) but that age, grade, status, courtship, territoriality, play, mood, states of health and of alarm or well-being are completely and intricately patterned and learned. To be viable members of their social groupings, fish, birds, mammals, and man must engage in significant symbolization—must learn to recognize, receive, and send ordered messages. In other words, the individual must learn to behave in appropriate ways which permit the other members of the group to recognize and anticipate his behavior. Society is that way in which behavior is calibrated so that existence is not a process of continuous and wasteful trial and error.

9

PERFORMANCES

Erving Goffman

BELIEF IN THE PART ONE IS PLAYING

When an individual plays a part he implicitly requests his observers to take seriously the impression that is fostered before them. They are asked to believe that the character they see actually possesses the attributes he appears to possess, that the task he performs will have the consequences that are implicitly claimed for it, and that, in general, matters are what they appear to be. In line with this, there is the popular view that the individual offers his performance and puts on his show "for the benefit of other people." It will be convenient to begin a consideration of performances by turning the question around and looking at the individual's own belief in the impression of reality that he attempts to engender in those among whom he finds himself.

At one extreme, one finds that the performer can be fully taken in by his own act; he can be sincerely convinced that the impression of reality which he stages is the real reality. When his audience is also convinced in this way about the show he puts on—and this seems to be the typical case—then for the moment at least, only the sociologist or the socially disgruntled will have any doubts about the "realness" of what is presented.

At the other extreme, we find that the performer may not be taken in at all by his own routine. This possibility is understandable, since no one is in quite as good an observational position to see through the act as the person who puts it on. Coupled with this, the performer may be moved to guide the conviction of his audience only as a means to other ends, having no ultimate concern in the conception that they have of him or of the situation. When the individual has

Erving Goffman is professor of sociology at the University of Pennsylvania. He is the author of *The Presentation of Self in Everyday Life, Stigma, Relations in Public, Interaction Ritual,* and *Frame Analysis.*

no belief in his own act and no ultimate concern with the beliefs of his audience, we may call him cynical, reserving the term "sincere" for individuals who believe in the impression fostered by their own performance. It should be understood that the cynic, with all his professional disinvolvement, may obtain unprofessional pleasures from his masquerade, experiencing a kind of gleeful spiritual aggression from the fact that he can toy at will with something his audience must take seriously. . . .[1]

I have suggested two extremes: an individual may be taken in by his own act or be cynical about it. These extremes are something a little more than just the ends of a continuum. Each provides the individual with a position which has its own particular securities and defenses, so there will be a tendency for those who have traveled close to one of these poles to complete the voyage. Starting with lack of inward belief in one's role, the individual may follow the natural movement described by Park:

> It is probably no mere historical accident that the word person, in its first meaning, is a mask. It is rather a recognition of the fact that everyone is always and everywhere, more or less consciously, playing a role . . . It is in these roles that we know each other; it is in these roles that we know ourselves.[2]
>
> In a sense, and in so far as this mask represents the conception we have formed of ourselves—the role we are striving to live up to—this mask is our truer self, the self we would like to be. In the end, our conception of our role becomes second nature and an integral part of our personality. We come into the world as individuals, achieve character, and become persons.[3]

While we can expect to find natural movement back and forth between cynicism and sincerity, still we must not rule out the kind of transitional point that can be sustained on the strength of a little self-illusion. We find that the individual may attempt to induce the audience to judge him and the situation in a particular way, and he may seek this judgment as an ultimate end in itself, and yet he may not completely believe that he deserves the valuation of self which he asks for or that the impression of reality which he fosters is valid. Another mixture of cynicism and belief is suggested in Kroeber's discussion of shamanism:

> Next, there is the old question of deception. Probably most shamans or medicine men, the world over, help along with sleight-of-hand in curing and especially in exhibitions of power. This sleight-of-hand is sometimes deliberate; in many cases awareness is perhaps not deeper than the foreconscious. The attitude, whether there has been repression or not, seems to be as toward a pious fraud. Field ethnographers seem quite generally convinced that even shamans who know that they add fraud nevertheless also believe in their powers, and especially in those of other shamans: they consult them when they themselves or their children are ill.[4]

FRONT

I have been using the term "performance" to refer to all the activity of an individual which occurs during a period marked by his continuous presence before a particular set of observers and which has some influence on the observers. It will be convenient to label as "front" that part of the individual's performance which regularly functions in a general and fixed fashion to define the situation for those who observe the performance. Front, then, is the expressive equipment of a standard kind intentionally or unwittingly employed by the individual during his performance. For preliminary purposes, it will be convenient to distinguish and label what seem to be the standard parts of front.

First, there is the "setting," involving furniture, décor, physical layout, and other background items which supply the scenery and stage props for the spate of human action played out before, within, or upon it. A setting tends to stay put, geographically speaking, so that those who would use a particular setting as part of their performance cannot begin their act until they have brought themselves to the appropriate place and must terminate their performance when they leave it. It is only in exceptional circumstances that the setting follows along with the performers; we see this in the funeral cortège, the civic parade, and the dreamlike processions that kings and queens are made of. In the main, these exceptions seem to offer some kind of extra protection for performers who are, or who have momentarily become, highly sacred. These worthies are to be distinguished, of course, from quite profane performers of the peddler class who move their place of work between performances, often being forced to do so. In the matter of having one fixed place for one's setting, a ruler may be too sacred, a peddler too profane. . . .

If we take the term "setting" to refer to the scenic parts of expressive equipment, one may take the term "personal front" to refer to the other items of expressive equipment, the items that we most intimately identify with the performer himself and that we naturally expect will follow the performer wherever he goes. As part of personal front we may include: insignia of office or rank; clothing; sex, age, and racial characteristics; size and looks; posture; speech patterns; facial expressions; bodily gestures; and the like. Some of these vehicles for conveying signs, such as racial characteristics, are relatively fixed and over a span of time do not vary for the individual from one situation to another. On the other hand, some of these sign vehicles are relatively mobile or transitory, such as facial expression, and can vary during a performance from one moment to the next.

It is sometimes convenient to divide the stimuli which make up personal front into "appearance" and "manner," according to the function performed by the information that these stimuli convey. "Appearance" may be taken to refer to those stimuli which function at the time to tell us of the performer's social statuses. These stimuli also tell us of the individual's temporary ritual state, that is, whether he is engaging in formal social activity, work, or informal recreation, whether or not he is celebrating a new phase in the season cycle or in his life-cycle. "Manner" may be taken to refer to those stimuli which function at the time to warn us of the interaction role the performer will expect to play in the oncoming situation. Thus a haughty, aggressive manner may give the impression that the performer expects to be the one who will initiate the verbal interaction and direct its course. A meek, apologetic manner may give the impression that the performer expects to follow the lead of others, or at least that he can be led to do so. . . .

However specialized and unique a routine is, its social front, with certain exceptions, will tend to claim facts that can be equally claimed and asserted of other, somewhat different routines. For example, many service occupations offer their clients a performance that is illuminated with dramatic expressions of cleanliness, modernity, competence, and integrity. While in fact these abstract standards have a different significance in different occupational performances, the observer is encouraged to stress the abstract similarities. For the observer this is a wonderful, though sometimes disastrous, convenience. Instead of having to maintain a different pattern of expectation and responsive treatment for each slightly different performer and performance, he can place the situation in a broad category around which it is easy for him to mobilize his past experience and stereo-typical thinking. Observers then need only be familiar with a small and hence manageable vocabulary of fronts, and know how to respond to them, in order to orient themselves in a wide variety of situations. Thus in London the current tendency for chimney sweeps and perfume clerks to wear white lab coats tends to provide the client with an understanding that the delicate tasks performed by these persons will be performed in what has become a standardized, clinical, confidential manner.

There are grounds for believing that the tendency for a large number of different acts to be presented from behind a small number of fronts is a natural development in social organization. Radcliffe-Brown has suggested this in his claim that a "descriptive" kinship system which gives each person a unique place may work for very small communities, but, as the number of persons becomes large, clan segmentation becomes necessary as a means of providing a less complicated system of identifications and treatments.[5] We see this tendency illustrated in factories, barracks, and other large social establishments. Those who organize these establishments find it impossible to provide a special cafeteria, special modes of payment, special vacation rights, and special sanitary facilities for every line and staff status category in the organization, and at the same time they feel that persons of dissimilar status ought not to be indiscriminately thrown together or classified together. As a compromise, the full range of diversity is cut at a few crucial points, and all those within a given bracket are allowed or obliged to maintain the same social front in certain situations.

In addition to the fact that different routines may employ the same front, it is to be noted that a given social front tends to become institutionalized in terms of the abstract stereotyped expectations to which it gives rise, and tends to take on a meaning and stability apart from the specific tasks which happen at the time to be performed in its name. The front becomes a "collective representation" and a fact in its own right.

When an actor takes on an established social role, usually he finds that a particular front has already been established for it. Whether his acquisition of the role was primarily motivated by a desire to perform the given task or by a desire to maintain the corresponding front, the actor will find that he must do both.

Further, if the individual takes on a task that is not only new to him but also unestablished in the society, or if he attempts to change the light in which his task is viewed, he is likely to find that there are already several well-established fronts among which he must choose. Thus, when a task is given a new front we seldom find that the front it is given is itself new.

Since fronts tend to be selected, not created, we may expect trouble to arise when those who perform a given task are forced to select a suitable front for themselves from among several quite dissimilar ones. Thus, in military organizations, tasks are always developing which (it is felt) require too much authority and skill to be carried out behind the front maintained by one grade of personnel and too little authority and skill to be carried out behind the front maintained by the next grade in the hierarchy. Since there are relatively large jumps between grades, the task will come to "carry too much rank" or to carry too little. . . .

I have suggested that social front can be divided into traditional parts, such as setting, appearance, and manner, and that (since different routines may be presented from behind the same front) we may not find a perfect fit between the specific character of a performance and the general socialized guise in which it appears to us. These two facts, taken together, lead one to appreciate that items in the social front of a particular routine are not only found in the social fronts of a whole range of routines but also that the whole range of routines in which one item of sign-equipment is found will differ from the range of routines in which another item in the same social front will be found. Thus, a lawyer may talk to a client in a social setting that he employs only for this purpose (or for a study), but the suitable clothes he wears on such occasions he will also employ, with equal suitability, at dinner with colleagues and at the theater with his wife. Similarly, the prints that hang on his wall and the carpet on his floor may be found in domestic social establishments. Of course, in highly ceremonial occasions, setting, manner, and appearance may all be unique and specific, used only for performances of a single type of routine, but such exclusive use of sign-equipment is the exception rather than the rule.

DRAMATIC REALIZATION

While in the presence of others, the individual typically infuses his activity with signs which dramatically highlight and portray confirmatory facts that might otherwise remain unapparent or obscure. For if the individual's activity is to become significant to others, he must mobilize his activity so that it will express *during the interaction* what he wishes to convey. In fact, the performer may be required not only to express his claimed capacities during the interaction but also to do so during a split second in the interaction. Thus, if a baseball umpire is to give the impression that he is sure of his judgment, he must forgo the moment of thought which might make him sure of his judgment; he must give an instantaneous decision so that the audience will be sure that he is sure of his judgment.[6]

It may be noted that in the case of some statuses dramatization presents no problem, since some of the acts which are instrumentally essential for the completion of the core task of the status are at the same time wonderfully adapted, from the point of view of communication, as means of vividly conveying the qualities and attributes claimed by the performer. The roles of prizefighters, surgeons, violinists, and policemen are cases in point. These activities allow for so much dramatic self-expression that exemplary practitioners—whether real or fictional —become famous and are given a special place in the commercially organized fantasies of the nation. . . .

Similarly, the proprietor of a service establishment may find it difficult to dramatize what is actually being done for clients because the clients cannot "see" the overhead costs of the service rendered them. Undertakers must therefore charge a great deal for their highly visible product—a coffin that has been transformed into a casket—because many of the other costs of conducting a funeral are ones that cannot be readily dramatized.[7] Merchants, too, find that they must charge high prices for things that look intrinsically expensive in order to compensate the establishment for expensive things like insurance, slack periods, etc., that never appear before the customers' eyes.

The problem of dramatizing one's work involves more than merely making invisible costs visible. The work that must be done by those who fill certain statuses is often so poorly designed as an expression of a desired meaning, that if the incumbent would dramatize the character of his role, he must divert an appreciable amount of his energy to do so. And this activity diverted to communication will often require different attributes from the ones which are being dramatized. Thus to furnish a house so that it will express simple, quiet dignity, the householder may have to race to auction sales, haggle with antique dealers, and doggedly canvass all the local shops for proper wallpaper and curtain materials. To give a radio talk that will sound genuinely informal, spontaneous, and relaxed, the speaker may have to design his script with painstaking care, testing one phrase after another, in order to follow the content, language, rhythm, and pace of everyday talk.[8] Similarly, a *Vogue* model, by her clothing, stance, and facial expression, is able expressively to portray a cultivated understanding of the book she poses in her hand; but those who trouble to express themselves so appropriately will have very little time left over for reading. As Sartre suggested: "The attentive pupil who wishes to *be* attentive, his eyes riveted on the teacher, his ears open wide, so exhausts himself in playing the attentive role that he ends up by no longer hearing anything."[9] And so individuals often find themselves with the dilemma of expression *versus* action. Those who have the time and talent to perform a task well may not, because of this, have the time or talent to make it apparent that they are performing well. It may be said that some organizations resolve this dilemma by officially delegating the dramatic function to a specialist who will spend his time expressing the meaning of the task and spend no time actually doing it. . . .

IDEALIZATION

It was suggested earlier that a performance of a routine presents through its front some rather abstract claims upon the audience, claims that are likely to be presented to them during the performance of other routines. This constitutes one way in which a performance is "socialized," molded, and modified to fit into the understanding and expectations of the society in which it is presented. I want to consider here another important aspect of this socialization process—the tendency for performers to offer their observers an impression that is idealized in several different ways.

The notion that a performance presents an idealized view of the situation is, of course, quite common. Cooley's view may be taken as an illustration:

> If we never tried to seem a little better than we are, how could we improve or "train ourselves from the outside inward?" And the same impulse to show the world a better or idealized aspect of ourselves finds an organized expression in the various professions and classes, each of which has to some extent a cant or pose, which its members assume unconsciously, for the most part, but which has the effect of a conspiracy to work upon the credulity of the rest of the world. There is a cant not only of theology and of philanthropy, but also of law, medicine, teaching, even of science—perhaps especially of science, just now, since the more a particular kind of merit is recognized and admired, the more it is likely to be assumed by the unworthy.[10]

Thus, when the individual presents himself before others, his performance will tend to incorporate and exemplify the officially accredited values of the society, more so, in fact, than does his behavior as a whole.

To the degree that a performance highlights the common official values of the society in which it occurs, we may look upon it, in the manner of Durkheim and Radcliffe-Brown, as a ceremony—as an expressive rejuvenation and reaffirmation of the moral values of the community. Furthermore, in so far as the expressive bias of performances comes to be accepted as reality, then that which is accepted at the moment as reality will have some of the characteristics of a celebration. To stay in one's room away from the place where the party is given, or away from where the practitioner attends his client, is to stay away from where reality is being performed. The world, in truth, is a wedding. . . .

NOTES

1. Perhaps the real crime of the confidence man is not that he takes money from his victims but that he robs all of us of the belief that middle-class manners and appearance can be sustained only by middle-class people. A disabused professional can be cynically hostile to the service relation his clients expect him to extend to them; the confidence man is in a position to hold the whole "legit" world in this contempt.

2. Park 1950:249

3. Park 1950:250.

4. Kroeber 1952:311.

5. Radcliffe-Brown, *Oceania I*:440.

6. Pinelli 1953:75.

7. Material on the burial business used throughout this report is taken from Robert W. Habenstein, "The American Funeral Director" (unpublished Ph. D. dissertation, Department of Sociology, University of Chicago, 1954). I owe much to Mr. Habenstein's analysis of a funeral as a performance.

8. Hilton 1953:399–404.

9. Sartre 1956:60.

10. Cooley 1922:352–53.

10

SOCIAL DRAMAS AND RITUAL METAPHORS

Victor Turner

In this chapter I shall trace some of the influences that led to the formulation of concepts I developed in the course of my anthropological field work and to consider how they may be used in the analysis of ritual symbols. In moving from experience of social life to conceptualization and intellectual history, I follow the path of anthropologists almost everywhere. Although we take theories into the field with us, these become relevant only if and when they illuminate social reality. Moreover, we tend to find very frequently that it is not a theorist's whole system which so illuminates, but his scattered ideas, his flashes of insight taken out of systemic context and applied to scattered data. Such ideas have a virtue of their own and may generate new hypotheses. They even show how scattered facts may be systematically connected! Randomly distributed through some monstrous logical system, they resemble nourishing raisins in a cellular mass of inedible dough. The intuitions, not the tissue of logic connecting them, are what tend to survive in the field experience. I will try later to locate the sources of some insights that helped me to make sense of my own field data.

The concepts I would like to mention are: "social drama," "the processual view of society," "social anti-structure," "multivocality," and "polarization of ritual symbols." I mention these in the order of their formulation. All are pervaded by the idea that human social life is the producer and product of time, which becomes its measure—an ancient idea that has had resonances in the very different work of Karl Marx, Emile Durkheim, and Henri Bergson. Following Znaniecki, the renowned Polish sociologist, I had already come, before doing field work, to insist on the dynamic quality of social relations and to regard Comte's

---

Victor Turner is professor of anthropology and social thought at the University of Chicago. He is author of *The Forest of Symbols*, *The Ritual Process*, and *Dramas, Fields, and Metaphors*.

distinction between "social statics" and "social dynamics"—later to be elaborated by A. R. Radcliffe-Brown and other positivists—as essentially misleading.
The social world is a world in becoming, not a world in being (except insofar as
"being" is a description of the static, atemporal models men have in their heads),
and for this reason studies of social structure *as such* are irrelevant. They are
erroneous in basic premise because there is no such thing as "static action." That
is why I am a little chary of the terms "community" or "society," too, though
I do use them, for they are often thought of as static concepts. Such a view
violates the actual flux and changefulness of the human social scene. Here I would
look, for example, to Bergson rather than, say, to Descartes, for philosophical
guidance.

However, I am alive to the virtues of Robert A. Nisbet's warning in *Social
Change and History*[1] about the use of "becoming" and similar notions, such as
"growth" and "development," which rest fundamentally on organic metaphors.
Nisbet has drawn our attention to a whole metaphorical family of sociological and
sociophilosophical terms such as "genesis," "growth," "unfolding," "development," on the one hand, and "death," "decadence," "degeneration," "pathol-
ogy," "sickness," and so on, which take off originally from the Greek idea of
"physis." This term literally means "growth," from φύ-ειτ, to produce, Indo-
European root BHU. It is the "key concept of Greek science," φύσικη meant
"natural science," as in physiology, physiognomy, and so on. This family also
derives from the Roman and Latinized European basic concept of nature, the
Latin translation or rather mistranslation of *physis.* "Nature" is from "natus"
meaning "born," with overtones of "innate," "inherent," "immanent," from the
Indo-European root GAN. The "nature" family is cognate with the "gen" family,
generate, genital, general, gender, genus, generic, and with the Germanic kind,
kin, kindred. All these terms "have immediate and unchallengeable reference to
the organic world, to the life-cycles of plants and organisms,"[2] where they are
literal and empirical in meaning. But "applied to *social* and *cultural* phenomena
these words are not literal. They are *metaphoric.* "[3] Hence they may be misleading; even though they draw our attention to some important properties of social
existence, they may and do block our perception of others. The metaphor of social
and cultural systems as machines, popular since Descartes, is just as misleading.

I am not opposed to metaphor here. Rather, I am saying that one must pick
one's root metaphors carefully, for appropriateness and potential fruitfulness. Not
only Nisbet but Max Black, the Cornell philosopher, and others have pointed out
how "perhaps every science must start with metaphor and end with algebra; and
perhaps without the metaphor there would never have been any algebra."[4] And,
as Nisbet says:

> Metaphor is, at its simplest, a way of proceeding from the known to the unknown.
> [This corresponds, curiously, with the Ndembu definition of a symbol in ritual.] It
> is a way of cognition in which the identifying qualities of one thing are transferred
> in an instantaneous, almost unconscious, flash of insight to some other thing that

is, by remoteness or complexity, unknown to us. The test of essential metaphor, Philip Wheelwright has written, is not any rule of grammatical form, but rather the quality of semantic transformation that is brought about.[5]

Metaphor is, in fact, metamorphic, transformative. "Metaphor is our means of effecting instantaneous fusion of two separated realms of experience into one illuminating, iconic, encapsulating image."[6] It is likely that scientists and artists both think primordially in such images; metaphor may be the form of what M. Polanyi calls "tacit knowledge."

The idea of society as being like a "big animal" or a "big machine," as James Peacock has pithily put the matter,[7] would be what Stephen C. Pepper has called a "root metaphor."[8] This is how he explains the term:

> The method in principle seems to be this: A man desiring to understand the world looks about for a clue to its comprehension. He pitches upon some area of common-sense fact and tries if he cannot understand other areas in terms of this one. The original area then becomes his *basic analogy* or *root metaphor*. He describes as best he can the characteristics of this area, or if you will, "discriminates its structure." A list of its structural characteristics becomes his basic concepts of explanation and description. [E.g., the gen-words, the kin words, the nature words.] We call them a set of categories [a possibly exhaustive set of classes among which all things might be distributed]. . . . In terms of these categories he proceeds to study all other areas of fact whether uncriticized or previously criticized. He undertakes to interpret all facts in terms of these categories. As a result of the impact of these other facts upon his categories, he may qualify and readjust the categories so that a set of categories commonly changes and develops. Since the basic analogy or root metaphor normally (and probably at least in part necessarily) arises out of common sense [which is the normal understanding or general feeling of mankind, but for anthropologists this operates in a specific culture], a great deal of development and refinement of a set of categories is required if they are to prove adequate for a hypothesis of unlimited scope. Some root metaphors prove more fertile than others, have greater power of expansion and adjustment. These survive in comparison with the others and generate the relatively adequate world theories.[9]

Black prefers the term "conceptual archetype" to "root metaphor," and defines it as a "systematic repertoire of ideas by means of which a given thinker describes, by *analogical extension,* some domain to which those ideas do not immediately and literally apply."[10] He suggests that if we want a detailed account of a particular archetype, we require a list of key words and expressions, with statements of their interconnections and their paradigmatic meanings in the field from which they were originally drawn. This should then be supplemented by analysis of the ways in which the original meanings become extended in their analogical use.

The illustration Black offers of the influence of an archetype on a theorist's work is of exceptional interest to me, for this very case had a profound effect on my own early attempts to characterize a "social field." Black examines the writings of the psychologist Kurt Lewin whose "field theory" has been fruitful in generating hypotheses and stimulating empirical research. Black finds it "ironical" that Lewin

> formally disclaims any intention of using models. "We have tried," he says, "to avoid developing elaborate models; instead we have tried to represent the dynamic relations between the psychological facts by mathematical constructs at a sufficient level of generality." Well [Black goes on], there may be no specific models envisaged; yet any reader of Lewin's papers must be impressed by the degree to which he employs a vocabulary indigenous to *physical* theory. We repeatedly encounter such words as "field," "vector," "phase-space," "tension," "force," "valence," "boundary," "fluidity"—visible symptoms of a massive archetype awaiting to be reconstructed by a sufficiently patient critic.[11]

Black is not upset about all this on the ground of general principles of sound method. He feels that if an archetype, confused though it may be in details, is sufficiently rich in implicative power it may become a useful speculative instrument. If the archetype is sufficiently fruitful, logicians and mathematicians will eventually reduce the harvest to order. "There will always be competent technicians who, in Lewin's words, can be trusted to build the highways 'over which the streamlined vehicles of a highly mechanized logic, fast and efficient, can reach every important point on fixed tracks.' "[12] There, of course, we have another uninhibited flood of metaphors.

Nisbet, too, as well as Black and Pepper, holds that "complex philosophical systems can proceed from metaphorical premises." For example, Freudianism, he says, "would have little substance left once stripped of its metaphors"[13]—Oedipus complex, topographical and economic models, defense mechanisms, Eros and Thanatos, and so on. Marxism, too, sees social orders as "forming embryonically" in the "wombs" of preceding orders, with each transition akin to "birth," and requiring the assistance of the "midwife," force.

Both Black and Nisbet admit the tenacity as well as the potency of metaphors. Nisbet argues that what we usually call revolutions in thought are

> quite often no more than the mutational replacement, at certain critical points in history, of one foundation-metaphor by another in man's contemplation of universe, society, and self. Metaphoric likening of the universe to an *organism* in its structure will yield one set of derivations; derivations which become propositions in complex systems of philosophy. But when, as happened in the 17th Century, the universe is likened instead to a *machine*, not merely physical science but whole areas of moral philosophy and human psychology are affected.[14]

I believe it would be an interesting exercise to study the key words and expressions of major conceptual archetypes or foundation metaphors, both in the periods during which they first appeared in their full social and cultural settings and in their subsequent expansion and modification in changing fields of social relations. I would expect these to appear in the work of exceptionally liminal thinkers—poets, writers, religious prophets, "the unacknowledged legislators of mankind"—just before outstanding limina of history, major crises of societal change, since such shamanistic figures are possessed by spirits of change before changes become visible in public arenas. The first formulations will be in multivocal symbols and metaphors—each susceptible of many meanings, but with the core meanings linked analogically to the basic human problems of the epoch which may be pictured in biological, or mechanistic, or some other terms—these multivocals will yield to the action of the thought technicians who clear intellectual jungles, and organized systems of univocal concepts and signs will replace them. The change will begin, prophetically, "with metaphor, and end, instrumentally, with algebra." The danger is, of course, that the more persuasive the root metaphor or archetype, the more chance it has of becoming a self-certifying myth, sealed off from empirical disproof. It remains as a fascinating metaphysics. Here, root metaphor is opposed to what Thomas Kuhn has called "scientific paradigm," which stimulates and legitimates empirical research, of which it is indeed the product as well as the producer. For Kuhn, paradigms are "accepted examples of actual scientific practice—which includes law, theory, application and instrumentation together—which provide models from which spring coherent traditions of scientific research"[15]—Copernican astronomy, Aristotelian or Newtonian "dynamics," wave optics, and others. My own view of the structure of metaphor is similar to I. A. Richards' "interaction view"; that is, in metaphor "we have two thoughts of different things *active* together and supported by a single word, or phrase, whose meaning is a resultant of their *interaction.*"[16] This view emphasizes the dynamics inherent in the metaphor, rather than limply comparing the two thoughts in it, or regarding one as "substituting" for the other. The two thoughts are active together, they "engender" thought in their coactivity.

Black develops the interaction view into a set of claims:

1. A metaphorical statement has two distinct subjects—a principal subject and a "subsidiary" one. Thus if one says—as Chamfort does in an example cited by Max Black—that "the poor are the negroes of Europe," "the poor" is the principal subject and the "negroes" the subsidiary one.

2. These subjects are best regarded as "systems of things," rather than things as elements. Thus, both "poor" and "negroes" in this metaphorical relation are themselves multivocal symbols, whole semantic systems, which bring into relation a number of ideas, images, sentiments, values, and stereotypes. Components of one system enter into dynamic relations with components of the other.

3. The metaphor works by applying to the principal subject a system of "associated implications" characteristic of the subsidiary subject. In the metaphor cited, for instance, the "poor" of Europe could be regarded not only as an oppressed class, but also as sharing in the inherited and indelible qualities of "natural" poverty attributed to black Americans by white racists. The whole metaphor is thereby charged with irony and provokes a rethinking of the roles both of the (European) poor and the (American) blacks.

4. These "implications" usually consist of commonplaces about the subsidiary subject, but may, in suitable cases, consist of deviant implications established ad

hoc by the author. You need have only proverbial knowledge, as it were, to have your metaphor understood, not technical or special knowledge. A "scientific model" is rather a different kind of metaphor. Here "the maker must have prior control of a well-knit theory," says Black, "if he is to do more than hang an attractive picture on an algebraic formula. Systematic complexity of the source of the model and capacity for analogical development are of the essence."[17]

5. The metaphor selects, emphasizes, suppresses, and organizes features of the principal subject by implying statements about it that normally apply to the subsidiary subject.

I have mentioned all this merely to point out that there are certain dangers inherent in regarding the social world as "a world in becoming," if by invoking the idea "becoming" one is unconsciously influenced by the ancient metaphor of organic growth and decay. Becoming suggests genetic continuity, telic growth, cumulative development, progress, etc. But many social events do not have this "directional" character. Here the metaphor may well select, emphasize, suppress, or organize features of social relations in accordance with *plant* or *animal* growth processes, and in so doing, mislead us about the nature of the *human* social world, *sui generis*. There is nothing wrong with metaphors or, *mutatis mutandis*, with models, provided that one is aware of the perils lurking behind their misuse. If one regards them, however, as a species of liminal monster, such as I described in *The Forest of Symbols*,[18] whose combination of familiar and unfamiliar features or unfamiliar combination of familiar features provokes us into thought, provides us with new perspectives, one can be excited by them; the implications, suggestions, and supporting values entwined with their literal use enable us to see a new subject matter in a new way.

The "becoming" metaphor fits fairly well, despite the apparent quarrel between functionalists and cultural evolutionists, with the structural-functionalist orthodoxy or paradigm, that gave rise to what Kuhn would have called the "normal science" of British social anthropology when I went into the field. For functionalism, as Nisbet has argued, following Wilbert Moore, from Durkheim through Radcliffe-Brown to Talcott Parsons, tried to present a unified theory of order *and* change based on a biological metaphor—it tries to draw the *motivational* mechanisms of change from the same conditions from which are drawn the concepts of *social order.* In other words, we have here the biological notion of immanent causation, an inner growth principle, as well as a homeostatic control mechanism. The simple, like the grain of mustard seed, *grows* into the complex, through various preordained stages. There are various micromechanisms of change in each specific sociocultural system, just as in modern evolutionary theory there are in biological entities and colonies, such as tensions, strains, discrepancies, and disharmonies, which are internal, endogenous to them, and provide the motor causes for change. In the social process—meaning by "process" here merely the general course of social action—in which I found myself among the Ndembu of Zambia, it was quite useful to think "biologically" about "village life-cycles" and "domestic cycles," the "origin," "growth," and "decay" of villages, families and lineages, but not too helpful to think about change as *immanent* in the structure of Ndembu society, when there was clearly "a wind of change," economic, political, social, religious, legal, and so on, sweeping through the whole of central Africa and originating *outside* all village societies. The functionalists of my period in Africa tended to think of change as "cyclical" and "repetitive" and of time as structural time, not free time. With my conviction as to the dynamic character of social relations I saw movement as much as structure, persistence as much as change, indeed, persistence as a striking aspect of change. I saw people interacting, and, as day succeeded day, the consequences of their interactions. I then began to perceive a form in the process of social time. This form was essentially *dramatic*. My metaphor and model here was a human esthetic form, a product of *culture* not of nature. A cultural form was the model for a social scientific concept. Once more I have to admit a debt to Znaniecki (I am also indebted to Robert Bierstedt's seminal article,[19] for the following summary of his views), who, like some other social thinkers, was disposed to maintain the neo-Kantian distinction between two kinds of system—natural and cultural—which exhibit differences not only in composition and structure, but also—and most importantly—in the character of the elements that account for their coherence. Natural systems, Znaniecki always argued, are objectively given and exist independently of the experience and activity of men. Cultural systems, on the contrary, depend not only for their meaning but also for their existence upon the participation of conscious, volitional human agents and upon men's continuing and potentially changing relations with one another. Znaniecki had his own label for this difference. He called it the "humanistic coefficient," and it is this concept that sharply separated his approach from that of most of his contemporaries on the American scene. Everywhere in his work he emphasized the role of conscious agents or actors— an emphasis which his opponents were inclined to criticize as the "subjective" point of view. It is persons as the objects of the actions of others, however, not as subjects, that meet his criteria for sociological data. Among the sources of these data Znaniecki listed the personal experiences of the sociologist, both original and vicarious; observation by the sociologist, both direct and indirect; the personal experience of other people; and the observations of other people. This emphasis supported his use of personal documents in sociological research. This whole approach I continue to find most congenial.

I felt that I had to bring the "humanistic coefficient" into my model if I was to make sense of human social processes. One of the most arresting properties of Ndembu social life in villages was its propensity toward conflict. Conflict was rife in the groups of two dozen or so kinsfolk who made up a village community. It manifested itself in public episodes of tensional irruption which I called "social dramas." Social dramas took place in what Kurt Lewin might have called "aharmonic" phases of the ongoing social process. When the interests and attitudes of groups and individuals stood in obvious opposition, social dramas did seem to me to constitute isolable and minutely describable units of social process. Not every social drama reached a clear resolution, but enough did so to make it possible to state what I then called the "processional form" of the drama. I had no thought, at that time, of using such a "processual unit," as I came to call the genus of which "social drama" is a species, in cross-societal comparison. I did not think it to be a universal type, but subsequent research—including work for a paper on "An Anthropological Approach to the Icelandic Saga"[20]—has convinced me that social dramas, with much the same temporal or processual structure as I detected in the Ndembu case, can be isolated for study in societies at all levels of scale and complexity. This is particularly the case in political situations, and belongs to what I now call the dimension of "structure" as opposed to that of "communitas" as a generic mode of human interrelatedness. Yet there is communitas, too, in one stage of the social drama, as I hope to show, and perhaps the capacity of its successive phases to have continuity is a function of communitas.

Not all processual units are "dramatic" in structure and atmosphere. Many belong under the rubric of what Raymond Firth has called "social organization" and defines as "the working arrangements of society . . . the process of ordering of action and of relations in reference to given social ends, in terms of adjustments resulting from the exercise of choices by members of the society."[21] Among these "harmonic" processual units would be what I call "social enterprises," primarily economic in character, as when a modern African group decides to build a bridge, school, or road, or when a traditional Polynesian group, like Firth's Tikopia, decides to prepare tumeric, a plant of the ginger family, for ritual dye or other purposes;[22] either group is concerned with the outcomes of these decisions on social relations within the group over time. Here individual choice and considerations of utility are discriminating features.

A recent book by Philip Gulliver,[23] which is a microanalysis of social networks (another interesting metaphor to be probed with reference to how it is used by anthropologists) in two small local communities among the Ndendeuli people of southern Tanzania, also represents a conscious attempt to describe dynamic processes over a period in nondramatic terms. Gulliver wished to direct especial attention and give added emphasis to the cumulative effect of an endless series of incidents, cases, and events that might be quite as significant in affecting and changing social relationships as the more dramatic encounters. Lesser events, he argues, serve gradually to set the stage for the bigger encounters. Gulliver urges that careful attention should be paid to "the continuum of interaction amongst a given collection of people."[24] He warns that we should not "concentrate so greatly on conflict situations that we neglect the equally important situations of cooperation—though the latter are likely to be less dramatic."[25] I agree with Gulliver, though I share Freud's view that disturbances of the normal and regular often give us greater insight into the normal than does direct study. Deep structure may be revealed through surface anti-structure or counter-structure. I will not here follow up Gulliver's interesting views on such formulations as "action-set," "network," "decision making," "role playing," and others. He has a lot of sturdy wisdom on those—but they would take us from the main themes. Gulliver cautions against the view, familiar since Weber, that

> assumes a rationality in men that we know by experience is often absent. Men can misconceive a situation and its possibilities, they can be stimulated by high emotion or by depression to make moves and decisions that otherwise they might not, they can be stupid, obstinate, short-sighted, or they may be calculating, alert, intelligent, or something in between. Yet social scientists often ignore these critical factors which affect decision-makers.[26]

In the social drama, however, though choices of means and ends and social affiliation are made, stress is dominantly laid upon loyalty and obligation, as much as interest, and the course of events may then have a tragic quality. As I wrote in my book *Schism and Continuity* (1957), in which I began to examine the social drama, "the situation in an Ndembu village closely parallels that found in Greek drama where one witnesses the helplessness of the human individual before the Fates; but in this case [and also in the Icelandic one, as I have found] the Fates are the necessities of the social process."[27] Conflict seems to bring fundamental aspects of society, normally overlaid by the customs and habits of daily inter-course, into frightening prominence. People have to take sides in terms of deeply entrenched moral imperatives and constraints, often against their own personal preferences. Choice is overborne by duty.

Social dramas and social enterprises—as well as other kinds of processual units—represent sequences of social events, which, seen retrospectively by an observer, can be shown to have structure. Such "temporal" structure, unlike atemporal structure (including "conceptual," "cognitive," and "syntactical" structures), is organized primarily through relations in time rather than in space, though, of course, cognitive schemes are themselves the result of a mental process and have processual qualities. If one were able to arrest the social process as though it were a motion film and were then to examine the "still," the coexisting social relations within a community, one would probably find that the temporary structures were incomplete, open-ended, unconsummated. They would be, at most, on their way to an ending. But if one had the science-fiction means of penetrating into the minds of the arrested actors, one would undoubtedly find in them, at almost any endophysical level existing between the full brightness of conscious attention and the darker strata of the unconscious, a set of ideas, images, concepts, and so on, to which one could attach the label "atemporal structures." These are models of what people "believe they do, ought to do, or would like to do."[28] Perhaps in individual cases these are more fragmentary than structural, but if one were to look at the whole group one would find that what ideas or norms an individual lacks or fails to put into systematic relation with other ideas, other individuals do possess or have systematized. In the intersubjective collective representations of the group one would discover "structure" and "system," "purposive action patterns" and, at deeper levels, "categorical frames." These individual and group structures, carried in people's heads and nervous systems, have a steering function, a "cybernetic" function, in the endless succession of social events, imposing on them the degree of order they possess, and indeed, dividing processual units into phases. "Structure is the order in a system," as Marvin Harris has said. The phase structure of social dramas is not the product of instinct but of models and metaphors carried in the actors' heads. It is not here a case of "fire finding its own form," but of form providing a hearth, a flue, and a damper for fire. Structures are the more stable aspects of action and interrelationship. What the philosopher John Dewey has called the "more rapid and irregular events" of the social process are converted into "slower and regular rhythmic events" through the cybernetic effects of cognitive and normative/structural models. Some of the "regular rhythmic events" can be measured and expressed in statistical form. But here we shall be first of all concerned with the shape, the diachronic profile of the social drama. I would like to stress as strongly as I can that I consider this processual approach decisive as a guide to the understanding of human social behavior. Religious and legal institutions, among others, only cease to be bundles of dead or cold rules when they are seen as phases in social processes, as dynamic patterns right from the start. We have to learn to think of societies as continuously "flowing," as a "dangerous tide . . . that never stops or dies. . . . And held one moment burns the hand," as W. H. Auden once put it. The formal, supposedly static, structures only become visible through this flow which energizes them, heats them to the point of visibility—to use yet another metaphor. Their very stasis is the effect of social dynamics. The organizational foci of temporal structures are "goals," the objects of action or effort, not "nodes," mere points of diagrammatic intersection or lines of rest. Temporal structure, until at rest and therefore atemporal, is always tentative; there are always alternative goals and alternative means of attaining them. Since its foci are goals, psychological factors, such as volition, motivation, span of attention, level of aspiration, and so on, are important in its analysis; contrastingly, in atemporal structures these are unimportant, for such structures reveal themselves as already exhausted, achieved, or, alternatively as axioms, self-evident cognitive or normative frames to which action is subsequent and subordinate. Again, since the goals significantly include social goals, the study of temporal structures involves the study of the communication process, including the sources of pressures to communicate within and among groups; this leads inevitably to the study of the symbols, signs, signals, and tokens, verbal and nonverbal, that people employ in order to attain personal and group goals.

Social dramas, then, are units of aharmonic or disharmonic process, arising in conflict situations. Typically, they have four main phases of public action, accessible to observation. These are:

1. Breach of regular, norm-governed social relations occurs between persons or groups within the same system of social relations, be it a village, chiefdom, office, factory, political party or ward, church, university department, or any other perduring system or set or field of social interaction. Such a breach is signalized by the public, overt breach or deliberate nonfulfillment of some crucial norm regulating the intercourse of the parties. To flout such a norm is one obvious symbol of dissidence. In a social drama it is not a crime, though it may formally resemble one; it is, in reality, a "symbolic trigger of confrontation or encounter," to use Frederick Bailey's terms. There is always something altruistic about such a symbolic breach; always something egoistic about a crime. A dramatic breach may be made by an individual, certainly, but he always acts, or believes he acts, on behalf of other parties, whether they are aware of it or not. He sees himself as a representative, not as a lone hand.

2. Following breach of regular, norm-governed social relations, a phase of mounting *crisis* supervenes, during which, unless the breach can be sealed off quickly within a limited area of social interaction, there is a tendency for the breach to widen and extend until it becomes coextensive with some dominant cleavage in the widest set of relevant social relations to which the conflicting or antagonistic parties belong. It is now fashionable to speak of this sort of thing as the "escalation" of crisis. If it is a social drama involving two nations in one geographical region, escalation could imply a stepwise movement toward antagonism across the dominant global cleavage between communist and capitalist camps. Among the Ndembu, the phase of crisis exposes the pattern of current factional intrigue, hitherto covert and privately conducted, within the relevant social group, village, neighborhood, or chiefdom; and beneath it there becomes visible the less plastic, more durable, but nevertheless gradually changing basic Ndembu social structure, made up of relations that have a high degree of constancy and consistency—that are supported by normative patterns laid down in the course of deep regularities of conditioning, training, and social experience. Even beneath these cyclical structural changes, other changes in the ordering of social relations emerge in social dramas—those, for example, resulting from the incorporation of the Ndembu into the Zambian nation, the modern African world, the Third World, and the whole world. I discuss this aspect briefly in the Kamahasanyi case in *The Drums of Affliction*.[29] This second stage, *crisis*, is always one of those turning points or moments of danger and suspense, when a true state of affairs is revealed, when it is least easy to don masks or pretend that there is nothing rotten in the village. Each public crisis has what I now call liminal characteristics, since it is a threshold between more or less table phases of the social process, but it is not a sacred limen, hedged around by taboos and thrust away from the centers of public life. On the contrary, it takes up its menacing stance in the forum itself and, as it were, dares the representatives of order to grapple with it. It cannot be ignored or wished away.

3. This brings us to the third phase, *redressive action*. In order to limit the spread of crisis, certain adjustive and redressive "mechanisms," (and here I joyfully borrow a metaphor from physics) informal or formal, institutionalized or ad hoc, are swiftly brought into operation by leading or structurally representative members of the disturbed social system. These mechanisms vary in type and complexity with such factors as the depth and shared social significance of the breach, the social inclusiveness of the crisis, the nature of the social group within

which the breach took place, and the degree of its autonomy with reference to wider or external systems of social relations. They may range from personal advice and informal medication or arbitration to formal juridical and legal machinery, and, to resolve certain kinds of crisis or legitimate other modes of resolution, to the performance of public ritual. The notion of "escalation" can apply to this phase also: in a complex, industrial society, for example, antagonists might move a dispute up from a court of lower jurisdiction to the supreme court through intervening judicial stages. In the Icelandic *Njál's Saga,* escalation characterizes the set of dramas that make up the saga. It begins with simple breaches of local order, minor crisis, and informal redress, mainly at the level of household communities in a small region of the South Quarter of tenth-century Iceland, which cumulate, despite temporary settlement and adjustment of claims, until, finally, a public breach that triggers the tragic main drama takes place: a *goði,* or priest chieftain, who is also a good man, is killed wantonly by his foster brother, the most intransigent of Njál's sons. The resulting crisis phase involves a major cleavage between factions consisting of the major lineages and *sibs* (here meaning bilateral vengeance and blood-compensation groups) in southern and southeastern Iceland, and the parties seek redress at the Althing and Fifth Court, the general assembly of Icelanders. *Njál's Saga* pitilessly reveals how Iceland just could not produce the adequately sanctioned judicial machinery to handle large-scale crisis, for inevitably, the Althing negotiations break down, and there is regression to crisis again, sharpened crisis, moreover, that can only be resolved by the total defeat and attempted annihilation of one party. The fact that though there was a general assembly of Icelanders there was no Icelandic nation was represented by the absence of national laws with teeth in them, the teeth of punitive sanctions jointly applied by the leading men of all four Quarters. I have discussed elsewhere[30] some of the various historical, environmental, and cultural reasons why the Icelandic commonwealth failed to become a state, lost its independence (in 1262), and accepted Norwegian overlordship. I was set on the track of these reasons by treating the saga literature as a series of social dramas. The sagas reveal that local feuds which could only be transiently contained by enlightened individuals generated forces over time which sundered Iceland and revealed the weakness of its uncentralized, acephalous polity. When one is studying social change, at whatever social level, I would give one piece of advice: study carefully what happens in phase three, the would-be redressive phase of social dramas, and ask whether the redressive machinery is capable of handling crises so as to restore, more or less, the status quo ante, or at least to restore peace among the contending groups. Then ask, if so, how precisely? And if not, why not? It is in the redressive phase that both pragmatic techniques and symbolic action reach their fullest expression. For the society, group, community, association, or whatever may be the social unit, is here at its most "self-conscious" and may attain the clarity of someone fighting in a corner for his life. Redress, too, has its liminal features, its being "betwixt and between," and, as such, furnishes a distanced replication and critique of the events leading up to and composing the "crisis." This replication may be in the rational idiom of a judicial process, or in the metaphorical and symbolic idiom of a ritual process, depending on the nature and severity of the crisis. When redress fails there is usually regression to crisis. At this point direct force may be used, in the varied forms of war, revolution, intermittent acts of violence, repression, or rebellion. Where the disturbed community is small and relatively weak vis-à-vis the central authority, however, regression to crisis tends to become a matter of endemic, pervasive, smoldering factionalism, without sharp, overt confrontations between consistently distinct parties.

4. The final phase I distinguished consists either of the *reintegration* of the disturbed social group or of the social recognition and legitimization of irreparable schism between the contesting parties—in the case of the Ndembu this often meant the secession of one section of a village from the rest. It frequently happened then that after an interval of several years, one of the villages so formed would sponsor a major ritual to which members of the other would be expressly invited, thus registering reconciliation at a different level of political integration. I describe one such ritual, Chihamba, in *Schism and Continuity*[31] and how it functioned to reconcile the sponsoring village, Mukanza, with several other villages, including one formed by the fission of one of its previous component sections.

From the point of view of the scientific observer the fourth phase—that of temporary climax, solution, or outcome—is an opportunity for taking stock. He can now analyze the continuum synchronically, so to speak, at this point of arrest, having already fully taken into account and represented by appropriate constructs the temporal character of the drama. In the particular case of a "political field," for example, one can compare the ordering of political relations which preceded the power struggle erupting into an observable social drama with that following the redressive phase. As likely as not, as Marc Swartz and I pointed out in the Introduction to *Political Anthropology*,[32] the scope and range of the field will have altered; the number of its parts will be different; and their magnitude will be different. More importantly, the nature and intensity of the relations between parts, and the structure of the total field, will have changed. Oppositions may be found to have become alliances, and vice versa. Asymmetric relations may have become egalitarian ones. High status will have become low status and vice versa. New power will have been channeled into old and new authority and former authority defenestrated. Closeness will have become distance, and vice versa. Formerly integrated parts will have segmented; previously independent parts will have fused. Some parts will no longer belong to the field, others will have entered it. Institutionalized relationships will have become informal; social regularities will have become irregularities. New norms and rules may have been generated during attempts to redress conflict; old rules will have fallen into disrepute and have been abrogated. The bases of political support will have altered. Some components of the field will have less support, others more, still others will have fresh support, and some will have none. The distribution of the factors of legitimacy will have changed, as also the techniques used by leaders to gain compliance. These changes can be observed, ascertained, recorded, and in some cases their indices can even be measured and expressed in quantitative terms.

Yet through all these changes, certain crucial norms and relationships—and other seemingly less crucial, even quite trivial and arbitrary—will persist. The explanations for both constancy and change can, in my opinion, only be found by systematic analysis of *processual* units and temporal structures, by looking at phases as well as atemporal systems. For each phase has its specific properties, and each leaves its special stamp on the metaphors and models in the heads of men involved with one another in the unending flow of social existence. In keeping with my explicit comparison of the temporal structure of certain types of social processes with that of dramas on the stage, with their acts and scenes, I saw the phases of social dramas as cumulating to a climax. I would point out too that at the linguistic level of "parole," each phase has its own speech forms and styles, its own rhetoric, its own kinds of nonverbal languages and symbolisms. These vary greatly, of course, cross-culturally and cross-temporally, but I postulate that there will be certain important generic affinities between the speeches and languages of the crisis phase everywhere, of the redressive phase everywhere, of the restoration of peace phase everywhere. Cross-cultural comparison has never applied itself to such a task because it has limited itself to atemporal forms and structures, to the products of man's social activity abstracted from the processes in which they arise, and, having arisen, which they channel to a varying extent. It is much easier to prop onself on the "paradigmatic" crutch, coolly remote from the vexatious competitiveness of social life. Such cross-cultural comparison, moreover, cannot be made until we have many more extended-case studies. An extended-case history is the history of a single group or community over a considerable length of time, collected as a sequence of processual units of different types, including the social dramas and social enterprises mentioned already. This is more than plain historiography, for it involves the utilization of whatever conceptual tools social anthropology and cultural anthropology have bequeathed to us. "Processualism" is a term that includes "dramatistic analysis." Processual analysis assumes cultural analysis, just as it assumes structural-functional analysis, including more static comparative morphological analysis. It negates none of these, but puts dynamics first. Yet in the order of presentation of facts it is a useful strategy to present a systematic outline of the principles on which the institutionalized social structure is constructed and to measure their relative importance, intensity, and variation under different circumstances with numerical or statistical data if possible. In a sense the social activities from which one elicits a "statistical structure" can be characterized as "slow process," in that they tend to involve the regular repetition of certain acts, as distinct from the rapid process seen, for example, in social dramas, where there is a good deal of uniqueness and arbitrariness. All is in motion but some social flows move so slowly relatively to others that they seem almost as fixed and stationary as the landscape and the geographical levels under it, though these too, are, of course, forever in slow flux. If one has the data to analyze a sequence of crucial processual units over, say, twenty or thirty years, one can see changes even in the slow processes, even in societies thought of as "cyclical" or "stagnant," to use the favorite terms of some investigators. But I do not want to present here methods of studying social processes— I have given examples of this in *Schism and Continuity*,[33] *The Drums of Affliction*, the analysis of the *Mukanda* rites in *Local-Level Politics*, and in various papers. This approach is an abiding concern of mine, and within it I made my first attempt to produce a paradigm for the analysis of ritual symbols. Nor do I wish just now to discuss the theory of conflict which obviously influences my "dramatistic" formulation.

I want rather to do something quite different, as far different as "anti-structure" is from "structure," though processualism would see both terms as intrinsically related, perhaps even as not contradictory in the ultimate, nondualistic sense. A mathematical equation needs its minus signs as well as its pluses, negatives as well as positives, zeros as well as numbers: the equivalence of two expressions is affirmed by a formula containing negations. It may be said that positive structuralism can only become processualism by accepting the concept of social anti-structure as a theoretical operator. There is nothing really mystical about this. For example, Znaniecki argued with reference to what he called "cultural systems":

> The people who share a certain set of interconnected systems (and among these systems there are usually also certain social groups—territorial, genetic or telic) may be more or less conscious of this fact, and more or less willing to influence one another for the benefit of their common civilization and to influence this civilization for their mutual benefit. This consciousness and willingness, in so far as they exist, constitute a social bond uniting these people over and above any formal social bonds which are due to the existence of regulated social relations and organized social groups. . . . If the term "community" is limited to the humanistic reality embracing such phenomena . . . as the development of new cultural ideals and attempts at their realization apart from organized group action, . . . there is no doubt but that a "community" in this sense can be scientifically studied, and that sociology is the science to study it as one of the specifically social data.[34]

Here we have what I would call "communitas" or social antistructure (since it is "a bond uniting . . . people over and above any formal social bonds," that is, "positive" structure) being regarded as a reputable object of scientific study. In my recent work I have been struck by the way in which pilgrimages exemplify such anti-structural communities—perhaps Znaniecki had observed communitas in its Polish setting most vividly made visible at the hilly shrine of Our Lady of Czestochowa, as I have seen it in its Mexican setting at the basilica of Our Lady of Guadalupe, and more recently at the remote shrine of Our Lady of Knock in County Mayo, Ireland.

In a sense, the "social drama" concept is within the brackets of positive structural assertions; it is concerned mainly with relations between persons in their status-role capacity and between groups and subgroups as structural segments. "Conflict" is the other side of the coin of "cohesion" here, with "interest" the motive binding or separating these persons, these men in servitude to structural rights and obligations, imperatives, and loyalties. But, as Znaniecki pointed out, there is a bond uniting people over and above their formal bonds. Therefore one should not limit one's inquiry to a particular social structure but look for the grounds of action in generic communitas. This was the reason that prompted me to begin the research that has so far resulted in only a few publications, one of which was *The Ritual Process* (1969). The reader should not think that I have forgotten the importance of the sociology of symbols. There are symbols of structure and symbols of anti-structure, and I wish to consider first the social bases of both. Like Znaniecki, I looked for evidences of the development of new cultural ideals and attempts at their realization and at various modes of social behavior that did not proceed from the structural properties of organized social groups. I found in the data of art, literature, philosophy, political and juridical thought, history, comparative religion, and similar documents far more suggestive ideas about the nature of the social than in the work of colleagues doing their "normal social science" under the then prevailing paradigm of structural functionalism. These notions are not always put forward with direct or obvious reference to social relations—often they are metaphorical or allegorical—sometimes they appear in the guise of philosophical concepts or principles, but I see them as arising in the experience of human coactivity, including the deepest of such experiences. For example, I have recently been paying attention to the notion that the familiar distinction made in Zen Buddhism between the concepts *prajñā* (which very approximately means "intuition") and *vijñāna* (very roughly, "reason" or "discursive understanding") are rooted in the contrasting social experiences I have described, respectively, as "communitas" and "structure." Briefly to recapitulate the argument in *The Ritual Process*, the bonds of communitas are anti-structural in that they are undifferentiated, equalitarian, direct, nonrational (though not *ir*rational), I-Thou or Essential We relationships, in Martin Buber's sense. Structure is all that holds people apart, defines their differences, and constrains their actions, including social structure in the British anthropological sense. Communitas is most evident in "liminality," a concept I extend from its use in Van Gennep's *Les Rites de passage* to refer to any condition outside or on the peripheries of everyday life. It is often a sacred condition or can readily become one. For example, the world over, millenarian movements originate in periods when societies are in liminal transition between different social structures.

With these distinctions in mind let us now look at what Suzuki Daisetz Teitaro, probably the greatest scholar in Zen studies writing English, has to say about the *prajñā/vijñāna* contrast. Suzuki (1967) writes:

> To divide is characteristic of *vijñana*, (discursive understanding,) while with *prajñā* (intuition) it is just the opposite. *Prajñā* is the self-knowledge of the whole, in contrast to *vijñāna,* which busies itself with parts. *Prajñā* is an integrating principle,

while *vijñāna* always analyzes. *Vijñāna* cannot work without having *prajñā* behind it; parts are parts of the whole; parts never exist by themselves, for, if they did, they would not be parts—they would even cease to exist.[35]

This "wholeness" of *prajñā* resembles Znaniecki's idea of "community" as the real source of the interconnection of cultural and social systems and subsystems. These cannot be interconnected on their own level, so to speak; it would be misleading to find their integration there—what unites them is their common ground in living community or communitas. Other explanations are specious and artificial, however ingenious, for partness can never by itself be made into wholeness—something additional is required. Suzuki expresses this with exceptional clarity as follows:

> *Prajñā* is ever seeking unity on the grandest possible scale, so that there could be no further unity in any sense; whatever expressions or statements it makes are thus naturally beyond the order of *vijñāna*. *Vijñāna* subjects them to intellectual analysis, trying to find something comprehensible according to its own measure. But *vijñāna* cannot do this for the obvious reason that *prajñā* starts from where *vijñāna* cannot penetrate. *Vijñāna*, being the principle of differentiation, can never see *prajñā* in its oneness, and it is because of the very nature of *vijñāna* that *prajñā* proves utterly baffling to it.[36]

Prajñā, as Suzuki understands it, would be the source of "foundation"—or root metaphors, since these are eminently synthetic: on them *vijñāna* then does its work of discriminating the structure of the root metaphor. A metaphor is a "*prajñā*-artifact," if you like, a system of categories derived from it would be a "*vijñāna*-artifact." Blaise Pascal's distinction between *l'esprit de finesse* and *l'esprit de géometrie* may represent something similar.

I would probably differ from Suzuki in some ways and find common ground with Durkheim and Znaniecki in seeking the source of both these concepts in human social experience, whereas Suzuki would probably locate them in the nature of things. For him communitas and structure would be particular manifestations of principles that can be found everywhere, like *Yin* and *Yang* for the Chinese. Indeed, *prajñā*,—intuition—is its becoming conscious of itself. Yet we find him identifying *prajñā* with the Primary Man *(gennin)* in "his spontaneous, free-creating, non-teleological activities"; he also declares that *prajñā* is "concrete in every sense of the term. . . . [and therefore] the most dynamic thing we can have in the world."[37] These (and other) characteristics seem to me to be ways of talking about human experiences of that mode of coactivity I have called communitas.

I had not read Suzuki, though I had seen quotations from his writings, before I wrote *The Ritual Process*, but in that book, on the basis of experiences and observations in the field, social experience as a person, readings in the experiences of others, and the fruits of discussion with others I came up with several statements about communitas that resemble Suzuki's on *prajñā*. For example: communitas is society experienced or seen as "an unstructured or rudimentarily structured and relatively undifferentiated *comitatus*, community, or even communion of equal individuals."[38] Also: "communitas is a relationship between concrete, historical, idiosyncratic individuals," "a direct, immediate and total confrontation of human identities."[39] In other passages I link communitas with spontaneity and freedom, and structure with obligation, jurality, law, constraint, and so on.

But though one would have to bring within the scope of the paradigm "structure" many features of the social drama, and the other Kurt Lewin-based concepts I used, to describe the Kenneth Burkean "scene" on which the "actors" played out their "acts" with regard to certain "purposes"—such as "field," "locomotion," "positive and negative valence," and the like, still some of its aspects escape into the domain of anti-structure, and even of communitas. For instance, after showing the various structural strategies employed by the main political faction of Mukanza Village to prevent the ambitious Sandombu from making good his claim to the headmanship, notably their accusation that he had slain his classificatory mother by sorcery, I show how when his rivals had forced him into exile they began to repine, for reasons of communitas. Their consciences began to trouble them over him, as often happens when people deny their past experiences of communitas. They began to think: was he not blood of their blood, born from the same womb (the very term used for a matrilineal group) as they? Had he not been part of their corporate life? Had he not contributed to their welfare, paying for the education of their children, finding jobs for their young men when he was a foreman on a government road gang for the PWD? His plea to return was allowed. A new misfortune led to a new divination, which found, *inter alia*, that Sandombu had not been guilty of the sorcery of which he had been accused, that an outsider had caused the woman's death. A ritual was performed, for which Sandombu paid a goat. He planted a tree symbolic of matrilineage unity to his dead mother's sister, and he and his main antagonists prayed there to the shades and were reconciled. Powdered white clay, symbolizing the basic values of Ndembu society—good health, fertility, respect for elders, observance of kinship dues, honesty, and the like, briefly a master symbol of structure imbued with communitas—was sprinkled on the ground round the tree and the several kinds of kin present were anointed with it. Here clearly it was not mere self-interest or the letter of the law that prevailed but its spirit, the spirit of communitas. Structure is certainly present but its divisiveness is muted into a set of interdependencies: it is seen here as a social instrument or means, neither as an end in itself nor as providing goals for competition and dissidence. One might also postulate that the coherence of a completed social drama is itself a function of communitas. An incomplete or irresoluble drama would then manifest the absence of communitas. Consensus on values, too, is not the basic level here. Consensus, being spontaneous, rests on communitas, not on structure.

The term "anti-structure" is only negative in its connotations when seen from the vantage point or perspective of "structure." It is no more "anti" in its essence than the American "counter-culture" is merely "counter." "Structure" may just as legitimately be viewed as "anti" or at least as a set of limitations, like William Blake's "limit of opacity." If one is interested in asking some of the questions formulated in the earliest days of sociology, and now relegated to the philosophy of history, such as, "Where are we going?" or "Where is society going?" or "Whither goes the world?" it might be well to see structure as limit rather than as theoretical point of departure. The components of what I have called anti-structure, such as communitas and liminality, are the conditions for the production of root metaphors, conceptual archetypes, paradigms, models for, and the rest. Root metaphors have a "thusness" or "thereness" from which many subsequent structures may be "unpacked" by *vijñāna* consciousness or *l'esprit de géometrie*. What could be more positive than this? For metaphors share one of the properties I have attributed to symbols. I don't mean multivocality, their capacity to resonate among many meanings at once like a chord in music, though root metaphors are multivocal. I mean a certain kind of polarization of meaning in which the subsidiary subject is really a depth world of prophetic, half-glimpsed images, and the principal subject, the visible, fully known (or thought to be fully known component), at the opposite pole to it, acquires new and surprising contours and valences from its dark companion. On the other hand, because the poles are "active together" the unknown is brought just a little more into the light by the known. To be brought fully into the light is the work of another phase of liminality: that of imageless thought, conceptualization at various degrees of abstractness, deduction both informal and formal, and inductive generalization. Genuine creative imagination, inventiveness, or inspiration goes beyond spatial imagination or any skill in forming metaphors. It does not necessarily associate visual images with given concepts and proportions. Creative imagination is far richer than imagery; it does not consist in the ability to evoke sense impressions and it is not restricted to filling gaps in the map supplied by perception. It is called "creative" because it is the ability to create concepts and conceptual systems that may correspond to nothing in the senses (even though they may correspond to something in reality), and also because it gives rise to unconventional ideas. It is something like Suzuki's view of *prajñā* in its purity. This is the very creative darkness of liminality that lays hold of the basic forms of life. These are more than logical structures. Every mathematician and every natural scientist would, I think, agree with Mario Bunge that

> without imagination, without inventiveness, without the ability to conceive hypotheses and proposals, nothing but the "mechanical" operations can be performed, i.e., the manipulations of apparatus and the application of computation algorithms, the art of calculating with any species of notation. The invention of hypotheses, the devising of techniques, and the designing of experiments, are clear cases of imaginative, [purely "liminal"] operations, as opposed to "mechanical" operations. They are not purely logical operations. Logic *alone* is as incapable of leading a person to new ideas as grammar *alone* is incapable of inspiring poems and as theory of harmony *alone* is incapable of inspiring sonatas. Logic, grammar, and musical theory enable us to detect formal mistakes and good ideas, as well as to develop good ideas, but

they do not, as it were, supply the "substance," the happy idea, the new point of view.[40]

This is the "flash of the fire that can." To revert to Suzuki's interpretation of the Zen vocabulary,[41] *vijñāna* alone is incapable of leading a person to new ideas. Yet in the social and natural worlds as we know them both *vijñāna* and *prajñā* are necessary for scientific theories, poems, symphonies, for intuition and reasoning or logic. In the area of social creativity—where new social and cultural forms are engendered—both structure and communitas are necessary, or both the "bound" and the "unbound." To view "societas" as human process, rather than as an atemporal timeless or eternal system modeled either on an organism or a machine, is to enable us to concentrate on the relationships, existing at every point and on every level in complex and subtle ways, between communitas and structure. We must devise approaches that safeguard both archmodalities, for in destroying one we destroy both and must then present a distorted account of man with man. What I call liminality, the state of being in between successive participations in social milieux dominated by social structural considerations, whether formal or unformalized, is not precisely the same as communitas, for it is a sphere or domain of action or thought rather than a social modality. Indeed, liminality may imply solitude rather than society, the voluntary or involuntary withdrawal of an individual from a social-structural matrix. It may imply alienation from rather than more authentic participation in social existence. In *The Ritual Process* I was mostly concerned with the social aspects of liminality, for my emphasis was still on Ndembu society. There liminality occurs in the middle phase of the rites of passage which mark changes in a group's or individual's social status. Such rites characteristically begin with the subject's being symbolically killed or separated from ordinary secular or profane relationships, and conclude with a symbolic birth or reincorporation into society. The intervening liminal period or phase is thus betwixt and between the categories of ordinary social life. I then tried to extend the concept of liminality to refer to any condition outside, or on the peripheries of, everyday life, arguing that there was an affinity between the middle in sacred time and the outside in sacred space. For liminality among the Ndembu is a sacred condition. Among them, too, it is one in which communitas is most evident. The bonds of communitas, as I said, are anti-structural in the sense that they are undifferentiated, equalitarian, direct, nonrational (though not irrational), I-Thou relationships. In the liminal phase of Ndembu rites of passage, and in similar ties the world over, communitas is engendered by ritual humiliation, stripping of signs and insignia of preliminal status, ritual leveling, and ordeals and tests of various kinds, intended to show that "man thou art dust!" In hierarchical social structures communitas is symbolically affirmed by periodic rituals, not infrequently calendrical or tied in with the agricultural or hydraulic cycle, in which the lowly and the mighty reverse social roles. In such societies, too, and here I begin to draw my examples from European and Indian history, the religious ideology of the powerful idealizes humility, orders of religious specialists undertake ascetic lives, and *per contra*, cult groups among those of low status play with symbols of power and authority. The world over, millenarian and revivalistic movements, as I mentioned earlier, originate in periods when societies are in liminal transition between major orderings of social structural relations. In the second half of *The Ritual Process* I gloss my illustrations from the traditional cultures of Africa, Europe, and Asia with comments on modern culture, referring briefly to Leo Tolstoy, Mahatma Gandhi, Bob Dylan, and such current phenomena as the Chicago Vice Lords and the California Hell's Angels. In 1970–1971 in Chicago a number of our seminar papers explored further aspects of communitas and liminality in connection with such topics as bureaucratic corruption in India and the Hindu tradition of gift-giving (Arjun Appadurai), trickster myths in Africa (Robert Pelton), Russian populism in the nineteenth century (Daniel Kakulski), countercultural communes (David Buchdahl), and symbol and festival in the "Évènements de Mai–Juin 1968," the Paris student uprising (Sherry Turkel). All these stimulating contributions contained a number of symbols of anti-structure, both as liminality and communitas. One student of Russian literature, Alan Shusterman, presented a paper on another type of liminality. His paper, called "Epileptics, Dying Men and Suicides: Liminality and Communitas in Dostoevsky," showed how in the Christian tradition as represented in Dostoevsky's Russia, "the lack of communitas . . . creates both an unviable liminality and the feeling of despair." His argument extended the application of the concept of liminality to ranges of data I have not myself taken into account. But with regard to this question of the contrast between the liminalities of solitude and communitas much remains to be said. Many existentialist philosophers, for example, view what they term "society" as something inimical, hostile to the authentic nature of the individual. Society is what some of them term the "seat of objectivity" and therefore antagonistic to the subjective existence of the individual. To find and become himself, the individual must struggle to liberate himself from the yoke of society. Society is seen by existentialism as the captor of the individual, very much in the same way as Greek religious thought, particularly in the mystery cults, viewed the body as the captor of the soul. To my mind these thinkers have failed to make the analytical distinction between communitas and structure; it is structure they seem to be talking about when they speak as Martin Heidegger does of the social self as the "unauthentic part of human-being." But they are really addressing themselves to a communitas of "authentic individuals" or trying to liberate such individuals from social structure. One might ask who is the audience of these prolific if alienated prophets of uncommunication? But this is diverging from my main topic, which is to consider the relations between social drama, processual analysis, anti-structure, and semantic study of ritual symbols.

Since I regard cultural symbols including ritual symbols as originating in and sustaining processes involving temporal changes in social relations, and not as timeless entities, I have tried to treat the crucial properties of ritual symbols as being involved in these dynamic developments. Symbols instigate social action.

The question I am always asking the data is: "How do ritual symbols work?"

In my view they condense many references, uniting them in a single cognitive and affective field. Here I will refer the reader to my Introduction to *Forms of Symbolic Action*.[42] In this sense ritual symbols are "multivocal," susceptible of many meanings, but their referents tend to polarize between physiological phenomena (blood, sexual organs, coitus, birth, death, catabolism, and so on) and normative values of moral facts (kindness to children, reciprocity, generosity to kinsmen, respect for elders, obedience to political authorities, and the like). At this "normative" or "ideological" pole of meaning, one also finds reference to principles of organization: matriliny, patriliny, kingship, gerontocracy, age-grade organization, sex-affiliation, and others. The drama of ritual action—the singing, dancing, feasting, wearing of bizarre dress, body painting, use of alcohol or hallucinogens, and so on, causes an exchange between these poles in which the biological referents are ennobled and the normative referents are charged with emotional significance. I call the biological referents, insofar as they constitute an organized system set off from the normative referents, the "orectic pole," "relating to desire or appetite, willing and feeling," for symbols, under optimal conditions, may reinforce the will of those exposed to them to obey moral commandments, maintain covenants, repay debts, keep up obligations, avoid illicit behavior. In these ways *anomie* is prevented or avoided and a milieu is created in which a society's members cannot see any fundamental conflict between themselves as individuals and society. There is set up, in their minds, a symbiotic interpenetration of individual and society. All this would fit in admirably with Durkheim's notion of morality as essentially a social phenomenon. But I am suggesting that this process only works where there is already a high level of communitas in the society that performs the ritual, the sense that a basic generic bond is recognized beneath all its hierarchical and segmentary differences and oppositions. Communitas in ritual can only be evoked easily when there are many occasions outside the ritual on which communitas has been achieved. It is also true that if communitas can be developed within a ritual pattern it can be carried over into secular life for a while and help to mitigate or assuage some of the abrasiveness of social conflicts rooted in conflicts of material interest or discrepancies in the ordering of social relations.

However, when a ritual does work, for whatever reason, the exchange of qualities between the semantic poles seems, to my observation, to achieve genuinely cathartic effects, causing in some cases real transformations of character and of social relationships. I refer, for example, to the extended case history of an Ndembu patient in a series of curative rituals, Kamahasanyi by name, in *The Drums of Affliction*,[43] for an illustration of this. The exchange of qualities makes desirable what is socially necessary by establishing a right relationship between involuntary sentiments and the requirements of social structure. People are induced to want to do what they must do. In this sense ritual action is akin to a sublimation process, and one would not be stretching language unduly to say that its symbolic behavior actually "creates" society for pragmatic purposes—including in society both structure and communitas. More than the manifestation of cognitive paradigms is meant here. Paradigms in ritual have the orectic function of impelling to action as well as to thought. What I have been doing in all this, perhaps, is trying to provide an alternative notion to that of those anthropologists who still work, despite explicit denials, with the paradigm of Radcliffe-Brown and regard religious symbols as reflecting or expressing social structure and promoting social integration. My view would also differ from that of certain anthropologists who would regard religion as akin to a neurotic symptom or a cultural defense mechanism. Both these approaches treat symbolic behavior, symbolic actions, as an "epiphenomenon," while I try to give it "ontological" status. Hence my interest in ritualization in animals. Of course, there remains the problem, to which I cannot claim to have given any satisfactory answer, and which several of my critics have mentioned (for example, Charles Leslie in a perceptive review of *The Ritual Process*), not of "why people continue to create symbolic ritual systems in a world full of secularization processes, but of why these systems ever go stale or become perverted, and of why people lose belief, often with anxiety, fear and trembling, but also with a sense of liberation and relief."[44] Here I would point to the long endeavor of Emile Durkheim to establish the reality of the object of faith which in his view has always been society itself under innumerable symbolic guises, without accepting the intellectual content of traditional religions. Traditional religions were doomed in his eyes by the development of scientific rationalism, but he believed that his theory would save what it seems to be destroying by showing that in the last analysis men have never worshiped anything other than their own society. Yet it is clear that Durkheim's "religion of society" like Auguste Comte's "religion of humanity" has never had much appeal to the mass of ordinary mankind. I cite these authors because both clearly felt the need of quickly converting their "sense of liberation" into a moral, even pseudoreligious system, a curious egolatry. Here I think the whole matter of symbolism is very relevant, as is the matter of what is symbolized. And here, too, I think the distinction between communitas and social structure has a contribution to make.

NOTES

1. Nisbet 1969:3–4.
2. Nisbet 1969:3–4.
3. Nisbet 1969:4. Turner's italics
4. Black 1962:242.
5. Wheelwright 1969:4.
6. Wheelwright 1969:4.
7. Peacock 1969:173.
8. Pepper 1942:39–29.
9. Pepper 1942:91–92.
10. Black 1962:241.
11. Black 1962:241.
12. Black 1962:242.
13. Nisbet 1969:5.
14. Nisbet 1969:6.
15. Kuhn 1962:10.
16. Richards 1936:93.
17. Black 1962:239.
18. Turner 1967.
19. Bierstedt 1968:599–601.
20. Turner 1971.

21. Firth 1964:45.
22. Firth 1967:416–464.
23. Gulliver 1971.
24. Gulliver 1971:354.
25. Gulliver 1971:354.
26. Gulliver 1971:356–357.
27. Turner 1957:94.
28. Richards 1939:160.
29. Turner 1968a.
30. Turner 1971.
31. Turner 1957:288–317.
32. Turner and Swartz 1966.
33. Turner:1968b.
34. Znaniecki 1936: Chapter 3.

35. Suzuki 1967:66–67.
36. Suzuki 1967:67.
37. Suzuki 1967:80.
38. Suzuki 1967:96.
39. Suzuki 1967:131–132.
40. Bunge 1962:80.
41. But not Nagarjuna's; he sees logic and intuition as essentially equal expressions of the only adequate stance toward *prajñā*, silence.
42. Turner 1970.
43. Turner 1968a: Chapters 4–6.
44. Leslie 1970:702–704.

PART FOUR

SHAMANISM, TRANCE, MEDITATION

INTRODUCTORY NOTE

Performances occur in everyday life. But the opposite is also true: performances occur in extraordinary places, invoking such force that special techniques are necessary to control and hedge them; special preparations are required to take performers to a peak experience and to bring them back from it. Parallel techniques are necessary for audiences. Theatres may be thought of as precincts where realities are doubled, tripled, multiplied: for a great performer does not stop being herself even as she becomes another. The paradox of acting is that in watching a Joan MacIntosh play Mother Courage by Brecht one does not see MacIntosh less, but more, even as you see into Mother Courage herself.

Shamanism is the oldest technique of theatrical performing. Primary shamanism originated in paleolithic times in central Asia (and perhaps in southwest Europe), and spread throughout Eurasia, across the bridge to Alaska, and down into all of both New World continents. Shamanism is also found in Africa, Australia, New Guinea—everywhere. Probably it arose independently in several places. The techniques of shamanism are singing, dancing, chanting, costuming, story telling. The shaman goes on a journey, or is transformed into other beings, or represents the struggle among beings. In any case, multiple realities are superimposed, much as in the decorated caves of Europe, Africa, and Australia paintings are superimposed on each other. Like the actor in the Western tradition, the shaman is both himself and others at the same time. The audience is engaged at a very deep level; participation is a necessary condition for the shaman's feats.

For the past four hundred years theatre in the West has become an adjunct of the industrial process. Plays are produced, they are repeated as long as there are customers, actors are meat displayed in the shop window. This kind of theatre has always been resisted on at least two levels. Popular entertainments, including popular religion, maintain old rituals and a close interaction among performers and spectators. And the avant-garde or experimental theatre depends on practices which are traditional in many parts of the world. When The Performance Group

123

went to India in 1976 we found more in common with Kathakali, Jatra, and village performances than with the Indian "modern theatre" which was derived from nineteenth-century Britain.

The section which follows does not include selections from some key texts. We recommend Weston La Barre's *The Ghost Dance,* Mircea Eliade's *Shamanism,* Claude Lévi-Strauss's "The Sorcerer and His Magic," S. Giedion's *The Eternal Present: The Beginnings of Art,* and Andreas Lommel's *Shamanism: The Beginnings of Art.* Peter T. Furst's "The Roots and Continuities of Shamanism" (*artscanada* magazine, December 1973/January 1974) is a good popular overview of the subject.

11

THE SHAMAN'S TENT OF THE EVENKS

A. F. Anisimov

Depending on the occasion, the shamanistic performance *(kamlanye)* took place among the Evenks either in the ordinary dwelling-tent or in a special structure, the shaman's tent. The search for lost reindeer, the shaman's performance before a journey, the foretelling of the future, and other analogous activities of the shaman were usually held in an ordinary tent. Performances on more important occasions were usually conducted in a special tent. On two sides of this tent stood a row of wooden figures, representations of shamanistic spirits symbolizing the mythical shamanistic clan-river. The number of spirit-figures varied according to the "powers" of the shaman, but the type of construction was always the same. . . .

The shamanistic tree, *turu*, was an inseparable attribute in any shamanistic performance, whether it was held in an ordinary tent or in a special structure, the *shevenchedek*. The *turu* was a tall young larch. It was placed in the center of the shaman's tent, with its top drawn through the smoke hole, or laid over the tent with the top covering the smoke hole. It played, on the one hand, the role of guardian-spirit of the tent and, on the other, served the shaman as a larch tree ladder for his journey into the upper world. During intervals between shamanistic activities, the shaman's spirit-helpers rested on its branches and gathered strength. In the shamans' concepts, the *turu* larch symbolized the shamanistic world-tree. . . .

The shaman's tent was built gradually. While the shaman fasted and, by means of hunger, excessive smoking, and other similar methods, prepared himself to carry out the performance, the other clansmen built the framework of the tent. After two or three days the shaman dispatched his *khargi* (one of his souls transformed into a totem animal) to the shaman ancestor-spirits in the lower

---

A. F. Anisimov is a senior member of the State Museum of Ethnology of Leningrad. He has published extensively on the Evenks.

world, and through this animal-double, the chief spirit-helper of the shaman, learned their will and received advice relative to the forthcoming shamanistic activities. This was outwardly manifested by the shaman's going into a neurotic sleep accompanied by vivid dreams.

The shaman's dream was interpreted by him as communication with his animal-double (the totem) with his ancestor-spirits (known to us from previous works as mythical beings of a dual nature—half-animal, half-human—of the type of the Australian *alcheringa* [sic)]. Depending on the results of this communication, the shaman determined the sequence in the construction of the tent. After this, the performance proper began.

The whole construction complex of the shaman's tent was divided into three parts: the tent proper and two "galleries"—the *darpe* and the *onang*. The *darpe* always oriented to the east of the entrance to the tent, and the *onang* to the west. The tent was built in the usual way, but of much larger dimensions in order to accommodate all the clansmen. The entrance of the tent was oriented to the east. In the center of the tent a small fire was kindled. Through the smoke hole hung a slim young larch, symbolizing the *turu* or world-tree. The lower end (or butt) of the *turu* was placed next to the fire pit. . . . On the side opposite the entrance, there stood a small platform [raft] made of wooden images of salmon trout spirits. On this sat the shaman, floating down the shamanistic river into the lower world —the *khergu*. His drum served him in this case as a boat, and his shaman's drumstick as a paddle. If the action took place on dry land, a skin from the forehead of wild deer, elk, and bear was spread out under the shaman. To the shaman's right and left were arranged wooden representations of knives, bear spears, a young larch with its butt split three ways, and images of the pike and the trout [*mayga*], one on each side. Some of these spirits served the shaman as weapons in the struggle against alien and inimical spirits; others (the trout and the pike) constituted his guard. The circle of ground occupied by the tent symbolized the middle world, or in other cases was interpreted as the shaman's island in the middle of the mythical shamanistic clan-river, the headwaters of which were thought to be in the upper world *(ugu),* the middle course of which ran on the earth (*dulyu,* "the middle world"), and the mouth of which was in the lower world *(khergu).*

To the east, opposite the entrance to the tent, the *darpe* was set up—a long row of living young larches and various figures of shamanistic spirits. At the opposite end of the tent the *onang* was set up. If the first, the *darpe*, symbolized the head of the river, the upper world, and the tent the middle world, then the *onang* embodied the lower world, the river of the dead, and accordingly it was constructed from dead wood—a wind-fallen tree. Around the *darpe* stood the *nelget,* small poles made of young larches torn out of the earth with their roots. The *nelget* were stuck in the earth by their tops with their roots pointing upward. In this position they represented the shamanistic tree of the upper world, which, in Evenk concept, grows with its roots upward, in the upper earth, and with its top pointing towards men (towards the middle world). In winter, when it was impossible to uproot a larch, it was felled and the butt split with a wedge, so as to give the appearance of branching roots. In the opposite row, the *onang*, the *nelget* stood with roots downward because the shamanistic tree of the lower world was thought to be located below the middle earth and hence must grow with roots pointing downward. All this is explained by the fact that besides the one principal shamanistic tree which, like the shamanistic clan-river, connected all three worlds in a unified mythical shamanistic world of the spirits (the roots of this tree, according to the shamans, were in the lower world, and its top reached the outermost part—the sky—of the upper world), the Evenks also recognized the existence of shamanistic trees, specific and proper only to each of the three worlds. Under their roots, it was thought, the shaman rested and gathered strength and knowledge, whenever he happened to be in one of the other worlds. In this respect, the significance of these trees is similar to that of the great shamanistic tree. In the middle earth, where men live, these trees correspond to the shaman's larch, in which dwells the shaman's external soul—his animal-double. The shaman's drum and his other accoutrements were made from the wood of this tree. In concepts connected with the shamanistic river, the functions of the shamanistic trees are taken over by the islands where there live spirits—female shamans, the guardians and proprietresses of the clan's mythical road, the river.

On top of the *nelget* were laid long, thin larches. In the *darpe* their roots were pointed to the east (towards the upper world), in the *onang* to the west. In the *darpe*, between the larch poles *(nelget)*, were set the anthropomorphic figures of shamanistic spirits *(khomoken)*. According to the shamans, they were the chief watchmen of the road to the upper world and guardians of the *omi*, souls of the clansmen; they live on the banks of the mythical clan river and vigilantly guard all entrances to the clan's storehouse of souls—*omiruk* (lit. "receptacle of souls"). In addressing them, the shaman called them grandmothers, grandfathers, ancestors, forefathers, guardians of the clan. In Evenk, *khomoty* means bear. In this connection, let us recall that the figure of a bear in human form occurs in the shamanistic rugs of the Evenks, where bears are drawn in the role of the chief spirit-lord among other zoomorphic totem-spirits. Addressing them as ancestor-spirits, forefathers, and guardians of the souls of the clan is quite natural if we keep in mind the undoubted totemic base of the bear cult among the Evenks.

In the center of the *darpe*, [reaching] from one end to the other, stood wooden representations of *kalir*, mythical giant wild reindeer. The *kalir* was thought to be the shaman's most powerful spirit. In the shamanistic performance he undertook all the most difficult assignments of the shaman, appearing in the role of a supreme animal, in that of a fighting bull of incomparable strength and exceptional dexterity, and as herd-leader of all the other shamanistic spirits. On the backs of the *kalir* were arranged rows of figures of the shamanistic spirits, *delbon* or salmon trout. These swam in the shamanistic river, guarding the approaches to the clan's storehouse of souls. Two huge figures of spirits, the *gutken* (pike), were placed before the entrance to the tent. In the mid-portion of each figure a square opening was cut, symbolizing the entrance to the upper world. These spirits were thought to be the watchmen and guardians of the doors from the middle to the upper world. Between them stood two anthropomorphic figures of the spirits *(khomoken)* and between these were laid, parallel or crosswise, two bars or simply larchwood sticks, forming the *ugdupka* or entrance (gate) to the middle world. After the participants in the shamanistic ceremony had entered the tent, squeezing through the *darpe* and the *ugdupka,* the sticks (bars) were lowered or crossed and the entrance to the middle world was considered closed. On either side of the *darpe* and around the circumference of the tent were placed live young larches forming an unbroken wall which, according to the shamans, guarded or covered up the mythical shamanistic clan-river.

On the side opposite the *darpe* (i.e., on the western side of the tent) the *onang* was arranged, symbolizing the lower reaches of the mythical shamanistic clan-river. Beside the *onang* stood dry spirit-larches, watchmen of the shaman, and numerous figures of birds—loons, ducks, geese—and other shamanistic spirits, guarding the clan's road to the lower world. Beside the tent stood two anthropomorphic figures *(sheven)* representing any two of the closest ancestor-spirits of the shaman which he had called from the land of *khergu* [the lower world] to guard the entrance to the world of the dead. Beyond these were placed two huge blocks of wood representing *shegan,* eelpouts. They lay across the *onang* barring the exit and entrance to the land of the dead. The eelpouts gulped down like frogs any spirits inhabiting the lower world who might attempt to pass its bounds, penetrate into the middle earth among people, and cause harm to them. In the center of the *onang* was a very large figure of the mythical shamanistic elk, and on both sides of the elk, figures of Siberian stags [marals]. On these was placed a large figure of a salmon trout with several openings (traps) and beside this stood, like a paling, dried larches with figures of shamanistic bird-spirits at the tops. This whole construction, in its over-all appearance, was reminiscent of a fishweir. After the shaman had succeeded in capturing an evil spirit, he placed it in the trap formed by spirit-helpers, from which no evil spirit, he thought, could escape. The pernicious spirits *(bumumuk)* were thought to be zoomorphic and were represented most often in the form of ermines or stoats, the Siberian ferret, wolves, wolverines, and other spirits under the control of shamans from other clans. At the rear of the whole group of figures of the *onang* stood charred figures of anthropomorphic watchmen-spirits of the shaman armed with spears, the so-called *mugdenne (mu,* "water"; *mugdy,* "deep," "fluid"; *mugdo,* "trunk," "stump"). They guarded the mouth of the mythical shamanistic clan-river and prevented the spirits of hostile shamans from entering the territory of the clan through the lower world by the clan's mythical shamanistic pathway, the river.

To the southeast of the *darpe* stood the *turu* with sacrifices hung on it— colored fabrics and skins of sacrificed reindeer. The *turu* was along larchwood pole with the butt driven into the ground, tied for security by a thong to a tall larch stump. At the top of the pole there was a small crosspiece to which was fastened a cloth—white or red for the supreme deity and black for the spirit of the earth or the taiga, and also for the spirits of the lower world. The sacrificial hide hung down from the top of the crosspiece, [its] head facing the south or east. In this case the *turu* was thought of as the road to upper deities. The sun and the moon were also included among the representations of this complex. The sun was represented by a circle carved on a stick and the moon by a half-circle or circle covered with symbolic ornaments (often in the form of two or three notches). The other images of deities and spirits were made in the form of anthropomorphic figures called by the general term *khomokor* (cf. *khomoty*, bear).

A generalized picture of the shaman's tent, and the *onang* and *darpe* attached to it, is shown in Figure 11.1, which represents a *shevenchedek* in cross-section. The number of images of shamanistic spirits, their position, and other arrangements varied according to the powers of the shaman and the character of the ceremony.

If the shamanistic performance took place in an ordinary tent, the figures of shamanistic spirits were few; in the middle of the tent stood a sapling larch symbolizing the shamanistic world-tree; beside the entrance were placed two figures representing watchmen-spirits *(deli);* next to the tent, the figure of a pike guarding the tent from evil spirits; and around the tent, figures of birds on sticks, guarding the tent "from the air." On the south side, [stood] the *turu* adorned with the sacrificial hide and "banners." Not far from it was the sacred reindeer dedicated to the supreme deity. On more important occasions, in addition to the figures mentioned, a small *darpe* was built beside the dwelling-tent in the form of a peak-roofed hut made of young larches, and on the opposite side, an *onang,*

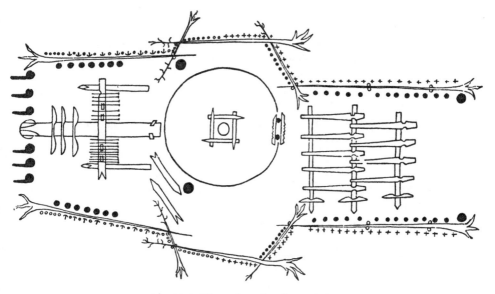

Fig. 11.1: Floor plan of a shaman's tent

likewise simplified. In the *anang* performance (to conduct the souls of the dead to the world of the dead) and in memorial feasts (the feeding of the souls of ancestors), blood sacrifices were brought to the beings of the lower world and, accordingly, the head of a sacrificed reindeer was placed on a pole among the spirit-images in the *onang*. In performances connected with the birth of a person and the guarding of his soul from the designs of evil spirits, a *turu* was placed on either side of the *darpe*. At the top of the *turu* were several crosspieces (the number depending on the number of shamanistic worlds). On the highest of them were placed figures of the souls of clansmen in the form of small sticks with crude likenesses of human heads and shoulders. The upper crosspiece of the *turu* symbolized the upper world and the anthropomorphic figures, the clan storehouse for the souls. In the center of the images, an analogous anthropomorphic figure was placed, this representing the soul of the person for whom the performance was being conducted.

Apparently, then, the ideas connected with the shaman's tent are associated, on the one hand, with the shamanistic tree *(turu)* and, on the other hand, with the mythical shamanistic clan-river.

In regard to the views connected with the shamanistic tree, the concept of the tree as a shamanistic world-tree is, first of all, essential. In the Evenk view it is connected with the three shamanistic worlds—upper, middle, and lower—and was thought of as the shaman's road from one world to another. . . . Reincarnation is conceived as passage into another world—the world of the ancestor-spirits—and resurrection as a return to the world of people. At the same time, reincarnation is thought of as a trial by fire or similar procedure, in short, traits characteristic of the totemistic form of initiation. The totemistic sources of this complex of concepts can be clearly traced also in its other facets. The ancestor-spirits of the shaman are imagined as living at the base of the clan tree and are associated with its base—the root, the beginning. These spirits were conceived as feminine spirits and are reflected in a generalized way in the form of the mother-mistress of the clan tree. This generalized figure is thought of in terms of a mother-beast. The passage of the shaman's soul (at the moment he is selected by the spirits) into this tree and his reincarnation is a spirit—the animal-double—are conceived as the temporary death of the man-shaman and his transformation into a beast. His appearance on earth is conceived of as the reincarnation of beast in man. . . .

As for the ideas about the mystical shamanistic clan-river (the meaning of which appears in the shaman's tent and the attached *darpe* and *onang*), it must be emphasized that the importance of the river is similar (in its functions) to the shamanistic tree *turu*. The shamanistic clan-river *mumongi khokto bira* (lit. "watery river-road") was thought of by the Evenks as the shaman's road to the upper and lower worlds, uniting all three shamanistic worlds—upper, middle, and lower—into one shamanistic clan-world, the universe. On the upper reaches of this river, identifiable with the upper world *(ugu buga)*, was the clan's storehouse for the souls of clansmen *(omi)* awaiting reincarnation. The middle world *(dulu* dulugu buga) was in the middle flow of the river. Here dwelt men, inhabiting the middle earth (the taiga). The lower world (khergu ergu buga) was associated with the lower course of the river and was conceived of as the land of the dead (buni~bukit). The land of the dead clansmen was at the mouth of the river. This land was imagined by the living as a clan camp, with pronounced autocratic features: when the shaman carried out the ceremony of conducting the soul of the deceased to the land of the dead and brought it to the mouth of the shamanistic clan-river, and entreated that the dead man be received into the camp of his fellow clansmen, he was met by the mistress of the land of the dead, who took the deceased into her clan.

If the shamanistic clan-river is basically similar to the shamanistic world-tree, then how, one may ask, are we to explain the origin of these similar ideas?

With the development of animistic beliefs, the totemist's concepts of his relationship to his totem were, so to speak, dichotomized. On the one hand, he thought of himself as a descendant of a mythical animal-primogenitor; on the other, as an animal whose spirit united with him during initiation (i.e., the ceremony of receiving the totem). Shternberg wrote:

> The Australian considers himself a man, that is, a member of a given clan, and at the same time insists that he is the same mythical animal-ancestor from which his clan is descended; finally, besides these, he considers himself the animal which is his totem. For example, if his totem is the kangaroo, he considers himself in the first place a part of his clan, in the second, a kangaroo, and in the third (since both kangaroos and men are descended from mythical ancestors who were half-animal and half-human), he is at the same time a descendant of the mythical ancestor.[1]

The psychology, strange at first glance, by which the personality is split in its relation to the totem, is a result of the fact that these conceptual forms themselves differ as to the time of their origin. The concept of mythical ancestors, half-human, half-animal, especially in the more archaic of its forms, that of the "mother-animal" or the fecund beast, is characteristic of the early (primary) phase of totemism; the view of the inclusion of the spirit into a totem is connected with the development of animistic beliefs. However, if the idea that the spirit of the totem enters into man lies at the base of the identification of man with totem, then, from this point of view, man was also a being of dual nature, thought to possess a second essence invisible to the eyes.

Ideas of birth and death, understood as the result of the reincarnation of the soul, originally bore the character of purely spatial concepts: death is a journey in one direction, towards the mother, the place of birth, and a transformation into a beast. Birth is a journey in the opposite direction and the reincarnation of the totem-beast-spirit in a man. The traces of these ancient beliefs are most clearly retained in the traditional forms of address to the slain bear, which the Ainus used in the rites of the bear festival. Addressing their parting words to the bear, the Ainus said that he (the bear) was about to go to the mother, by the road leading to the rising sun. There is his home. There from ancient times live people

—ancestors—and from there his mother must send to men a bear like him. The words from a parting address to the bear, in which it is said that on the road leading to the rising sun, to the mother's house, his (the bear's) birds "crow-grandfathers will cry joyfully around him,"[2] bear witness to the fact that this maternal place of birth is thought of as the matrilocal settlement of a matrilineal group and that the beings living there are totems. Among the Evenks these concepts were connected, as we have seen, with ideas about the world-tree of life, and birth, with ideas which were a later transformation of concepts concerning the totemistic centers.

Different in meaning and in time of origin, the mythical world of spirits and deities surrounding the *turu* larch in the shaman's tent, in the form of plastic images, obviously personifies this complex process of historical transformation of ancient notions about totemistic centers into the complex structure of the shaman's tent. . . .

The construction of the shaman's tent and also the preparation of the shamanistic spirit-images were generally done by the whole camp, as a rule by the men. According to the character of the shamanistic spirit-images, their number and order of arrangement in the *darpe* and *onang,* those present attempted to guess the shaman's intentions, the content of the impending performance, the significance for the clan of unexpected events. There arose among the clansmen lively conversations, creating that mood in the participants which, the shamans insisted, was absolutely essential to any important performance. It is essential to realize that in this preliminary stage, before the shamanistic activity proper, those present already felt the strong impact of the whole situation. In any case, when the ceremony began, many seriously maintained that they saw and sensed realistically everything that the shaman described by his actions.

With the coming of darkness, the shaman went into the shaman's tent, lit in it a small fire, and, imitating the cry of a loon, began to gather the clansmen for the fulfillment of the shamanistic activity. The members of the camp, one after the other, made their way along the *darpe* into the tent, wiggled past the huge images of salmon trout supposedly guarding the entrance from the upper world into the middle world (the tent), wiggled through the *ugdupka* [gate], and took seats in the pose characteristic of nomads (legs tucked under them) along the sides of the tent. When the last of them had wiggled through the *ugdupka,* small planks attached to it, representing spirit-watchmen, were lowered or placed across it and the entrance to the tent was considered closed. The journey which the participants in the ritual made was similar, in the shaman's words, to the movement of the souls *(omi)* out of the clan storehouse for souls *(omiruk).*

We shall describe the performance on the basis of our field notes, written from first-hand impressions during the 1931 expedition.

In the middle of the tent a small fire burned. The tent was in semi-darkness. Along the sides sat the clansmen, talking softly. A pervasive feeling of expectation of something extraordinary heightened the nervous excitement, still more strengthening the mystical mood. Opposite the entrance the shaman sat. His pinched, nervous face pale; he, silent, alert, irritable, moved his shoulders, gently swaying from side to side. His face twitched, his hands trembled. To the right and left lay the images of spirits—the salmon trout, the *mayga*, two pole-knives, fish-spears, a splintered larchwood pole. The fire was surrounded on four sides by shamanistic spirit-images, salmon trout. At a sign given by the shaman, his assistant took from the *tursuk* the shaman's ritual robes—the robe, the breast-piece, footwear, the cap (for minor shamans, a headband; for chief shamans of clans, besides the cap, an iron "crown" with a representation of reindeer horns), and mittens. The assistant then got the drum, warmed it over the fire for better sound, and quietly tested it to see that it was ready for action. Then he began to dress the shaman. The clothed shaman sat down on a small wooden platform which represented the shamanistic spirits of fish; he held the drum in his left hand, placed it on his left knee, held in his right hand the drumstick, and struck it against the outer side of the drum. The conversation broke off in mid-word. The shamanistic ceremony had actually begun.

The fire was damped. The drum sounded in the semi-darkness. The clansmen, pressing themselves against the sides of the tent, awaited the shaman's words with palpitating hearts. The most impressionable and those with the strongest imaginations looked with wide-open and protruding eyes at the grim figure of the shaman. Swaying slowly from side to side in time to the drum, the shaman began the invocatory song to the spirits in a quiet melodious voice full of inner feeling.

The invocatory shamanistic songs of the Evenks were always rhymed, rhythmic, full of clear and beautiful metaphors, and always accompanied by a rhythmical refrain. When the shaman had sung a verse of the song, those present repeated it in chorus. Then the shaman beat on the drum at regular intervals, accompanying the sound by the singing of a couplet, and led a rhythmical refrain, matching the note of the drum. Those present joined him. The drum again replaced the refrain. The second verse of the song followed; everything was repeated again in the same order.

In an improvised song of summons to the spirits, the shaman addressed his spirit-helpers, calling them to his aid in the struggle against the spirit of the disease. Addressing each of his spirits in turn, the shaman vividly described for the listeners its form, adorning it with all manner of comparisons, listing its services to the clan and the characteristics of its supernatural power. The shaman related in the song where the spirit was at the time, what it was doing, whether it obeyed the shaman's summons willingly or unwillingly, and, finally, how the spirit, submitting to the shaman's demands, left his clan territory and came to the shaman in the tent. At this moment, the song ceased and the sounds of the drum were gradually muffled, becoming a soft roll. The listeners with bated breath awaited the appearance of the spirit. The ensuing silence was broken by a sharp blow on the drum, changing into a short roll. In the silence following this, the voices of the spirits could be clearly heard: the snorting of beasts, birdcalls, the whirring of wings, or others, according to the spirit appearing before the shaman at the moment. Such conjuring tricks were not achieved by all shamans,

however, but only by the virtuosi in this line—the *khogdy shaman* (great shaman). The sound of the drum was unexpectedly interrupted. The shaman yawned
broadly, receiving into himself the spirit which had come, and again struck the
drum. Well warmed over the fire, the drum sounded long, filling the half-darkness
with sound. Those attending sat there under the impression of the appearance
of the spirit, deafened by the incessant rolling of the drum. Then the drumming
ceased. The shaman began the invocatory song to the next spirit. Rousing themselves from their torpor, the watchers picked up the shaman's words and everything began again in the same order, until all of the shaman's spirits were
gathered.

Having gathered the spirits, the shaman distributed his orders among them in
accordance with the order of the images of the *darpe* and the *onang:* some he
ordered to guard the tent, others to be watchman on all the pathways of the
shaman's activity, still others to remain with him to carry out his orders. Among
the shaman's spirits, the *khargi* or animal-double of the shaman filled one of the
first places. Under guard of the whole group of spirits the shaman sent the *khargi*
to the lower world to learn the cause of the clansman's illness. The sound of the
drum became thunderous, the shaman's song more agitated. The *khargi,* accompanied by the other spirits, headed for the lower world by way of the shamanistic
world-tree. There he found the *mangi,* the chief ancestor-spirit of the shaman,
and learned from him everything of interest. In the less important cases it was
sufficient for this purpose to turn to the nearest ancestor-spirit of the shaman,
most often to the one whom the particular shaman had succeeded on earth. But
cases were not rare in which the *mangi* proved incapable of establishing the cause
of the disease, and the shaman was compelled to send the *khargi* for the same
purpose to the upper world, to the supreme deity.

The journey of the *khargi* to the other world is described in the shaman's songs
in such fantastic form, so deftly accompanied by motions, imitations of spirit-
voices, comic and dramatic dialogues, wild screams, snorts, noises, and the like,
that it startled and amazed even this far from superstitious onlooker. The tempo
of the song became faster and faster, the shaman's voice more and more excited,
the drum sounded ever more thunderously. The moment came when the song
reached its highest intensity and feeling of anxiety. The drum moaned, dying out
in peals and rolls in the swift, nervous hands of the shaman. One or two deafening
beats were heard and the shaman leaped from his place. Swaying from side to
side, bending in a half-circle to the ground and smoothly straightening up again,
the shaman let loose such a torrent of sounds that it seemed everything hummed,
beginning with the poles of the tent, and ending with the buttons on the
clothing. Screaming the last parting words to the spirits, the shaman went further
and further into a state of ecstasy, and, finally, throwing the drum into the hands
of his assistant, seized with his hands the thongs connected to the tent pole and
began the shamanistic dance—a pantomime illustrating how the *khargi,* accompanied by the group of spirits, rushed on his dangerous journey fulfilling the
shaman's commands. The drumstick in the skillful hands of the shaman's assist-

ant beat out a furious roll. The accompaniment reached its highest point. The voices and snorts of beasts and the like were heard in the tent. Under the hypnotic influence of the shamanistic ecstasy, those present often fell into a state of mystical hallucination, feeling themselves active participants in the shaman's performance. The shaman leaped into the air, whirled with [the help of] the tent thongs, imitating the running and flight of his spirits, reached the highest pitch of ecstasy, and fell foaming at the mouth on the rug which had been spread out in the meanwhile. The assistant fanned the fire and bent over the shaman's stiffened, lifeless body. The latter, representing at this moment his *khargi* in the land of the *khergu* (the world of the dead), was outside of this seeming corpse. The assistant, fearing that the shaman might not return to the land of *dulu* (the middle world), persuaded him to return as quickly as possible from the lower world, orienting himself by the light of the fire which he (the assistant) had kindled in the tent. The shaman began to show signs of life. A weak, half-understandable babble was heard—the barely audible voices of the spirits. This signified that the *khargi* and the spirits accompanying him were returning to the middle world. The shaman's assistant put his ear to the shaman's lips and in a whisper repeated to those present everything that the shaman said was happening at the time to the *khargi* and his spirits. The shaman's weak, barely audible whisper changed into a loud mutter, unconnected snatches of sentences, and wild cries. The helper took the drum, warmed it over the fire, and started to beat it, entreating the shaman (that is, his *khargi*) not to get lost on the road, to look more fixedly at the light of the tent fire, and to listen more closely for the sound of the drum. The drum sounded faster and louder in the hands of the assistant; the shaman's outcries became ever clearer and more distinct. The drum sounded still louder, calling the shaman, and finally became again the accompaniment of ecstasy. The shaman leapt up and began to dance the shamanistic pantomime dance symbolizing the return of the *khargi* and his attendant spirits to the middle world *(dulu)*. The shaman's dance became more and more peaceful, its movements slow. Finally, its tempo slowed, the dance broke off. The shaman hung on the thongs, swaying from side to side in time with the drum. Then, in recitative, he told the onlookers about the *khargi*'s journey to the other world and about the adventures that had happened. Freeing himself from the thongs, the shaman returned to his place. He was given the drum. The shaman's song was again heard. The shaman transmitted the advice of the ancestor-spirits as to how the evil spirit of the disease should be fought, put the drum to one side, and paused. Someone from among the onlookers offered him a lit pipe. Pale and exhausted, the shaman began avidly to smoke pipe after pipe. With this the first part of the performance ended.

When he was rested, the shaman again took the drum and began to expel the spirit of the disease. At first he tried to persuade it to leave the patient's body voluntarily. The spirit refused. The long-continued discussion between the spirit and the shaman irritated the latter and turned into irrepressible outbursts of anger, cries, and threats. The sound of the drum again gathered strength. The shaman threw the drum to his assistant, leaped from his place, seized the thongs attached to the center-pole of the tent, and began to whirl around in a furious dance beside the patient, attempting to expel the spirit of the disease. Tired and powerless, the shaman returned again to his place, took the drum, and again struck up the song, asking his spirit-helpers what he should do next. On the advice of the *khargi* (the chief soul of the shaman, his animal-double), he began to expel the disease by fanning and rubbing the place of the illness with various parts of the bodies of animals and birds—hair from the neck of a reindeer, a piece of skin from the snout of a Siberian stag, a bear's forehead, the antler of a wild deer, skin from the forehead of a wolverine or a wolf, eagle feathers, and the like. But this also clearly showed itself to be insufficient. The irritated shaman denounced all manner of disease-spirits, sat down again, beat long and indignantly on the drum, and then, softening the blows, passed over to the usual melody and began to consult with his spirit-helpers on what he should do next. On the *khargi*'s advice he proposed that the disease-spirit pass into a sacrificed reindeer. Between the shaman and the disease-spirit there began again a long dialogue; the shaman praised the flavor of the reindeer's meat, of the different parts of its body, and derogated the body of the patient as much as he could. The disease-spirit held to the opposite opinion. Finally, the shaman succeeded somehow in persuading the disease-spirit to accept the ransom. The sacrificial reindeer was brought into the tent. The sacrificial rope was fastened around the reindeer's neck and the loose end of it put into the patient's hand. To the sound of the drum, the patient, turning the end of the thong over in his hands, began to twist it. At the moment when the twisted rope pulled the reindeer's head, one of the men standing beside it killed the animal with a knife-blow. This meant that the disease-spirit ran across the twisted rope into the reindeer and struck it. The reindeer was skinned. The skin was hung up as a sacrifice to the supreme deity; the heart was given to the shaman, who seized on it and avidly bit into it. The shaman spat out a piece of reindeer heart into a hole made in one of his spirit-images, stoppered the hole with a wooden plug, and carried the image into the *onang*, ordering his spirit-helper to take the captured disease-spirit into the abyss of the lower world. But often the disease-spirit fooled the shaman and remained in the patient's body. Then the shaman spread out the skin of the killed reindeer under the patient, smeared the blood of the reindeer on the diseased part, and began to wheedle the disease-spirit out with the scent of blood. As soon as the spirit crawled out, wishing to taste the reindeer's blood, the shaman threw himself on the patient, licked off the smeared blood from the body, and spat it into the hole (cavity) in one of his spirit-idols, which took the disease-spirit into the abyss of the lower world. At other times, complicating the circumstances of the action, the shaman said that the disease-spirit would not come to this bait. Then the shaman, annoyed, once more threw himself on the drum. It sounded loudly in his hands, deafening the disease-spirit with abuse and threats. The shaman gathered all his spirit-helpers. These surrounded on all sides the disease-spirit residing in the person. The shaman began an account, fascinating for its fantastic content, of the battle between the shaman's zoomorphic spirit-helpers and the disease-spirit. The latter hid itself in the contents of the stomach. Then, the most cunning of the shaman's spirits, the goose, pushed his beak into the patient's stomach and with it caught the cause of the disease. The shaman and his spirits celebrated. The joyful, deafening sound of the drum rang out. The clansmen attending the ceremony sighed with relief, but the joy showed itself to be premature. The disease-spirit tore itself from the goose's beak and threw itself in the direction of the onlookers. They were stunned with horror. However, another of the shaman's spirits, the splintered pole symbolizing the shamanistic tree, was in the runaway's path. The pole seized the disease-spirit, squeezed it into its wooden body, and under guard of two wooden watchmen *(kotó)* came over to the shaman. The third and most fascinating part of the performance began.

The shaman's spirits, as followed from his songs and actions, were surrounding the captured, disease-spirit in a dense ring, showering it with the most malicious jokes, ridicule, profanity, and threats. The spirits pinched it, nibbled at it, pulled at its legs, spat; the most irritated of them urinated and defecated on it, and so on. The tent rang with the sound of the drum, exclamations, the wild cries of the shaman imitating the voices of his spirit-helpers. The sound of the drum again reached a peak of intensity. The shaman tore himself from his place, seized the thongs attached to the tent pole, and threw himself into a dance frantic in its rhythm and intensity. Behind him two men held the thongs. The drum in the hands of the shaman's assistant groaned and died out in a thunder of beats. Wild screams, the snorting of beasts, bird voices rushed about the tent with the shaman. From under his feet flew brands, coals, hot ashes, but no one paid attention to this. With their cries the onlookers tried to help the shaman. The ecstasy of the shaman and the onlookers reached its highest pitch; the captured disease-spirit was taken into the lower world by the shaman's spirits to be thrown into the abyss. On the brink of the lower world, the loon or another of the shaman's spirit-birds swallowed the disease, flew with it over the abyss, and there expelled it through the anal opening. After this the shaman and his spirits returned to the middle world, barricading as they went all the passages from the lower world. When they reached the middle earth *(dulu)*, the shaman's dance ended. The shaman returned to his place. He was given the drum. To its sound he recounted to those present all the particulars of the expulsion of the disease-spirit into the abyss of the *buni* (world of the dead). A pause ensued and the shaman and his spirits rested.

The fourth part of the performance represented the clan vengeance of the shaman and his spirits on the shaman of the hostile clan. The shaman's *khargi* learned from his ancestor-spirits who had sent the evil spirits to the clan. Exclamations of indignation and threats descended from all sides onto the evil alien shaman. The shamanistic spirits of the clan made up a group of zoomorphic monsters and under the leadership of the shaman's *khargi* set out to avenge themselves on the clansmen of the shaman who had sent the disease-spirit.

The following and concluding part of the performance was dedicated to the gods of the above. A reindeer was offered them in sacrifice. The skin of the sacrificed animal was hung on a long, thin larch at the altar *(turu)* and its meat was eaten by all of those present. In a special song addressed to the gods, the shaman thanked the protectors of the clan for the help received. He then performed a special dance symbolizing his journey to the gods of the upper world. He climbed up, supposedly, by the *turu* into the upper world and walked along the earth of the upper world, passing the heavens one after the other, to the *Amaka sheveki,* the supreme god. The shaman gave him for safekeeping the soul of the patient—a small wooden image of a man attached to the top of the *turu* larch. The *Amaka* entrusted the guarding of the patient's soul to the spirit of the shaman. The shaman's return journey to the earth of the *dulu* (middle world) was represented in the form of a strenuous, joyous, noisy dance of ecstasy. Then the shaman went to the altar, stood beside the spread-out skins of sacrificed reindeer, and pronounced a long *moliurtyn*—an improvised prayer to the Christian deities.

Having arrived back in the tent, the shaman, at the request of those present, began to divine by means of his rattle and a reindeer scapula. The clansmen, in turn, set forth their desires. The shaman threw his rattle up in the air and, from the way it fell, determined whether or not the desire would be fulfilled. Then he took the shoulder blade of the sacrificed reindeer, laid hot coals on it, blew on them, and predicted according to the direction and character of the cracks in the bone what awaited his clansmen in the future.

At the end of the performance the shaman's tent was abandoned. The reindeer-skin covering (lap rug) was taken from it but everything else remained in place.

—Translated by Dr. and Mrs. Stephen P. Dunn

NOTES

1. Shternberg 1956.
2. Pilsudskiy 1914:120–121.

12

THE SHAMANISTIC ORIGINS OF POPULAR ENTERTAINMENTS

E. T. Kirby

A special category of theatrical activity includes types of performance that appear to be unrelated, or only indirectly related, to each other and to drama proper. Rope-walking, conjuring, juggling, sword-swallowing, and other such acts associated with the wandering mountebank, the fairground, circus ring, side-show, and music hall represent particularized skills developed as a means of popular entertainment. One link with drama is an origin of clowning and comic performance and activity of this type. Tumblers figure prominently in the Chinese theatre, and the Italian *commedia dell'arte* was probably created by acrobats. The techniques of the stage magician contributed to the illusionism of nineteenth-century drama, and trained animal acts were employed in its hippodrome-like spectacle. Performances of this kind, such as acrobatics or magic acts, when practiced as popular entertainments, seem to relate to the esthetics of drama only through the use of skill and through a common theatricality; they seem independent of considerations of narrative form or of the representation or enactment of another reality. To regard them as a category of theatrical activity, therefore, is to deal with aspects of dramatic theory that have been largely neglected.

One ancient center for the diffusion of acrobatics appears to have been the Near East, Crete, and Greece. However, Indian and Chinese magic acts, juggling, and acrobatics exerted a very strong influence upon later European performance, as did the acrobatics of the wandering, shamanist gypsies. These activities represent an aspect of the social acculturation process which provided opportunities for itinerant entertainers—a stratum or horizon of phenomena that various cultures have in common. At this level, performance is essentially secular in nature and motivated by economic considerations. But in the Chinese and Indian centers of diffusion we find clear evidence of an antecedent level of

E. T. Kirby is professor of theatre at the State University of New York, Brockport. He is the author of *Ur-Drama: The Origins of Theatre*.

performance in which the same acts are associated with the fakir and the religious mendicant. Beneath this stratum and at the origin of the phenomena, certain of the performances are directly associated with rites of exorcism and curing of disease.

Many popular entertainments may be traced back to this single source—the rituals of shamanism, which were functional rituals of similar pattern that operated within a variety of metaphysical systems. In a sense, then, shamanistic ritual was the "great unitarian artwork" that fragmented into a number of performance arts, much as Wagner believed had been the case with ancient Greek tragedy. Very different types of performance, such as magic acts, acrobatics, puppetry, and fire-eating can be shown to have derived from, or at least been preceded by, the phenomena of such rituals, and thus provide the framework for a general theory of origins.

It is only recently that something of the extent, nature, and significance of shamanist phenomena has become known. Shamanist ritual occurs or has occurred virtually the world over, among the most different and distantly separated peoples or cultures, and can be traced back in prehistoric times. It is the preeminent characteristic of primitive metaphysical systems. Similarities in the rituals practiced in different cultures must be due to parallel development, with similar phenomena produced independently by similar needs. Shamanism is, in this very important sense, archetypal.

Essentially, shamanism may be defined as the practice of trance for the purpose of curing the sick, although this is a limited definition. The shaman may also practice such related functions as divination or contact with spirits of the dead, but trance-curing is fundamental and accounts, on the basis of function, for the wide distribution and independent creation of the rituals.

The shamanistic séance is aptly named. It is very like the séance of a medium in modern Western culture, with its levitation of tables, strange rappings, spectral apparitions, and voices from the dead. Eliade notes how in a Chukchee shaman's séance "suddenly the voices of the 'spirits' are heard from every direction; they seem to rise out of the ground or to come from very far away. . . . During this time, in the darkness of the tent, all sorts of strange phenomena occur: levitation of objects, the tent shaking, rain of stones and bits of wood, and so on."[1] Ventriloquism is one of the specialized forms of popular entertainment represented here in a primal mode. Anisimov describes how in an Evenk séance in Siberia "wild screams, the sporting of beasts, bird voices rushed about the tent with the shaman."[2] In South Africa, ventriloquism is associated with a pseudo-shamanism, performances developed from the functional rituals.[3] Shamans of the Algonquins used ventriloquism to represent rushing wind and the voices of spirits under ground and in the air.[4] Hallowell describes the characteristics of an Ojibwa séance as follows:

> When a conjurer undertakes to divine, a small structure is built and, upon entering
> it, he summons his spiritual helpers. They manifest themselves vocally, the voices

issuing from the conjuring lodge being distinguishable from the voice of the conjurer who kneels within. Each pawagan [spirit] upon entering the tent usually sings
a song and sometimes he names himself. . . . Another manifestation of their
presence is the movement of the lodge itself. From the time the conjurer enters
it is seldom still. It oscillates and sways from side to side, behaving in a most animate
fashion.[5]

As these phenomena and the appelation "conjurer" suggest, the shaman employs techniques similar to those of the stage magician. One sleight-of-hand trick
in particular is characteristic of shamanism the world over, the apparent extrac-
tion of the disease agent from the patient in the form of some material object
—a bone, stone, or tuft of fibres—that has been concealed in the shaman's mouth
or about his person and is produced at the crucial moment. That this simple trick
is a characteristic of rituals in different cultures is undoubtedly due to a need to
make the disease both tangibly and conceptually real within a system of causality
that can be dealt with by the shaman. Related tricks used by Algonquin shamans
include carved representations of snakes produced from a cloth bag that has been
shown to be empty, and one in which a bear's claw is made to hang "magically,"
suspended from the inverted surface of a mirror.[6] Alaskan shamans use a whole
range of sleight-of-hand tricks in their practices of curing:

One observer describes "driving a knife into the body without marking the skin;
bending a long, narrow piece of nephrite; swallowing a bead and later on recovering
it from another's ear or eye, and tricks with twine cut into lengths, chewing the
pieces, amid heaving of the chest and violent contortions, and drawing the twine
out entire."[7]

Among his tricks, the Alaskan shaman swallows eighteen inches of a smooth
stick, an act suggesting the origins of sword swallowing.[8] In the pseudo-shamanism of the Shango festival in Nigeria, sleight-of-hand is employed to extract yards
of cloth from beneath the shirt of an unsuspecting audience member.[9]

Such conjuring, an apparition of objects, is directly associated in shamanism with the techniques of the escape artist, just as such acts are similarly
associated on the variety stage. The Cree shaman allows himself to be
stripped nearly naked and tied tightly within an elk's skin. After a lengthy
incantation, he escapes suddenly from his bonds.[10] Ojibwa shamans "will permit themselves to be securely tied, placed within the jugglery, and a moment
later be at liberty and the cords at some other locality."[11] The practice is
also common throughout Alaska, where it is elaborated upon in terms of
spectacle and "real life drama."

Getting untied when he had been trussed in various ways and allowing himself to
be burnt were favorite shamanistic tricks around Norton Sound and south of the
Lower Yukon. In one such case, the shaman, bound and wearing a large mask, was
placed inside a crib of wood, which was set afire. However, his assistants secretly
substituted a log of wood for the shaman. At Cape Prince of Wales, instead of being

strangled, a shaman might be burnt, put down through a hole in the ice (where he supposedly remained for several months), or speared or knifed without injury.[12]

A Kwakiutl shaman appears to have her head cut off or to be run through with a sword. She is then sealed in a wooden box which is consumed in a fire until only bones remain, and the "spirit" of the woman then speaks from the fire. The trick is accomplished with a tunnel and kelp speaking tubes that extend beneath the fire. The woman later appears unharmed, of course.[13]

Escape from bonds is associated with the miraculous disappearance of the person, just as similar performances are aspects of stage illusionism and escape acts. One important example of such an act shows the direct connection between shamanism and modern illusionism: the "Indian basket trick," which originated in shamanist fakirism and became famous on the European variety stage. In this trick, a child is placed in an oblong basket that is tied with a belt and then pierced with a sword, which emerges dripping with blood. When the basket is opened, it is found to be empty, the escape of the person inside having been effected by means of a contrivance, a sliding double-bottom and back to the basket. Sponges hidden inside produce the blood.[14] The trick belongs in part to the category of magical death and revival that may derive from shaman initiation,[15] and which was characteristic, in particular, of North American shamanism. Illusionism like that of the stage magician was originally proof of the shaman's supernatural control over death, a corollary of his control over disease.

It is important to note that while the tricks are essentially fraudulent contrivances, just as are the illusions of modern magicians and escape artists, delusionary experience is associated with the shamanist séance and remains associated with tricks and illusionism during the phase of pseudo-shamanism. Not only is the performer, the shaman, in trance and undergoing delusionary experience, but so, to a degree, is the audience. If these are, as I believe, the characteristics of primal theatre, it is of consequence to dramatic theory—a point I will return to later— and an anthropological sequence is established in regard to a perception of illusion and deception. Shirokogoroff's account of a tungus séance is cited by I. M. Lewis as representative of his own study and is a classic analysis of the function of delusion in an archetypal form of shamanism:

> The rhythmic music and singing, and later the dancing of the shaman, gradually involve every participant more and more in a collective action. When the audience begins to repeat the refrains together with the assistants, only those who are defective fail to join the chorus. The tempo of the action increases, the shaman with a spirit is no more an ordinary man or relative, but is a "placing" (i.e., incarnation) of the spirit; the spirit acts together with the audience, and this is felt by everyone. The state of many participants is now near to that of the shaman himself, and only a strong belief that when the shaman is there the spirit may only enter him, restrains the participants from being possessed in mass by the spirit. This is a very important condition of shamanizing that does not however reduce mass susceptibility to the suggestion, hallucinations, and unconscious acts produced in a state of mass ecstasy. When the shaman feels that the audience is with him and follows him he becomes

still more active and this effect is transmitted to his audience. After shamanizing, the audience recollects various moments of the performance, their great psychophysiological emotion and the hallucinations of sight and hearing that they have experienced. They then have a deep satisfaction—much greater than that from emotions produced by theatrical and musical performances, literature and general artistic phenomena of the European complex, because in shamanizing, the audience at the same time acts and participates.[16]

It was this experience upon which the concept of catharsis was based by the ancient Greeks.

A particularly vivid example of the use of tricks and illusion as a ground for delusionary experience is provided by Ronald Rose's account of the phenomena that occur in Australian initiation rituals. The candidates are secluded at night, and their nerves are worked upon for awhile by their initiators; a masked figure, which might be the god Baieme, approaches them:

> He lay on his back. His body gave a shiver and his mouth opened. Some of the men gasped almost inaudibly. From his mouth, the boys saw a thing come forth, a live thing that was not a snake, nor was it a cord. But it looked like a cord and moved like a snake. Slowly it issued from the gaping, quivering jaws, the length of a man's finger but not so thick. It moved about on the man's face and became longer, almost as long as a man's arm. It left his mouth and crawled in the grass. Then it returned to the man's body.[17]

Later in the rituals, the adepts in magic, known as "clever men," put on a display of rope tricks and illusionary acts:

> Clever-men appeared to lie on their backs and clever-ropes exuded from their mouths, their navels. The cords seemed to rise into the air, and the old fellows climbed hand-over-hand up them to treetop height. Then some of them moved from the top of one tree to the top of another by means of the cords, which swayed out into space. The boy had been told that clever-men could travel vast distances in no time with the aid of such cords; now he was seeing for himself some of these marvelous things.
>
> Some of the doctors walked straight to the trunks of big eucalyptus trees and appeared to melt into them, reappearing a moment later on the other side.[18]

The boys are carefully prepared to be susceptible to the stimuli and suggestions of the ritual. A quartz crystal is used to hypnotize them or to deepen them in that state. It is difficult to tell how much is trickery and illusion and how much is delusion. The magicians who walk through trees probably do no more than step around them, and suggestion does the rest. The basis for the "clever-ropes" is more difficult to perceive. Perhaps the magicians climb actual ropes into the trees, but most of the experience is clearly delusionary. Rose was shown such a cord in the presence of an aborigine friend who believed that he saw it, while Rose saw nothing on the demonstrator's first effort, and the second consisted of carefully drawing a string of saliva out to the length of a few inches. Some of the accounts in his study suggest that phenomena are reported as occurring if in some way they can be conceived of as happening. That is, the delusion may be conceptual, accepting the symbolic meaning of the trick, rather than perceptual, actually seeing a delusionary occurrence, and the report of perception made on that basis. Any "sign" of a phenomenon is its manifestation. But there is a continuum of experience from one mode to the other, and the former is used to prepare initiates for the latter.

Other types of performance common to popular entertainments develop in the same way as conjuring, although the delusions associated with their first phase are essentially conceptual rather than perceptual. These performances originate as extensions of the shamanistic function in that area of his role most susceptible to broader social application, divination, and prognostication. Puppets, for example, appear to function first as miniature shamans. Carved human figures made by the Alaskan Eskimos become possessed by a spirit and are used in divination.[19] In Java, a puppet is put in trance, as it were, by a mirror held before it—a common practice with human shamans. It begins to "twitch convulsively, like a human being entering into a trance," and then divines, with movements of the head answering questions posed to it.[20] Jane Belo has sketched this aspect of the Javanese puppet complex:

> In Java, it was customary to construct a doll out of a dipper and a rice-steaming basket which was, by various measures, caused to be imbued with the spirit inhabiting a sacred site. Once animated, this puppet was able to dance and to give signs in answer to questions put to it, as a clairvoyant. In Bali, the *sanghyang déling* performance was a related development. Here two wooden puppets, on a string passed through a hole in their middles, would dance through the power of the spirits inbuing them.[21]

The Menominee shaman makes two small effigies dance by means of threads connected to his toes, demonstrating his magical power over them[22] and the Malemute shaman uses a fetish with wolf body and alligator-like head in his curing séances, causing it to move about beneath a parka and using ventriloquism to produce its growing. Shamanist puppetry reaches one of its point of highest development in the mechanical tableaux created throughout Alaska and the northwest.[23] There puppetry is practiced as an illusionism associated with magical deaths and escape acts. The degree to which the spectacles are thought to be spirit-presences is not apparent, but the principle is represented.

Fire-walking, fire-handling, and fire-eating are typical of the type of act once practiced on street corners, in fairs, carnivals, and circuses. The origin of this group of phenomena can also be identified with shamanist practice. It is so widespread and so characteristic of shamanism that Eliade considers a "mastery over fire" to be its "particular magic specialty."[24] One fundamental, cross-cultural source for these phenomena is a shamanist trance ritual of exorcism held at night about a glowing fire. The !Kung [sic] bushmen hurl burning brands into the darkness while shouting for the evil spirits to go away. The trance leads to paroxysms in which participants rush into the fire and scoop up hot coals, which they pour over themselves and scatter over the spectators.[25] Ceylonese exorcism rituals are based on ecstatic dancing with lighted torches, which are rubbed on the dancers' bodies, placed beneath their garments without igniting them, and put into their mouths.[26] Iroquois trance performers in masks scoop up and "juggle" live coals in their bare hands and scatter them upon spectators.[27] The pseudo-shamanism of the Shona of South Africa shows fire-handling as one specialization within a structured differentiation of shamanist ritual. Some of the practitioners "speak in foreign tongues, others are ventriloquists, and others again impress their clients by holding burning logs in their hands or live coals in their mouths."[28]

Similar practitioners remained as fakirs or mountebanks specializing in tricks with fire throughout Europe, Asia, and Africa. Albert A. Hopkins reproduces the illustration of a mountebank in England licking a red-hot bar of iron and describes the fire-eaters and related performances of the late nineteenth-century variety stage, acts which included the eating of burning tow, flaming oil, and lighted sponges. He describes experiments in protecting the skin against heat for the purpose of such acts, and it is certain that similar methods of deception were practiced in shamanist performances as well.[29]

The primary phase of the phenomena would not be a form of illusionism, however, but would be identified with those cases in which trance seems to protect participants against pain and is sometimes said to cure the wounds miraculously, as with the Moslem Darvishes who place glowing coals and irons in their mouths and wound themselves with iron instruments heated red-hot.[30] Self-torture, such as that associated with Indian fakirism, defines the esthetics of one type of popular entertainment in origin and in nature, and these same practices also partake of illusionism.

The element of actual danger is also present in acrobatic performances. These also appear to have originated in shamanist exorcism rituals. Wirz writes of the Ceylonese devil-dancers, who perform with fire, that they "begin to dance, first with slow, measured steps, then faster and faster, finally spinning round the dancing scene like tops, and somersaulting like circus clowns, and doing all kinds of acrobatics."[31] "Ground" or "carpet" acrobatics associated with tumbling appear to have developed from the convulsive nature of trance performance and the extreme muscular tensions that occur, in which it is as if the person is seized, shaken, and propelled by an alien force:

> The Impande dancer, who begins by dancing backward in a rapid shuffle, finally falls to the ground and rolls about with great abandon, swings heels over head, goes rigid, with the body a curve supported only by heels and crown of head. The majority of dances, no matter how sedate, climax in a period of violent action, the rhythm of the drums forcing a faster and faster pace, the feet moving at incredible speeds, arms shaking, head shaking, whole body in vibrant motion.[32]

Codification and stylization of convulsive trance movements seem to have led to the various stands, leaps, and movements of the "ground acrobats" of the circus. Arab acrobats, for example, have their own distinctive style, specializing in side leaps, leaps on one hand, and a twirling that "gives the impression of a spinning top motivated by the lash of a schoolboy."[33] Strehly describes the "diabolical zest" with which the whole troupe performs simultaneously, encouraged by their own stamping feet and clapping hands, a "veritable wild music, which stifles even the sound of the orchestra under their deafening clamor."[34] The behavior in general and the spinning dance in particular seem to relate Arab acrobatics to antecedent ecstatic performances, such as those of the "whirling Dervishes."

There is evidence that rope-walking and other equilibristic acts also had antecedents in shamanist practices. The shaman in India sits or stands on a swing made of a sword blade or with a bar studded with thorns or spikes. Siberian Votyak tradition describes rope-walking in a shamanistic initiation, an account that contains elements of fancy, hallucination, and actual performance:

> Inmar appears to the favored person at night, in company with a wizard who has already been enlightened, leads out the pupil, to the sound of the *gusli*, either into the fields, or to a deep ravine, or to rivers of enormous breadth over which strings are stretched. In the field, the pupil of the mysteries sees seventy-seven firs, the needle-shaped leaves of which are being counted by many wizards. . . . To test his abilities, the future *tuno* is made to dance on tight strings over the ravine several times; he that does not fall once will be the cleverest.[35]

This is most probably a stereotypical vision that occurred during shamanic initiation, but it seems also to have been based upon an actual performance. The shaman's "magical flight" to the "sky world" during trance is acted out by the Evenk shaman, who swings suspended from two thongs during the séance.[36]

Circus clowns are associated with acrobats. The identification of clowning and acrobatics goes back through the Italian *commedia dell'arte* and the Medieval mimes to the popular entertainments of ancient Greece and Rome. A single origin of both is suggested by the association. That would seem to be the shamanistic "demon play" that develops from the trance-dance séance. Clowning arises from a differentiation of the shaman's function as well as from representation of an antagonistic reality based on portrayal of spirits or demons of disease. One of the Zuñi clown societies, the Néwekwe, was a curing society, exercising the functions of the shaman.[37] It is thought that "curing was almost certainly a primary function" of clowns among the Yaqui and Mayo.[38] Among the Plains Indians, the "contrary" was often both clown and shaman. Ojibwa contraries masqueraded in grotesque costumes and practiced exorcism as a cure of sickness, particularly that caused by spirit possession, and the Canadian Dakota "consider the clown to be the most powerful of shamans."[39] These associations of shamans and clowning suggest an identity between the functions of the two groups. If the function of the comic, represented by the clown, is therapeutic, as well-known theories hold, there would be a basic reason for the identification with the shaman, the society's doctor. However, there is also evidence to show that the clown was originally the doctor's antagonist, a representation of spirits who were the sources of malignancy.

Gananath Obeyesekere has shown in detail how Ceylonese curing rituals, known as demon plays, evolved into partially comic performances. The demons, acted by masked performers, were originally representations of physical illness but then came to portray the psychological meanings of symptoms and psychosomatic and psychological illness in particular. One reason for this development would certainly be the realization, in the course of time and with the development of physical medicine, that shamanic rituals achieve a higher percentage of cures with psychological illness than they do with physical illness. But essential, perhaps determining, characteristics of comedy seem also to have played a primary role in this transformation. The Ceylonese clowns "express bizarre, psychotic thinking and sense confusion"[40] because these are aspects of the diseases they are representing and treating. However, they also do so because such forms of expression are characteristic of the comic. Recognition of this fact seems to have followed upon portrayals of bizarre and psychotic behavior, represented in all seriousness, which resulted in causing laughter rather than fear. Elements of fear remain significant in the demon plays. The awesome, violent, and horrible aspects of the demon are first emphasized, but when he appears in the performance his behavior is comic. Obeyesekere observes that "these *inversions* not only ease the interaction situation, but prevent the attitudes one has towards demons in ordinary life from being generalized to the ritual situation."[41] Fear is also used directly, clearly for purposes of therapeutic shock, in an episode in which the demon rushes suddenly and unexpectedly upon the patient. The comedy is functional, having some therapeutic effect, by making the symptoms laughable in terms of bizarre and psychotic behavior, and it also functions against psychological repression in general by acting out vulgarities that are not represented in sanctioned behavior.

In its primal phase, clowning is identified with the representation of the diseased and deformed. The Aztecs had comic performances in which the ill and crippled were represented; "deaf, lame, blind, deformed, or sick people, or sometimes merchants, mechanics, or prominent citizens were mimicked, burlesqued, and made fun of."[42] The six masked figures associated with the origins of the Yoruba Egungun masquerade are a hunchback, an albino, a leper, a prognathous individual, a dwarf, and a cripple.[43] In southern Nigeria, scrotal elephantiasis is considered a magical penalty inflicted on adulterers, and thus is an object of laughter. Plains Indian contraries are identified with grotesque mythological beings with anatomical distortions such as large flapping ears or enormous mouths.[44] Cherokee clowns called Boogers "distort their figures by stuffing abdomen, buttocks, or skins," and the humpback was characteristic of ancient Greek and Roman mimes, as it was of the Turkish Karagoz, of Pulcinella, Punch, and related clowning types.

The physically grotesque distortion that derives from the representation of disease and abnormality then becomes transposed into caricature of social types, the "merchants, mechanics, or prominent citizens," who are mocked in more developed comedy. Even then, comedy retains the characteristics of an exorcism or demon play. The face-painting in Chinese drama shows it to be derived from the demon play, and the social types who are represented with painted faces all have something in their character that is deserving of criticism; that is, they are to some degree still demons. The exorcism archetype in which unwanted comic characters are driven off, expelled from the world of the play, is the standard form in Greek Old Comedy, which most probably originated directly in the demon play, but it is also found in later drama with which it does not have direct association, such as the comedies of Restoration England, and hence demonstrates the characteristics of an archetype that can inform literature. Comedy represents the antagonist in social and psychological terms, but it is a pattern based on the shaman's antagonism to disease spirits, that which is to be driven away or eliminated.

These, then, are the shamanistic origins of popular entertainments—of ventriloquism, puppetry, conjuring and escape acts, acrobatics, acts like fire-eating, and clowning. They appear to be very different types of performance, but in their association with the shamanistic séance or exorcism certain generalizations can be made concerning their basic esthetic principles. These principles may be contrasted with those currently in favor as standards of dramatic or theatrical activity and which have consequently been applied to origins. It is commonly held that drama is inherently identified with an imitation of reality and that this may be traced back to imitative dances and actions, such as the miming of animals, used in magical control over that which is imitated. Dramatic imitation is also traced back to an instinct for role-playing and imitation in childhood. A second theory holds that dramatic activity is play, a manifestation of an instinct for play that is apparent in childhood and in the activities of primitive man. Neither theory has actual anthropological validity nor is either relevant in regard to the materials and concept of origin considered here.

At their origin, popular entertainments are associated with trance and derive from the practices of trance, not of childhood play or imitation. They do not seek to imitate, reproduce, or record the forms, of existent social reality. Rather, the performing arts that develop from shamanist trance may be characterized as the manifestation, or conjuring, of an immediately present reality of a different order, kind, or quality, from that of reality itself. Shamanist illusionism, with its ventriloquism and escape acts, seeks to break the surface of reality, as it were, to cause the appearance of a super-reality that is "more real" than the ordinary. The illusionism is directly associated with delusionary experience, which is inherently surreal and more intense, more "real," than ordinary experience. The principle of the "more real" as the virtual ground of reality links spectacular and fraudulent trickery with demonstrations of the body's "supernatural" physical abilities in the trance state. Acts in which real danger is either present or the product of illusion show themselves to be present before an audience as virtual reality, "more real" than imitation. It is for this reason that Zuñi clowns will kill and dismember a dog or drink urine in the course of their activities. Such actions and the grotesque physical deformities of clowns relate them directly to the freaks of nature also exhibited at carnivals and in circus side-shows. Once a form of the "sacred," they represent a challenge to reality by the surreal as virtuality. Like fragments of the archaic, shamanist ur-drama, these various acts remain, each in its own form, elements of the "marvelous," of the surreal, that has been perpetuated in popular entertainments.

NOTES

1. Eliade 1964:255.
2. Anisimov 1963:104.
3. Gelfand 1959:106.
4. Hoffman 1896:138–9.
5. Hallowell 1942:10.
6. Hoffman 1896:97, 99.
7. Lantis 1947:88.
8. Lantis 1947:88.
9. D.W.M. 1953:309.
10. Hoffman 1896:142.
11. Hoffman 1896:143.
12. Lantis 1947:88.
13. Boas 1966. Hawthorn 1967.
14. Hopkins 1967 (1897):46–7. Jennings 1882:430.
15. Eliade 1964:54–5.
16. Lewis 1971:53.
17. Rose 1956:103–4.
18. Rose 1956:104–5.
19. Lantis 1947:79.
20. Epton 1966:118–119.
21. Belo 1960:12.
22. Hoffman 1896:98.
23. Curtis 1970 (1915):211.
24. Eliade 1964:5.
25. Marshall 1969:376–7.
26. Halverson 1971:338–9.
27. Blau 1966:568.
28. Gelfand 1959:106.
29. Hopkins 1967 (1897).
30. Brown 1968 (1868):281.
31. Wirz 1954:134.
32. Colson n. d.:87.
33. Strehly 1903:287–8.
34. Strehly 1903:387–8.
35. Anisimov 1963:153.
36. Anisimov 1963:102.
37. Parsons and Beals 1934:494.
38. Parsons and Beals 1934:506.
39. Ray 1945:84–6.
40. Obeyesekere 1969:202.
41. Obeyesekere 1969:205.
42. Bancroft 1866 (Vol. 1):291.
43. Adedeji 1970:81.
44. Ray 1945:103.

13

TRANCE EXPERIENCE IN BALI

Jane Belo

A quite distinct type of trance manifestation was the group of *sanghyangs* performed in the mountain district around Selat, in the eastern section of Bali. These were folk plays, crude, earthy performances given without any elaborate and gilded costuming and paraphernalia but using the simple homely objects to be found around the house. A potlid might be the center of the performance, or a broom. The players might take the part of the domestic pig or the familiar monkey that lived in the trees round about, and they dressed for either role in the shaggy black needles from the sugar palm, tied in bunches to their bodies. No high-flown jargon relating to the gods and their imperial retinue was invoked to explain why Darja suddenly would go into trance and wallow in the mud like a pig, why Darma suddenly would climb a bamboo pole and swing from it like a monkey. Very little was said about the theoretical entering by spirits belonging to the gods' world. To questioning on this aspect of the performances the people gave vague and confused answers, qualifying all their suggested explanations with expressions of doubt and uncertainty. They were not concerned with known godly personalities to whom a chain of religious and legendary associations clung. It was just a fact: the men went into trance and behaved like that. The word used when the man passed into the state of trance was not *keraoehan* (entered) but *nados* or *nadi* (from *dados* and *dadi*, to become).

The people knew how to bring about this change of state and had known how for at least two generations—they said they had always known. They saw nothing remarkable in it. Only certain individuals went into trance, but they were ordinary human beings, and there was nothing remarkable about them either. The

Jane Belo (1904–1968) made her first trip to Bali in the 1920s. The field work for *Trance in Bali* dates from the 1930s. She is also author of *Bali: Temple Festival,* and *Bali: Ragda and Barong.*

only necessary qualification mentioned to us was that, as children, they should not have been bitten. They said: "Those become *sanghyangs* who are bold. But if they have been snapped at by a dog or by a pig and are wounded, usually, when they are smoked, they don't go in trance. If they have been snapped at by a dog or a pig but not wounded, they do go in trance when smoked."

Certain rather strict rules surrounded the giving of *sanghyang* performances. It had to be the harvest season, after the Oesaba festival in the Dalem temple. The moon had to be growing full: they were never given during the dark of the moon. They had to be given at nightfall, never in the daylight. Neither might the performers go on playing after about nine o'clock at night, for on no account were they to come in contact with dew.

Some of the performances were more delicate than others, less likely to succeed unless the greatest caution was exercised in the preparation for them. For the *sanghyang* snake and the *sanghyang* puppy, stage-property snake and puppy had to be constructed from fresh grass. "He who goes to seek for the grass must not be seen, and it must not be seen where he puts it. Moreover, the grass must be such as has not been eaten by cows, or by anything else." These performances, which were likely to fail if the gatherer of the materials had been observed, were called the most secret *(pijit)*.

A considerable crowd had to be present to insure that the trancer did not get out of hand. Once, they said, a man who had become a *sanghyang* pig escaped from the courtyard where he was playing and roamed the outskirts of the village all night long. They were not able to catch him until the morning. He had by that time ravaged the gardens, trampled and eaten the plants, which was not good for the village. He had also, being a pig, eaten large quantities of excreta he had found in the roadways, which was not good for him.

At the season for *sanghyangs*, performances might take place every night for several nights in succession and even in several different houses on the same night. In the village of Doeda it was said that every household had its *sanghyang*. The crowd that gathered was alert and attentive, the whole spirit like that for a game in which everyone would take part. Everyone would join in the singing which directed the trancers' performance. People would call out jibes to the performers, urging them on, taunting them with phrases known to infuriate them. The crowd enjoyed this very much indeed. When the time came to bring the act to an end, a whole group would fall upon the trancer, who struggled fiercely in convulsions precipitated by the attack. Amid great excitement, everyone would fall over everyone else in a headlong rough-and-tumble. Then they would set themselves to nursing the trancer back to normal consciousness. All would then be just as intent on caring for the man who was coming back to himself as they had been a few moments before in taunting and exciting the creature he had "become." In this land of rigidly formal trance séances, where mediums dressed in gilded cloth and jewels would sit in solemn conclave giving trance impersonations of the gods, it was surprising to come across such homely and undignified proceedings surrounding the practice of trance—a sort of adoles-

cent roughhouse. The odd thing was that the actual trance states achieved by
these techniques were quite as intense as those which were produced in the
elaborate settings and with all the aura of the godly presences hanging about
them.

The history of our connection with the *sanghyang* players of this district began
in September, 1937, when Walter Spies and I first learned of their existence.
Walter Spies had at the time been residing in Bali for some thirteen years and
had by study and exploration become thoroughly familiar with all the types and
variations of performances to be found throughout the island. To run across a
veritable nest of new forms unknown to him seemed an astounding discovery.
The people gave a list of twenty different varieties of *sanghyangs* practiced
locally:

sanghyang	*lelipi*	snake
"	*tjélèng*	pig
"	*koeloek*	puppy
"	*bodjog*	monkey
"	*seripoetoet*	(puppets of palm, on a string)
"	*memedi*	(evil spirit, steals children)
"	*tjapah*	(bit of woven palm)
"	*séla praoe*	(kind of potato)
"	*sampat*	broom
"	*dedari*	heavenly nymph
"	*lesoeng*	rice-pounding mortar
"	*kekerèk*	small bamboo object
"	*djaran gading*	yellow horse
"	*djaran poetih*	white horse
"	*tétèr*	(three-forked stick, tied to finger)
"	*dongkang*	toad
"	*penjoe*	turtle
"	*lilit linting*	(coiling)
"	*sémbé*	(oil lamps on a string)
"	*toetoep*	potlid

Only two of these corresponded with forms known in other parts of Bali, the
sanghyang dedari and *sanghyang memedi*. The others were all completely new,
as if, as sometimes happens in Bali, a sudden burst of creativity had at some time
given rise to a whole gamut of improvisations, which later became standardized
in the locality as traditional forms.[1]

Soon after we had heard of the new *sanghyangs*, we were able to persuade the
people to put on a trial performance of three kinds. They warned us that because
it was not the season, they were likely not to succeed. But taboos and restrictions
in Bali were not so stringent that they could not be got around by some sophistry
or other. The influence of the Hindu priests, past masters at this art, was no doubt

responsible for the lack of inflexibility. At any rate, the three performances came off to our entire satisfaction and to that of the audience.

During the subsequent harvest season I was away from Bali. Walter Spies, however, attended the festival and witnessed seventeen of the performances. Enchanted by them, he wrote to me the glowing description which I shall presently quote. GM, my Balinese secretary, accompanied him and made a complete record: descriptions of the procedure and the different properties, the texts of the songs, interviews with the chief players, and the comments of the villagers concerning the manifestations. Later GB, [Gregory Bateson], GM, and I saw a group of three *sanghyangs*, arranged for us, and only one of the three, in our opinion, failed to come off. Finally, we were able to arrange for Dr. van Wulfften Palthe, a psychiatrist, to be present at a performance of three of the varieties of *sanghyangs*, to examine the players before, during and immediately after the seizures, testing their pupillary reactions and the reflexes of the limbs. The results of his examinations were that pronounced physiological changes were observable in the subjects in the trance state. His observations also fully supported the villagers' claim to a localized effect (that is, an effect in one arm only, as if it were disconnected from the body) brought on by certain of the rituals. This was a most remarkable effect, it seems, of especial interest in medical circles and a parallel to symptoms of hysterical conversion. Dr. van Wulfften Palthe referred to this phenomenon particularly in his paper on possession[2]. . . .

COMMENTS OF THE VILLAGERS

At various times GM talked with the villagers asking for explanations and inquiring into the sensations of the players. He questioned Darja, Danna, Soekadi, and Soekani among the players, and Goja and Tabanan, who served as impresarios, organizing the performances and arranging for the necessary properties. The statements he elicited are scattered through his reports over two years' time. Nobody ever volunteered any explanations. Generally when he was sitting around waiting for a performance to begin, he would slip in a question about the *sanghyangs* and, as opportunity offered, would ask the same questions of other individuals. For convenience, we have grouped the statements here under two headings.

About the Gods and Going in Trance

September 9, 1937

GM: As, for instance, in *sanghyang dedari, sanghyang tjélèng, sanghyang memedi,* who is it who enters?

Goja: For *sanghyang dedari, dedari* [nymphs] enter. If it is *sanghyang* pig, it is a demon *(beboeta)* which enters; and if *sanghyang memedi,* it is a *memedi* [evil spirit] which enters. On this I am not clear, may I not be mistaken.

April 11, 1938

GM: That god Ratoe Pandé [Prince Blacksmith] whose shrine is in the house-temple [shrine before which players are blessed in preparation for the perform-ance], what god is that?

Tabanan: I think that is the shrine of Betara Seri [rice god], and that is why we have *sanghyangs* here in the harvest season. Mostly when it is not the harvest season they don't go in trance *(nados)*.

Walter Spies: Don't people here make *sanghyangs* at the time of pestilence?

Goja: We don't make *sanghyangs* here for that, because here in this district, in the villages of Doeda and Djangoe, we have never had pestilence. When it is the time of worship *(atji-atji)* in the Dalem temple, as now, we make *sangh-yangs.* It begins generally on the first day [during the bright moon]. The worship in the Dalem temple is in the tenth month.

April 13, 1938

GM: Try to tell us, what is the use of making *sanghyangs* here at the *Oesaba* season? In the West, in Oeboed, people make *sanghyangs* when there is pesti-lence. What is the reason here? When the *sanghyangs* are made, does the rice crop increase? If you don't make *sanghyangs,* is there no harvest?

Darma: It's because out of the past our inheritance is like that—that's why I can't explain it. Always and always we have had *sanghyangs.*

Tabanan: It belongs with the worship of Déwi Seri. If it's not the *Oesaba* season, we don't have *sanghyangs.*

GM (to Tabanan): What do you think, in *sanghyang* snake, who enters, god or demon?

Tabanan: Well, my thoughts are stupid. In *sanghyang* snake, perhaps it's the god of the snake which enters. And the others likewise, that's the way I think of it.

GM: Is there a shrine here, a place of the god of the snake?

Tabanan: There is no shrine for the god of the snake that I have seen, but a shrine for the god of the *sanghyang* pig, there is one, on the side of the pigsty.

April 11, 1938

GM: Here [in this district] what do people say when one loses consciousness, *keraoehan* (entered) or *kepangloeh?*

Darma and Goja: If it's *sanghyang,* we say nadi [become] here. Nobody says *sanghyang kepangloeh,* nor *keraoehan* either; *kerangsoekan* also not. Here, if it is in the temple, then only it's *kepangloeh.* For instance if we had a ceremony *(petirtaan)* in the temple and I were going to pray and as soon as I came into the temple I went in trance (*engsap* [lost consciousness]), that would be *kepan-*

gloeh here. And further, if anyone during his unconsciousness had tremors suddenly, that would be *kepangloeh*. As soon as he has lost consciousness, he has no feeling of his body, he babbles, of anything at all he may chatter. If there is a lack of a shrine in the temple, he may speak of that lack. For instance, if I from the beginning have been making use of a shrine for Ratoe Batoe Dawa and then I don't work upon it, the person in trance *(sang kepangloeh)* speaks of that. If someone is entered *(keraoehan)*, at any rate this is how I think of it, that is at the desire of the gods. Yes, for example, if I *nadi* [go in trance], and I am told by my brother this for instance: "Go somewhere or other and pick up something or other," and then I go to seek it and there it is, that's *keraoehan*. And again, for instance, if I should go to the woods and at once find and pick up a stone, and my brother should go in trance (*ketedoenan* [be come down into]) and he should say concerning my finding the stone, for instance, "That's it, use it for so and so!" like that.

GM: And who enters *sanghyangs*, god or demons?

Goja: From the beginning there have been gods of the *sanghyangs*. And there were also demons. Those three cannot be separated—god, demon, man—they cannot be broken off from each other. The way I think of it, first the man was entered *(asoekina)* by the demon, and after he had been entered by the demon, then he was entered by the god. Perhaps the god of the *sanghyangs* is Dedari Soetji [Pure Nymph].

The Performers' Sensations

All the performers questioned by GM said they had begun to go in trance as *sanghyangs* when they were young boys. Most of them could not remember anything about the first experience, what sort of *sanghyangs* it was they played, and they were not even sure where it happened—it was too long ago.

Of the players we studied particularly, Soekani, Soekadi, and Soekrena were brothers, the three eldest of a family of six boys whose father was also a *sanghyang* player in his time. The younger boys did not play *sanghyangs*. Soekani was the father of five children, the eldest about eight years old. Soekadi had four children, and Soekrena also five. Their younger brothers were unmarried.

Darja was the only *sanghyang* player in his immediate family. He was one of ten children, of whom only two elder sisters and one older brother survived. Darma, who spoke of Darja as his younger brother, was actually a cousin. These two often played together as a pair.

The following comments are from a conversation GM held with Soekani, Soekadi, and Darja:

June 10, 1939

GM (to Soekani): How long is it since you began to be a *sanghyang*?

Soekani: Since I had just become adolescent *(menèk teroena)* I've been playing *sanghyangs* . . . Maybe it's twenty years. Every time I'm smoked I just go in trance *(nados)*, only my thought [may be] half-conscious *(ngedap sepera)*. When it's the season *(Oesaba)* I really go in trance.

GM: What is the feeling like when you are beginning to be smoked?

Soekani: When I am just being smoked my ears are stopped up, hearing the song. After that I immediately lose consciousness (*lali* [forget]), I feel as if I were all alone. When I am about to come to myself (*éling* [remember]) suddenly I am in place (*megenah* [know where I am]). The song I hear, but if a different song is sung to me, I am angry; I am overcome. It's like that for a moment.

GM: You become all kinds of *sanghyangs*. What are your thoughts like, the same or different?

Soekani: My thoughts are the same being any *sanghyang*. My thoughts are to follow the song.

GM (to Soekadi): What do you feel like when you are beginning to be smoked?

Soekadi: In the beginning, overcome, pins and needles, burning, like that.

GM: When people sing, do you know it?

Soekadi: I hear the singing, but the people who are singing I don't see. I hear the song clearly, but people talking of other things I don't hear. When the song sung to me is changed, suddenly I'm angry, my thoughts are overcome. Then I am angry with the singers. Somehow or other, often I even trample on the singers. Whatever the song that is being sung to me, when I've had enough, I just get angry.

Darja thought perhaps his first experience was being *sanghyang* pig.

GM: What is your feeling when you are first smoked?

Darja: Somehow or other suddenly I lose consciousness. The people singing I hear. If people call out, calling me *"Tjit—tah!"* [pig call], like that, I hear it too. If people talk of other things, I don't hear it.

GM: When you are a *sanghyang* pig, and people insult you, do you hear it?

Darja: I hear it. If anyone insults me I am furious.

GM: When you've finished playing, how do you feel, tired or not?

Darja: When it's just over, I don't feel tired yet. But the next day, or the day after that, my body is sick. What's more, when I've become *sanghyang kekérèk* [lifting the firewood with the little finger], I am quite exhausted for even five days.

At another time, when they had been discussing *sanghyang* snake and puppy, GM asked Darja how he felt, when he went in trance.

Darja: When I've already gone in trance *(nadi)*, my thoughts are delicious *(lega pisan)*, but I do not remember [am not conscious of] it. What's more, my whole body is very hot. And then, if I am touched with holy water, my thoughts are like a crazy person's.

Darma: When the *sanghyang* dies [the snake and puppy, it will be remembered, were said to "die" when the life went out of them], my thoughts are absolutely dark. When that happens, like a crazy person, I don't know anything. If I am not touched by a person or by holy water, all of a sudden I go crazy.

In still another conversation:

GM (to Darma): When you become *sanghyang* snake, what is the feeling like, and where do you feel your body [to be]?

Darma: When I'm a *sanghyang* snake, suddenly my thoughts are delicious. Thus, my feelings (*bajoe* [strength]) being delicious, suddenly I see something like forest, woods, with many many trees. When my body is like that, as a snake, my feeling *(rasa)* is of going through the woods, and I am pleased.

GM: If you become a *sanghyang tjapah* [bit of woven palm], what does your body feel like, and where?

Darma: Then I feel I am in the house-temple, that's how my thoughts are. When I feel I'm in the house-temple, I don't know why, suddenly I'm delighted to be in the house-temple.

GM: That bit of woven palm, you feel that is your body?

Darma: For instance, if you are planting rice in the fields, don't you feel your place is low? That's how I feel, low, in the house-temple.

GM: And if you're a *sanghyang* puppy, what does your body feel like? Where do you feel yourself to be?

Darma: I've never been a *sanghyang* puppy. My younger brother there most often becomes that kind of *sanghyang*. I don't know what the feeling's like.

GM asks Darja the same question.

Darja: I just feel like a puppy. I feel happy to run along the ground. I am very pleased, just like a puppy running on the ground. As long as I can run on the ground, I'm happy.

GM (to Darma): And if you're a *sanghyang sélaperaoe* [kind of potato], where do you feel yourself to be, and like what?

Darma: I feel to be in the garden, like a potato planted in the garden. That's it, just like a potato in the garden.

GM: And if you are a *sanghyang* monkey, where do you feel as if you were? When you're a monkey, do you feel like the male or like the female?

Darma: My thoughts are like a monkey's. Then, like a monkey, I seek in the forest for fruit. As to my feeling, it falls to me to be the male, to my younger brother there [Darja] the female.

GM: And doesn't it come into your thoughts to make love there in the woods, the two of you?

Darma: Yes, to beat upon (*adoek* [literally, to beat up a mixture, a slang phrase for motions of copulation]) my mate. I don't go through with the copulation, but in my thoughts there is copulation. I have the feeling that we are many there in the woods, in the forest.

GM: And if you're a *sanghyang* broom, what's it like, and where do you feel?

Darma: Like sweeping filth in the middle of the ground. Like sweeping filth in the street, in the village. I feel I am being carried off by the broom, led on to sweep.

Before any of us had had a chance to witness many of the varieties of *sangh-yangs,* one of the trancers, Soekadi, described a number of them to GM, making the point that it was possible for only the hand to "go in trance," or the whole body. He ascribed the difference to the "smoking."

Speaking of *sanghyang sembé,* with the hanging lamps, he said:

"The *sanghyang* player takes hold of the *dapdap* branch with his right hand. Under that hand is placed a brazier, and the hand is smoked by the brazier. It also happens that even to his body he is smoked, then he altogether goes in trance. It may be that his body is smoked, it may also be that only his hand is smoked. If it is only his hand that is smoked, in a moment, if it works, only his hand has a tremor. If his entire body is smoked, his body and his hand, all together have a tremor."

Again, describing *sanghyang seripoetoet,* with the puppets on a string, he said:

"In this also the hand only may be smoked, or it may be even to his body. If it is only the hand that is smoked, he who is smoked can converse like someone who has not lost consciousness. But if it is even to his body that is smoked, he cannot converse."

Of *sanghyang sampat,* in which the broom is tied to the fingers, he said:

"For this one also, his hand with the broom only may be smoked, or his hand with his body. It is the same, if, for instance, only the hand is smoked, only the hand goes in trance."

I quote these three statements because it seems strange that nowhere did Soekadi mention a difference in intention or in sensation of the player himself. The whole matter was treated as a ritual event, in a ritual sequence. Yet in at least one instance, when GM saw the *sanghyang* with lamps, he noted that although only the hands of the players were placed over the braziers, one of them seemed to him to "go in trance with his whole body." His whole body had trembled during the performance, and afterward it was necessary to rub him all over.

On the whole, however, the introspective comments of these players are surprisingly satisfactory. They did not have the ring of the much-repeated phrases heard in other districts, where the people were more accustomed to discussing their trance experiences and where the more specific supernatural element was stressed. Darma's saying that he felt he was being "led on" by the broom is most expressive and exactly describes what seemed to be happening in all of the tied-to-the-finger performances. The hypnotic threshold, the selective awareness of certain stimuli and imperviousness to others irrelevant to the situation, well-known in hypnosis experiments, is illustrated in the players' remarks about hearing the song, but not hearing people talking of other things, not seeing the singers, but trampling upon them when angered. The feeling of lowness, which Darma described as delightful, fits in with the whole constellation of ideas about being mounted, being sat on, and so forth, wherein the pleasurable quality of the trance experience is connected with the surrendering of the self-impulses. This is one aspect of the trance state which seems to have reverberations in the trance vocabulary in whatever country these phenomena appear—and the aspect which is perhaps the hardest for non-trancers to grasp. Being a pig, a toad, a snake, or a creepy spirit are all enactments of the feeling of lowness in a very literal, childish, and direct manner. Recognizing this urge *to be low* as the foundation of some—probably not of all—trance phenomena makes understandable what we would otherwise be at a loss to explain. What could induce a grown man to wallow around in a mud puddle and eat filth, to hop about on all fours, or to slither over the ground on his belly, if he were in his right mind? Behavior that would be a degradation—animal-like behavior which the Balinese were careful to avoid in their current manners, and which was even institutionalized as a punishment for incest[3]—becomes in the trance state pleasurable and delightful.

Of another order are the feelings described by the *sanghyang* players as angry, being overcome *(iboek, boelèn)*, crazy *(boedoeh)*. These correspond to what the trancers with the kris often mentioned in other parts of Bali, the feeling of anger when they attacked the Witch. This is a particularly Balinese phrasing for the violent storm of emotion which showed itself in the convulsive fit. Very probably different cultures interpret in different terms the involuntary spasm which is basic and universal, surrounding the experience with an emotional setting in accord with the prevailing affective make-up of the people. This affective interpretation or coloring of the trance experience no doubt determines the mood in which what we have called the "somnambulistic" trance activity, the enacting of the role, takes place. The climax, as a cataclysmic discharge of nervous tension, might occur against a background of any strong emotion, anger, fear, sexuality—one might say that it is of the stuff of emotion, undifferentiated, and physiologically on too low a level to have a meaning in the terms human beings use to refer to *conscious* emotional states. None the less, trancers in any individual culture learn to perform from each other, they observe the trance behavior of their fellows before they ever themselves fall into trance—hence the distinct cultural patterning of the behavior in the somnambulistic states—and, when they are themselves asked to describe their feelings, they cannot help giving answers based upon their observation of their fellows and the conception of the trance phenomena accepted by the culture. To a Balinese, apparently, a man having a convulsive fit *looks* as if he were angry. MM [Margaret Mead] and GB have shown in a sequence of moving-picture film the resemblance between the temper tantrum set off in Balinese children by the teasing of an impervious mother and the "fit" the adult trance performers fall into when they attack with a kris the equally impervious Witch figure. The fit looks the same when the trancer has been wallowing in the mud as a pig or dashing about with a potlid tied to his finger. Again we hear "anger" spoken of by the trancers as the prevailing emotion of the final convulsive seizure. Yet from everything we know about such attacks we would be prepared to assume that the trancer could not possibly be conscious while in its throes; that he must be judging objectively from what he has observed in others—in other words, he may indeed *be* angry, during the fit, but he could not know it.

One can imagine a similar argument about the trance manifestations in Haiti —if we had the necessary collection of trancers' statements—but centering there on whether the basic emotion engulfing the trancer was sexual. Foreign observers tend to see a strong sexual undercurrent in Haitian trance activities. Because the culture phrases and interprets the phenomena in religious terms, some Haitians are at pains to deny any connection with sexuality. The Balinese too had ready explanations of the trance phenomena in terms of the religion. Yet the anger motif keeps recurring in the Balinese statements alongside the formal explanations.

It is significant that anger, in Bali, is not one of the emotions which it is customary to demonstrate in the normal state. The Balinese people are certainly not fiery-tempered. They appear to swallow whatever resentment they may feel, to express it only indirectly, as by endeavoring to get a *balian* to cast a spell on an enemy, or, in extreme cases, to let it burst out after a long period of brooding and nursing of a grievance, in the abnormal attack of violence known as *amok*. Compared with other peoples, who express anger more readily, they would appear to be either the most easy-going, good-tempered people imaginable—or incredibly consistent inhibitors of anger. Some Western psychologists, accustomed to freer demonstration of anger as "normal" behavior, would incline to the hypothesis that the habitually repressed anger finds a vent in the trance state, that it is at last released after being long pent up. Perhaps. We cannot be sure that such a mechanism, familiar in our culture, would apply in Balinese culture. We do not know whether for them it is merely customary not to show anger, or it is customary not to be angry. Certainly, beside them, Dutch, English, and American persons in Bali appear uncommonly irascible and short-tempered as a group —and have a reputation as such among the Balinese. It is not impossible that when the Balinese go in trance and have a violent fit of what they think of as anger, they are indulging in the luxury of an orgy of unfamiliar emotion.

Another point of particular import in Balinese culture is the reference to *place* in the statements of the *sanghyang* performers. One of the usual terms for the trance state in Bali is *paling*, that is, having lost the sense of direction. Here we have Soekani telling us that when he comes to himself "suddenly I am back in place." In his hypnosis experiments Dr. Milton H. Erickson has made a special study of the ways the subjects reorient themselves when coming out of trance. The change in orientation seems to be somehow essential in the trance state, as in the dream. I like very much Darma's description of the illusions of change of place he experiences in his various *sanghyang* roles—he is in the forest, in the house-temple, in the village street. The childlike pleasure he takes in these not-very-distant excursions, the simplicity of the illusion, are both touching and, somehow, revealing. The results of this entire interrogation came as a surprise to us: no one before had told us of such a transposition in space. GM had probably been instructed by us to inquire of the trancers *where the feeling began in the body (kenken rasané, toer didja rasaang beli ragan beliné?)*. The phrasing in Balinese not being any too clear, the subject answered by telling where he felt his body to be. GM then followed up this lead, asking about the illusion of displacement in other *sanghyang* performances. The statements he elicited tie up nicely with Soekani's remark that when he came to himself he was suddenly back in place. For the first time we have been told explicitly where the subject wandered to during his disorientation.

I think there can be no question but that these villagers were thoroughly adept at the practice of trance, so much so that they were able to slip into a state of half-consciousness almost instantaneously—a state in which they would experience certain sensations and have the feelings appropriate to the role they were playing, but would be sufficiently aware of these sensations and feelings to be able to recall them later. If conditions were propitious, if it was "the season" and all had gone well with the preparations, they might spontaneously fall into a deeper trance of which they would say, "I don't know anything," or "It is absolutely dark *(peteng).*" The audience understood well enough the possibilities of the situation and was master of a number of tricks to be played upon the subject, worthy of the professional stage hypnotist. They knew how to make a game of his suggestibility, humoring him, taunting him, and finally bringing about—if he failed to fall into it spontaneously—the convulsive attack in profound unconsciousness. Most remarkable was the inventiveness shown in all these varieties of *sanghyang,* the veritable spate of trance plays produced by this region, and, as GB remarked, the same freedom in the treatment, tendency to obscenity, and *innocence* which is characteristic of Balinese folk art.

NOTES

1. Gregory Bateson pointed out a parallel between the *sanghyang* performances of the Selat district and the wood carving of the village of Sebatoe. Here also there was an outburst of folk art, producing an enormous crop of wooden figures all outside the traditional forms in sculpture, expressing the free fantasies of the relatively unskilled villagers. In a very short time after the inception of this movement, the carvers had settled down to a recognizable style in the production of their little figures, and though they continued to experiment with ever more audacious and grotesque subjects, the rendering conformed to what could already be called "the Sebatoe tradition." Gregory Bateson and Margaret Mead collected some eight hundred of these figures.

2. Van Wulfften Palthe 1940:2123–53.

3. Belo 1935. Offending couples were forced, according to old custom, to crawl on all fours and to drink from a pig's drinking trough. Also, on February 23, 1937, during the stay of GB and MM in Bajoeng Gedé, we all witnessed the ritual penance of animal-like behavior imposed on an incestuous pair.

PART FIVE

RITES, CEREMONIES, PERFORMANCES

INTRODUCTORY NOTE

Almost all the activities of—what shall we call them?—primitives, Others, non-Westerners, communal peoples, those who have a living oral tradition—can be regarded as theatre. Too often anthropologists, who came as missionaries, or with trading parties, or as instruments of colonization and exploitation, saw in the Others only savagery, or a quaintness to be brought back to the British Museum (in one way or another). The view that all practices are "religious" avoids the problem of what religion is, especially in cultures where economic, social, political, and entertainment activities are integrated. To look again at the performances of the Others as theatre will, I think, give totally different, and deeper, insights.

This section could go on endlessly because everywhere in the literature are descriptions of performances. But we chose a few that tended toward examining these performances as performances. And we added to these selections Grotowski's vision of a modern theatre based on ritual techniques.

14

DESERT RITUALS AND THE SACRED LIFE

Richard A. Gould

The daily life of the Aborigines is rewarding but routine. There is a kind of low-key pace to the everyday round of living. In their ritual lives, however, the Aborigines attain a heightened sense of drama. Sharp images appear and colors deepen. The Aborigines are masters of stagecraft and achieve remarkable visual and musical effects with the limited materials at hand. Although some of the ritual practices seem at first glance to be bizarre and even sadistic, their ceremonial life is notable for meditation and sobriety rather than for frenzy.

There are several excellent scholarly accounts of Aboriginal religious and ritual practices as well as detailed descriptions of traditional beliefs and ceremonial organization.[1] Reading these in preparation for going into the field made me aware of the complexities of Aboriginal religion, but my understanding of the sacred life still seemed incomplete. I could not share in the emotional satisfaction brought about by these beliefs and practices. They seemed too much like intellectual exercises which left me impressed but unmoved. Instead of being exhilarated after I witnessed my first ceremonies, I felt depressed and inadequate to the task of understanding. What was wrong?

At first I blamed the Aborigines. These short dances and songs seemed like mere powderpuffs. How could anyone take such spiritual tidbits seriously? Since I knew that a complicated social organization and theology underlie the rituals, I was taken aback by the seeming insignificance of the pantomimes.

The fault was with my own understanding. Not until I saw the Aborigines in the desert, living under nomadic conditions in the regions they normally frequented, did I realize how deeply I had misjudged their religion. In time I watched many more ceremonies and participated in a few, and my understanding

---

Richard A. Gould is professor of anthropology at the University of Hawaii. *Yiwara* is based on field studies in Australia in the 1960s.

of and delight in them grew. Gradually I experienced the central truth of Aboriginal religion: that it is not a thing by itself but an inseparable part of a whole that encompasses every aspect of daily life, every individual, and every time—past, present, and future. It is nothing less than the theme of existence, and as such constitutes one of the most sophisticated and unique religious and philosophical systems known to man. Professor Emile Durkheim, a distinguished French sociologist, writing about forty years ago, contrasted the sacred and profane aspects of Aboriginal life.[2] If not interpreted too literally, this is a useful distinction for describing Aboriginal ceremonies, since separation of the sexes during important ceremonies and separation of daily activities from ritual actors and events function to varying degrees in most ceremonial activities. But I found Durkheim's framework more of a hindrance than a help in appreciating the Aboriginal religion. For me the striking thing was the absolute relevance of every part of it to the problems and situations of daily life. In a sense, everything within the Aborigines' environment is holy, not in some vague, pantheistic sense but in terms of concrete ties which the rituals use and revitalize.

Rather than attempt a formal description of Aboriginal religion, I prefer to describe certain rituals which I witnessed and which were illuminating and significant to me. Each is quite different from the others and each reveals a wide area of Aboriginal belief. There is much more to Aboriginal religion than these particular rituals, but since they epitomize the essential elements better than most they will serve as a guide to the general character of Aboriginal beliefs and ceremonies.

MARKS OF MANHOOD

The shouting had barely begun when a woman ran up to me saying, *"Malulu pitjangu* [The kangaroo-novice came]." I went out in time to see a young man with a string cord tied around his head walking out to the creekbed with a group of older men. This lad had left Warburton about a year ago with his maternal uncle and has now returned along with a group of men from the reserves at Ernabella and Musgrave Park in South Australia. In addition to these places he had also visited the reserve at Areyonga in Northern Territory. Now he is going out to the secluded camp where two other novices are living.

The three novices, all between about thirteen and sixteen years of age, know they will be circumcised soon, but exactly when and how they are not sure. They live together in a camp in the bush while their relatives in the main camp send food out to them. The one already mentioned has had the good fortune to make the "grand tour" with his mother's brother, visiting distant camps where he was shown sacred dances and taught sacred songs. The other two have been at the bush camp for about three months; their range of sacred knowledge when they are circumcised will be far less than his. However, since a large group of Warburton and Musgrave Park people is now gathered together, the prevailing sentiment is that all three boys should be operated on at the same time.

The novices have mixed feelings. They can imagine the pain only too well and are nervous and apprehensive. But they also know the whole community will be watching them and that their present behavior will be discussed for the rest of their lives. They are proud to have this opportunity to make a public show of their physical courage.

During their seclusion they are introduced to sacred dances and songs to an extent that they have never experienced before. The actual ordeal comes as the climax following a buildup lasting as long as five or six weeks. The songs and dances which the boys are taught are short and episodic. In highly abbreviated form they re-enact adventures and events in the lives of mythological beings that lived in the "dreamtime" *(tjukurpa)*. The Pitjantjara word indicates a kind of timeless mythical past during which totemic beings traveled from place to place across the desert performing creative acts. Some of these beings are natural species of the region, such as the opossum, kangaroo, echidna (spiny anteater), dingo, marsupial cat, bush turkey, emu, eagle, rabbit-eared bandicoot, bat, carpet snake, "mountain devil" lizard, magpie, and goanna, but there are other special ones, among them Wati Kutjara (the Two Men), Wanampi (the Water-snake), and Yula (Penis). The "tracks" or routes taken by these beings in the dreamtime lace the desert in all directions, often crossing and recrossing.[3] Although they lived in the past, the dreamtime beings are still thought of as being alive and exerting influence over present-day people. While the dancers prepare, the novices lie on the ground, face down, with eyes closed. When each dance begins they sit up but may not look directly at the performance. One lad holds his hand in front of his face and peers out between his fingers, while the others avert their eyes slightly to one side. They have not yet reached the level of sacred knowledge at which they can look directly at the dances without fear of illness.

Singing usually begins in the early afternoon and may continue until the next morning, then be resumed the next afternoon, and so on. The men sit in two circles, representing a division which runs through the entire society. One circle calls itself "sun," the other "shade." Each circle consists of men who belong to generations which alternate with those of the opposite circle. For example, I sit on the sun side with men of my own generation as well as those of my grandfather's and my grandson's generations (these generations are called *nganatarka*). Opposite me, in the shade circle, sit men of my father's and my son's generations (called *tarputa*). The men in each circle sit facing inward, and each man grasps a stick in front of him. During songs, rhythm is maintained by pounding the sticks on the ground. This rhythmic pounding is said to be the sound of the mythological kangaroos' tails thumping against the ground as they hopped from one place to the next in the dreamtime. After a while this pounding creates a depression in the soil underneath the stick, and each song-circle has a ring of these depressions radiating out like spokes on a wheel. These are said to be the sleeping grounds of the totemic kangaroos (the sleeping places of living kangaroos are easily recognized by just such a pattern, worn by their tails in the soil). Aside from sticks used to beat out a rhythm and simple percussion devices such as tapping a stick against a spearthrower, the desert Aborigines have no musical instruments.

Among most of the Ngatatjara every person belongs to one of six named categories or "sections."[4] White Australians sometimes call these "skin groups." Sections serve to regulate marriage, and they play a vital role in enabling widely separated groups or individuals to visit one another. They serve as a kind of "shorthand kinship"[5] which allows visitors, even those with distant or nonexistent kinship ties, to participate in ceremonies, seek out potential marriage partners, and share food and other necessities while far from home. The names of the sections also serve on occasion as personal names. The operation of this so-called six-section system (really four sections with six names) has been accurately depicted by the Australian missionary and linguist Wilfred H. Douglas.[6] . . .

Notice how generation-levels, marriage rules, and seating within the divisions are all correlated by this arrangement. This seating arrangement in opposed circles is conspicuous during the singing leading up to and during the circumcision ceremony. For other ceremonies the singers sit on different sides of the dance area but do not always form distinct circles.

The men performing and directing dances leading up to the final night belong to groups which the Australian anthropologist Mervyn Meggitt has aptly termed "cult-lodges."[7] Each of these groups consists of men who believe themselves to be descended in the male line from the same dreamtime being. Formally speaking, women are also members of these groups by virtue of descent, but they are not permitted to watch the dances or learn the sacred traditions. Instead, their male relatives act on their behalf at these ceremonies.

During the period leading up to the final rituals, sacred boards are brought out by the different cult-lodges from their respective caches and displayed to the other initiated men present. The incised designs are reverently contemplated as the lodge elders explain the story-lines depicted on each one. Sometimes additional paraphernalia, such as sacred stones and large pieces of incised pearlshell, are displayed at this time. They are then replaced in their respective caches.

The dances performed by the cult-lodges are moments in which the dreamtime past fuses with the present. The dancers feel a closeness of spirit with their totemic ancestors, becoming in the dance the being himself. At the conclusion of each dance a singer reaches out with his hand or a stick to touch a dancer, thereby breaking the spell and drawing the dancers back into the present.

Although short in themselves, these dances usually require several hours of preparation, mainly for decorating the dancers' bodies and the sacred paraphernalia carried or used in the dances. Members of each cult-lodge carry out these preparations with extreme care, with the older members supervising each detail and instructing younger members on the correct designs. While not as spectacular as the dance regalia seen in other parts of Aboriginal Australia, the preparations are thought by the Aborigines to be at least as important as the actual dances. This is not so much a matter of craftsmanship or artistry as propriety; that is, each design or piece of paraphernalia is judged by the older men in terms of whether or not it includes all the traditionally correct elements for the particular ceremony being performed. An appropriate design is called *tulku mulapa* (true [or "proper"] sacred tradition). A neat, carefully painted body design is enjoyed by the lodge members but is not required for the ceremony. In short, craftsmanship and artistry are permitted and even, in an informal way, encouraged, but only if they do not in any way violate the themes set down by tradition.

Activity begins early on the final day. With such a large group present the excitement is intense. At dawn the women and children sit together near the camp, wailing. The men stand apart and sing. The entire scene is covered with a pale blue haze left by the still-smoking fires of the night, and the strong shadows caused by the rising sun create a shimmering quality in the air not matched at any other time of day. After the songs the women and children are chased away by the shouts of the men, who retire to the dance ground to meet with the novices.

Immediately upon arrival at the dance ground the men divide into two circles and begin singing sacred songs about the dreamtime Kangaroo *(Malu)*. The novices are made to lie down, and blankets (acquired from the Mission) are placed over them. They remain under the blankets throughout the entire day except for brief moments when they are told to sit up and watch dances. This is an occasion for high spirits and camaraderie. With much hand-gesturing and use of a complicated kind of "double-talk" used on ceremonial occasions,[8] the men in the different song circles jest about what will befall the novices later in the day. Some of the finger gestures are graphic and exaggerated portrayals of how the boys' penes will be operated on, and these never fail to bring howls of laughter. The big joke, of course, is that the boys under the blankets can hear the bloodthirsty note of glee in the men's voices but can only guess (too rightly, in fact) what is so funny.

One man, circumcised a few years ago, is carried away by the enthusiasm of the moment and declares that he will be subincised right now. He is quickly grabbed by several men (his "brothers," both real ones and other men belonging to the same generation and section as himself) and held tightly as he is tilted backward, exposing his penis. The operator, an older man, steps forward and, using a sharp stone flake, cuts open the man's urethra from the meatus to a point about halfway to the scrotum. This is a fantastically painful operation, said to be even worse than circumcision, and the victim nearly passes out. But he sustains the entire operation without a murmur or cry and is quietly praised afterward for his fortitude. There is singing or other ritual attached to this operation. Afterward the victim stands close to a fire for a while to let the wound dry and then sits quietly off to one side for the rest of the day.

Meanwhile, other men have retired to a point in the bush where they cannot be observed directly. Using sharp, pointed sticks they reopen their own subincision wounds and line up in a semicircle on the dance ground facing the singers.

They perform a series of hopping dances back and forth directly in front of the novices, while the blood from their penis wounds splashes on their thighs. Then they too stand for a while by the fires to let their wounds dry. Immediately following this series of dances, I noticed some younger men running individually among the song-circles. Each would dart in and stand in front of an older man, lifting him up under the arms and embracing him tightly. According to Tindale, who witnessed a circumcision ceremony among Pitjantjara Aborigines in South Australia, in this practice the younger man embraces the man who held his penis during his circumcision.[9] It is a mark of public courtesy and appreciation by the younger man and is expected of him on this occasion. This ritual is followed by another hopping dance involving freshly reopened subincision wounds and an episode in which each of the novices is taken by a group of his classificatory brothers and tossed into the air (I was told that this was to let everyone see the boys), while everyone else in the gathering wails. After this the boys are hustled back under their blankets and the singing resumes.

For a little while at least there are no more dances or other activities, and I take advantage of the lull to collect my thoughts and try to assimilate what I had just seen. Although I have read about the practice of subincision and watched films of it, the first direct exposure is a grim experience. I know that more of this sort of thing will follow, and I try to understand why these men are willing to subject themselves to such excruciating ordeals.

Further dances follow, all re-enacting episodes from the travels of the totemic Two Kangaroos in the vicinity of Mount Davies, a prominent landmark in South Australia, about 180 miles east of the Warburton Mission, which has many sacred associations. For these dances, ocher and charcoal pigments are liberally applied to the dancers' bodies and, as a final touch, blood is sprinkled over the shoulders, chest, and back of each dancer, using either penis blood or blood taken from the basilic vein in the arm. The final dance portrays the totemic Echidna. This animal is a desert monotreme with quills that make it look like a small porcupine. It sometimes protects itself by digging into the ground in a series of jerky movements which always leave its quills facing upward for protection, and the dancer on this occasion is widely renowned for his ability to mimic these movements. His performance elicits great glee from the singers and adds a lighthearted touch to the proceedings.

Once again there is a lull in the activities, though singing continues without interruption. Portions of a couple of kangaroos which were cooked and divided yesterday are shared and eaten, and many of the men relax or talk among themselves. The atmosphere at times like these is like that of a men's club, with banter and easy conversation among peers and attention and respect by younger men toward the lodge elders. This is generally the case whenever cult-lodges assemble to prepare for ceremonial events, and young men who have not been initiated yearn to join in the camaraderie of these gatherings. Meanwhile the women and children return to the main camp from their temporary camp in the bush, and everyone awaits sunset and the final phase of the ceremony.

On most evenings nightfall comes quietly in the desert, but not now. Big fires are lighted as the women and children assemble in the place where they sat this morning. The men walk over from the dance ground and stand waiting. About 200 people are present. There is an air of excitement, with shouting and laughter, as everyone waits for darkness to fall. When are things going to start? There is some confusion, as there often is when an important event is about to occur. No one is in a position of authority to start the ceremony. The lodge elders have declared their readiness to proceed, but, like everyone else, they do not wish to be thought of as "bossy," so they procrastinate along with the rest. As a rule, the excitement at times like this must be allowed to build up to the point where everyone is impatient to act. Then an assertive man knows that his "bossiness" will be overlooked in favor of general approval about what needs to be done— in this case the boys' circumcision. In this case, the lead is taken by a small group of classificatory elder-brothers of one of the novices. Since there is no official leader or governing body in Aboriginal society, it takes a while for the matter to be decided. At long last the initiated men form into two tight bunches, one for the sun group, the other for the shade, and start for the dance ground.

The men in each group alternately run and walk toward the dance ground, grunting or shouting in unison as they go. When they arrive, each group runs back and forth across the large clearing where the ceremony will take place, then sits down in its circle and starts singing. The women and children follow the men and sit together at one end of the clearing. As the singing continues, several women get up and perform a simple dance, hopping stiffly with their heads and arms hanging limp. As soon as they finish, about a dozen men assemble at the opposite end of the clearing about 100 feet away. The women and men all pick up burning sticks from the fires and, with much shouting and histrionics, hurl the firebrands through the air at each other. This causes a brilliant effect, like fireworks. After a few minutes, the women send some young boys running across the clearing to the men, who toss them into the air and make them run back in a line. Finally the men sit down and return to their singing.

One man remains at each end of the clearing to build up an enormous bonfire, then these men, too, return to the song-circles. For a while the gathering becomes quiet, except for the singing which grows less excited and more carefully ca- denced. There is real tension at this point, with the women and children straining to see past the bonfires. Suddenly the three naked novices emerge from between the two fires, running in a line in perfect step with one another and with the rhythm of the singers. From a choreographic point of view this is a brilliantly engineered dramatic climax which would delight the most jaded ballet-goer. As the boys appear, the women and children begin to wail loudly, and before the boys reach the end of the clearing where everyone is seated, another electrifying sound is heard above the cries. A carved sacred board of medium size, called a bullroarer, is rotated rapidly through the air and as it spins it emits a weird, heart-stopping noise which is said to be the voice of the totemic Kangaroo. Even after I had seen this ceremony several times, the whir of the bullroarer always brought shivers up my spine. The effect on the women and children is dramatic —in a screaming mob they all run away from the dance ground and from the camp, back to their temporary camp in the bush.

Singing continues for a while as several men get up and perform a rapid backward dance with wildly vibrating knees. After they sit down, the two bonfires are built up, and again there is an air of expectancy. The bright glare of the fires acts as a curtain across the far end of the clearing. While the singing continues, a pair of unpainted naked men emerge, weaving back and forth across the clearing in a rapid, high-stepping dance. They skillfully control their movements in exact unison, and between them in an upright position is suspended a magnificent string cross constructed on an eight-foot spear. This piece of sacred paraphernalia is called *waniki*, and it is, for the duration of the ceremony, the actual body of the dreamtime Kangaroo. The novices see this exceedingly sacred item for the first time as they sit upright between the song-circles. The dancers pass swiftly in front of them, then zigzag their way back across the clearing and disappear behind the fires. Everything is done so expertly and happens so quickly that it hardly seems real. My subjective reaction to this episode was that at no other time I could recall did I feel more as if I had been in a dream while still awake, and I think this was exactly the dramatic intent of the performance. The action flowed silently, in perfect time with the rhythm of the singers, emerging out of the blackness between the fires at the end of the clearing and returning there, all in the space of perhaps thirty seconds. The absolute perfection of this presentation of the *waniki* was talked about among the men for weeks afterward.

Abruptly, the singing stops. A group of young men run forward and build a large bonfire, then settle themselves next to one another on their hands and knees to form a "human table" in front of it. One of the novices is picked up and carried by several of his *kuta* (elder brothers, real and classificatory) to the table. They lay him across it on his back. Another brother grips the boy's penis to keep it steady, and the operator (the novice's maternal uncle and also his potential father-in-law) steps forward. Still another brother draws the foreskin forward as far as he can. The operator then takes a stone knife and, either by slicing directly through or by cutting around a few times, removes the foreskin. A lad who has been troublesome as a youth or during his seclusion in novicehood may be punished at this time by prolonging the operation, but on this occasion and with the other two boys the operation proceeds without delay. The foreskin is passed to the boy's older brothers, who take it away and place it by the fire. If it wiggles while drying it is a sign that the boy will be unruly and a possible troublemaker (mainly in the sexual sense) as an adult. Then the dried foreskin is shared and eaten by the brothers. If the boy is mutilated during the operation, bleeds to death, or dies from an infection of the wound, these brothers have the duty of pursuing the circumciser and killing him. Meanwhile the boy is congratulated and led to the fire where he sits, letting the heat dry the wound.

Despite the intense pain, none of the three initiates cried out at any time. The ceremony is now over, and each novice, dazed from the operation, is quietly led away to a secluded place in the bush. Tomorrow the initiated men will meet with the novices in their camp and make sacred hair-buns *(pukutji)* which all of them, including the novices, will wear. While their wounds heal, the lads will remain in seclusion, wearing the hair-buns and keeping silent the whole time. The ordeal is over, and in several weeks they will return to camp as initiated men. . . .

LINKS TO THE LAND

My first efforts to understand the meaning of cult-lodges in Aboriginal life led me toward the strictly practical. It was apparent that some aspects of Aboriginal ceremonies were closely connected with important parts of daily life. For example, the discipline of the novices during seclusion and the rigors of physical pain during initiation helped instill an ability to withstand pain and isolation in general, abilities useful to any people who must live by foraging in a chancy and sometimes hostile environment. . . .

Another practical value, suggested by Tindale, is in learning the names and locations of watering places through contact with the myths about them.[10] These are first learned by novices in the instruction given to them during initiations, both in songs and dances and from the designs inscribed on sacred boards. As mentioned earlier, the designs carved on decorated spearthrowers also play a part in this instruction. Long sequences of named waterholes are memorized along with the stories (told in song) of the dreamtime events that occurred in these places. Initiates also sometimes visit the places connected with the sacred traditions. In watching young men in such situations, I have been impressed by their earnest efforts to absorb every detail of instruction. Having previously memorized the songs about the place, the initiate looks around carefully to make sure that every detail of topography and vegetation also registers on his consciousness. Even while departing, from time to time he casts a glance back over his shoulder, "back sighting" on the waterhole so that he will recognize it if he returns. The usefulness of this kind of knowledge to the desert people is obvious, and the cult-lodges, with their ordeals and instructions, help foster its recall and its transmission from one generation to the next.

These examples show that Aboriginal ceremonial life is not cut off from the practicalities of subsistence and daily living, even though much of the ceremony and ritual takes place in isolated settings, away from women and children. But although the knowledge and discipline promoted by the sacred life are useful to the Aborigines, I found that in interviews my informants never consciously expressed these practical ideas to support their views about the importance of the totemic cult-lodges in their lives. Before long I realized that I was dealing as much with feelings or sentiments as with strictly practical motives. The experience that gave me the greatest insight into the particular emotional appeal of the sacred life was my trip to Pukara.

Pukara is a sacred waterhole about 135 miles east of the Warburton Ranges Mission, in rugged sandhill country a few miles south of the Bell Rock Range. We reached it in the morning after a particularly rough cross-country trip. The weather was hot, and the tires on the Land-Rover, riddled by stakes after months of this kind of driving, required constant patching and repair. I made the trip with four Aborigines who had expressed a desire to perform a series of important rites at this place. Three were Pitjantjara-speakers and the fourth a Ngatatjara-speaker who "switched" dialects temporarily out of respect for the others. Along the way we stopped at a place where a vein of red ocher was exposed among the rocks. One of the men ground some of the ocher into powder and mixed it with the fat of an emu that had been killed during the trip. With this dark red pigment he drew a series of parallel lines across his chest. . . .

We rest at Pukara until around midday; then my four guides get up and start walking to the north in single file, away from the waterhole. I follow at the end of the line. . . .

Continuing our journey, we pass through a grove of mulga scrub and approach an area of low rocky formations between the sandhills. These rocky formations are covered with small desert mallee trees with long, pale green leaves hanging limp in the still, hot air. The rocks, probably sandstone of some kind, are pale yellow in color, and as soon as my guides see them they begin to wail loudly, kneeling and covering their eyes as they cry. This kind of wailing is fairly stereo-typed behavior among the desert Aborigines whenever someone is sick or has died.

The wailing continues for about five minutes. Then the men quietly rise and walk over to a cluster of eight small rockpiles, all formed from the yellow rock in the nearby outcrops. The largest of these piles stands to a height of 21 inches and is about 5 feet in diameter. Each pile has a space around it which the men proceed to clear of weeds and pebbles. I notice, too, that there is a hearth next to each rockpile. The men go off for a few minutes and return with firewood. This they place on four of the hearths, with each man at a separate rockpile. A branch is split and placed on the ground and thin wedges are inserted to hold the crack open and "nail" the branch to the ground. One man stands astride the branch to hold it down, while another places bits of dry kangaroo dung in the crack and lays the edge of his spearthrower across the branch at a point directly above the dry dung. He holds one end of the spearthrower and a third man kneels and takes hold of the other end. The two men saw vigorously back and forth with the spearthrower, working between the standing man's legs. In about twenty seconds a faint wisp of smoke appears from the dung inside the crack, and the men stop sawing and begin to blow on the smoldering dung, adding bits of dry grass to it as tinder. The faint glow spreads until the tinder is alight, and the burning tinder is then carried around to light the four fires.

Under nomadic conditions this is the only method the desert Aborigines have of making fire. Ordinarily, when I am traveling in the bush with Aborigines, I give them matches, but on this occasion I have used up my entire supply in vulcanizing tire-patches. Once on this trip, I even had to ask my companions to light a fire by this traditional method so I could make a tire-patch—one of the ironies that often occur when traveling in this region.

After lighting the fire, each man steps up to his rockpile and, using a small, sharpened stick, jabs at his subincised penis until the wound is reopened. When blood flows freely from the wound it is sprinkled over the rockpile. This accomplished, each man then stands for a few minutes by his fire to let the heat dry the wound and slow the flow of blood. These activities are carried on in a sober silence.

This completes the first part of the ritual, and the men form into single file and walk back to the waterhole, one of them carrying a firestick. Again, silence is maintained. The atmosphere throughout this episode is one of extreme reverence and meditation. From the time we arrived at the rockpiles the men have seemed deeply engrossed in contemplation, and I must be content with watching and recording what I see.

Back at Pukara, the man with the firestick uses it to ignite the dry brush surrounding the waterhole. In a few minutes all the brush and thorns that have accumulated since the place was last visited are burned off. The men stand around, contemplating the waterhole. They call me over and point out some of its features. The water smells vile, like marsh gas, and is black and oily in color. Nevertheless, the men find it drinkable. The waterhole lies in a natural depression or hole in a shelf of limestone at the edge of a dry lakebed. All around the lakebed are high sandhills, turning from pink to red as evening approaches. On the limestone surface at one side of the waterhole, there is a series of natural ripples or parallel grooves. These, I am told, are the chest scars of the totemic Wanampi Kutjara (Two Water-snakes) who visited this place in the dreamtime. The man who painted his chest with red ocher explains that he and the three other men are members of this cult-lodge and that he is the oldest man present. The red ocher on his chest represents the chest scars of the Water-snake-men (human and animal forms are largely interchangeable in these myths).

We make camp on the broad crest of a sandhill about 100 yards from the waterhole. That night the men explain their behavior at the rockpiles. Pukara, they say, is where the Two Water-snake-men came in the dreamtime after collecting and eating large quantities of sweet yellow *wama*. They became sick at this place and vomited out the contents of their stomachs onto the ground. The *wama* they vomited out turned to stone (*yapuringu*—became rock [in the dreamtime]), becoming the piles of yellow rock where the men sprinkled penis blood today. The Water-snake-men accomplished this transformation "by themselves" *(yungara)*, and today the spirit of these ancestral beings is alive and resides in the rockpiles.

The eldest man says that he and his son were both born near here. This place is their "dreaming," and he addresses his rockpile as *"ngayuku mama* [my father]"—meaning that he and his son both claim descent in the male line from the Water-snake spirit living within the rockpile. The three other men say that they were born at or near various other points along this same totemic track. Each of the other seven rockpiles is the paternal ancestor-spirit of a lodge member not with us on this trip, and the three men address the respective piles with kinship terms appropriate to their relationship to these absent members. Even though this place is not their own "dreaming" (that is, birthplace), as members of the same cult-lodge they have both the privilege and the duty of acting here on their relatives' behalf.

The wailing was a sign of sorrow over the illness of the totemic Water-snakes. The fires have no symbolic importance, but the sprinkling of penis blood is *kapi pinpa* (just like rain) in its importance in causing the actual grevillea flower—the source of *wama*, a highly prized and much-sought-after delicacy—to ripen and the plants to multiply.

In short, all members of this cult-lodge, whether they have their actual "dreaming" here or act on behalf of relatives (including women) who do, have the sacred duty of performing this rite, annually if possible. By doing so they temporarily re-enter the dreamtime (hence the deeply meditative behavior during and after the ritual), and the rockpiles become part of their own being. Even when they are not performing the ritual, a direct kinship tie always exists between the men and the rockpiles. Their general duties as lodge members also include keeping the area around the rockpiles clean, seeing to it that the piles themselves remain intact, and, of course, deciding on suitable novices to instruct in the traditions.

Anthropologists commonly refer to rituals of this kind as "increase" ceremonies. Meggitt, however, has correctly pointed out that this term is something of a misnomer: "It is worth noting . . . that the term 'increase,' although commonly used in the literature in relation to such rituals, is not strictly accurate. The participants are simply concerned to maintain the supplies of natural species at their usual level, to support the normal order of nature."[11]

In this case, the members of the totemic Wanampi Kutjara cult-lodge have acted to maintain the abundance of *wama* and regard the sprinkling of penis blood as an essential act in ensuring the ripening and continued fertility of this plant species. This ritual act benefits mainly the lodge members and their relatives, since these are the people who tend to forage and hunt in the general area around this sacred site, but it will also benefit any other people who may visit this region in search of food. Many "increase" ceremonies are also performed *in absentia* from the actual totemic site, generally when they are being shown to novices prior to an initiation ordeal.

At dawn the men get up and go directly to the waterhole. While one of them sweeps off the limestone shelf with an impromptu handbroom made of twigs and brush, the others climb into the water and begin removing handfuls of sticky black mud from the bottom. They splash around and laugh, obviously enjoying the mudbath. Now that the overgrowth is gone I can see a low embankment along the north side of the waterhole, and the men take their handfuls of mud and pile them on this mound. One takes a stick and starts poking around in the mud underneath the water. Soon he finds what he is looking for and begins lifting out pieces of smooth, naturally shaped rock and pieces of waterlogged wood and placing them on the swept area of limestone next to the pool. Forty-seven of these objects are dredged up and laid out to dry in the sun.

The work of removing mud from the waterhole is slow, but the embankment steadily grows higher until it stands almost 3 feet high and is completely coated with black slime. Meanwhile the pieces of stone and wood have dried and are being discussed by the men. They say that after recovering from their sickness at the site of the rockpiles the Two Water-snakes continued their dreamtime travels until they reached the present site of the waterhole. They entered the ground here, transforming themselves into the waterhole and also transforming various objects they had with them at the same time. They and these objects are said to reside in the waterhole today. Each of the pieces of wood and stone extracted from the mud is one of these transformed objects belonging to the Wanampi Kutjara. The men point out one piece, a waterlogged stick, which they tell me is a piece of firewood belonging to the totemic beings. Another stick is the Water-snakes' wooden club *(kupulu)*, and a piece of stone is one of their dogs. After being dried off and inspected, these objects are reverently replaced in the mud inside the waterhole.

Now the action proceeds rapidly. One man grinds a large quantity of red ocher and mixes it with water. Using his hand as a brush, he spreads the pigment over the rock rim of the pool, coating it thoroughly until the brilliant red color extends nearly all the way around (except for the spot below the mud-covered embankment). The other three men finish spreading the wet mud over the embankment and start inscribing serpentine designs in it, rather in the manner of fingerpainting. Before long the entire surface of the mound facing the waterhole is covered with these designs, which the men say represent the totemic Water-snakes. Pukara is now a spectacular sight. The black mud surface of the embankment, the bright red-ocher color of the waterhole rim, and the white of the swept limestone shelf combine to form a vivid contrast to the pale and dusty shades of the surrounding lakebed and nearby spinifex flats. It is an impressive transformation, and the men are proud of the results. In time, wind and rain will deface their handiwork, and vegetation will creep in and cover the site again, but the men have derived spiritual satisfaction from performing these acts and hope to return in another year to carry out their sacred duties once again. . . .

The anthropologists Ronald M. Berndt and Catherine H. Berndt point out that the myth of the totemic Water-snake, or, as it is often called, the Rainbow-snake, is widespread in Australia, particularly in Arnhem Land to the north and in the western and central deserts, where it is typically associated with rain and water.[12] For me, this ritual offered a firsthand awareness of something which the Berndts, Strehlow, and other scholars have mentioned in their writings—namely, the direct kinship ties which individuals have to particular sacred landmarks. These landmarks are nothing less than the bodies of the totemic beings, or items connected with them, transformed during the dreamtime into individual waterholes, trees, sandhills, ridges, and other physiographic features, as well as into rock alignments and sacred rockpiles, but still spiritually alive and influencing the present. The emotional sentiments of kinship are extended by the Aborigines to these sacred landmarks. Thus the sight of virtually every landmark, no matter how insignificant it may seem to the foreign visitor passing through the desert, brings deep emotional satisfaction to the Aborigine. No wonder Aborigines are able to find their way through this apparently featureless country, since their memories are constantly reinforced by spiritual ties with even the smallest rock outcrop.

An outsider might phrase this another way. The concept of the "dreaming" breaks down the separation of man and his physical environment. The desert Aborigines do not seek to control the environment in either their daily or their sacred lives. Rituals of the sacred life may be seen as the efforts of man to combine with his environment, to become "at one" with it. Deep feelings of belonging to a harmoniously ordered universe result from these apparently bizarre rituals, and a person's relationship to his "dreaming," carried on within the appropriate cult-lodge, becomes the core of his social and spiritual identity.

NOTES

1. Spencer and Gillen 1899; Spencer and Gillen 1927; Stanner 1963; Strehlow 1947; Meggitt 1962.
2. Durkheim 1961:52.
3. Berndt 1959:97–98.
4. Bates 1913:396–397. Elkin 1940:298, 315–326. There is evidence that sometime between 1913 and 1930 the Aborigines living near Laverton and Mount Margaret Mission (and perhaps Warburton as well, later on) modified their original four-section system into the present six-section arrangement.
5. Berndt and Berndt 1964:60.
6. Douglas 1964:126.
7. Meggitt 1962:68.
8. Hale 1967. This "double talk" is comparable in many ways to the ceremonial or "clowning" language of the Walbiri, called *tjiliwiri.*
9. Tindale 1935:205.
10. Tindale 1935:223.
11. Meggitt 1962:221.
12. Berndt and Berndt 1964:209.

15

THE THEATRE'S NEW TESTAMENT

Jerzy Grotowski

The very name "Theatre Laboratory" makes one think of scientific research. Is this an appropriate association?

The word research should not bring to mind scientific research. Nothing could be further from what we are doing than science in the strict sense, and not only because of our lack of qualifications, but also because of our lack of interest in that kind of work.

The word research implies that we approach our profession rather like the mediaeval wood carver who sought to recreate in his block of wood a form which already existed. We do not work in the same way as the artist or the scientist, but rather as the shoemaker looking for the right spot on the shoe in which to hammer the nail.

The other sense of the word research might seem a little irrational as it involves the idea of a penetration into human nature itself. In our age when all languages are confused as in the Tower of Babel, when all aesthetical genres intermingle, death threatens the theatre as film and television encroach upon its domain. This makes us examine the nature of theatre, how it differs from the other art forms, and what it is that makes it irreplaceable.

Has your research led you to a definition?

What does the word theatre mean? This is a question we often come up against, and one to which there are many possible answers. To the academic, the theatre is a place where an actor recites a written text, illustrating it with a series of movements in order to make it more easily understood. Thus interpreted the

---

Jerzy Grotowski is founder-director of the Polish Laboratory Theatre of Wroclaw, and is author of *Towards a Poor Theatre*. His most recent work rejects traditional theatres and ordinary relationships between spectators and performers.

theatre is a useful accessory to dramatic literature. The intellectual theatre is merely a variation of this conception. Its advocates consider it a kind of polemical tribune. Here too, the text is the most important element, and the theatre is there only to plug certain intellectual arguments, thus bringing about their reciprocal confrontation. It is a revival of the mediaeval art of the oratorical duel.

To the average theatre-goer, the theatre is first and foremost a place of entertainment. If he expects to encounter a frivolous Muse, the text does not interest him in the least. What attracts him are the so-called gags, the comic effects and perhaps the puns which lead back to the text. His attention will be directed mainly towards the actor as a centre of attraction. A young woman sufficiently briefly clad is in herself an attraction to certain theatre-goers who apply cultural criteria to her performance, though such a judgement is actually a compensation for personal frustration.

The theatre-goer who cherishes cultural aspirations likes from time to time to attend performances from the more serious repertoire, perhaps even a tragedy provided that it contains some melodramatic element. In this case his expectations will vary widely. On the one hand he must show that he belongs to the best society where "Art" is a guarantee and, on the other, he wants to experience certain emotions which give him a sense of self-satisfaction. Even if he does feel pity for poor Antigone and aversion for the cruel Creon, he does not share the sacrifice and the fate of the heroine, but he nevertheless believes himself to be her equal morally. For him it is a question of being able to feel "noble." The didactic qualities of this kind of emotion are dubious. The audience—all Creons —may well side with Antigone throughout the performance, but this does not prevent each of them from behaving like Creon once out of the theatre. It is worth noticing the success of plays which depict an unhappy childhood. To see the sufferings of an innocent child on the stage makes it even easier for the spectator to sympathize with the unfortunate victim. Thus he is assured of his own high standard of moral values.

Theatre people themselves do not usually have an altogether clear conception of theatre. To the average actor the theatre is first and foremost *himself*, and not what he is able to achieve by means of his artistic technique. He—his own private organism—*is* the theatre. Such an attitude breeds the impudence and self-satisfaction which enable him to present acts that demand no special knowledge, that are banal and commonplace, such as walking, getting up, sitting down, lighting a cigarette, putting his hands in his pockets, and so on. In the actor's opinion all this is not meant to reveal anything but to be enough in itself for, as I said, he, the actor, Mr. X, *is* the theatre. And if the actor possesses a certain charm which can take in the audience, it strengthens him in his conviction.

To the stage-designer, the theatre is above all a plastic art and this can have positive consequences. Designers are often supporters of the literary theatre. They claim that the décor as well as the actor should serve the drama. This creed reveals no wish to serve literature, but merely a complex towards the producer.

They prefer to be on the side of the playwright as he is further removed and consequently less able to restrict them. In practice, the most original stage-designers suggest a confrontation between the text and a plastic vision which surpasses and reveals the playwright's imagination. It is probably no mere coincidence that the Polish designers are often the pioneers in our country's theatre. They exploited the numerous possibilities offered by the revolutionary development of the plastic arts in the twentieth century which, to a lesser degree, inspired playwrights and producers.

Does this not imply a certain danger? The critics who accuse the designers of dominating the stage, put forward more than one valid objective argument, only their premise is erroneous. It is as if they blame a car for travelling faster than a snail. This is what worries them and not whether the designer's vision dominates that of the actor and the producer. The vision of the designer is creative, not stereotyped, and even if it is, it loses its tautological character through an immense magnification process. Nevertheless, the theatre is transformed—whether the designer likes it or not—into a series of living tableaux. It becomes a kind of monumental "camera oscura," a thrilling "laterna magica." But does it not then cease to be theatre?

Finally, what is the theatre to the producer? Producers come to the theatre after failing in other fields. He who once dreamed of becoming a playwright usually ends up as a producer.

The actor who is a failure, the actress who once played the young prima donna and is getting old, these turn to production.

The theatre critic who has long had an impotence complex towards an art which he can do no more than write about takes up producing.

The hypersensitive professor of literature who is weary of academic work considers himself competent to become a producer. He knows what drama is—and what else is theatre to him if not the realisation of a text?

Because they are guided by such varied psycho-analytic motives, producers' ideas on theatre are about as varied as it is possible to be. Their work is a compensation for various phenomena. A man who has unfulfilled political tendencies, for instance, often becomes a producer and enjoys the feeling of power such a position gives him. This has more than once led to perverse interpretations, and producers possessing such an extreme need for power have staged plays which polemicize against the authorities: hence numerous "rebellious" performances.

Of course a producer wants to be creative. He therefore—more or less consciously—advocates an autonomous theatre, independent of literature which he merely considers as a pretext. But, on the other hand, people capable of such creative work are rare. Many are officially content with a literary and intellectual theatre definition, or to maintain Wagner's theory that the theatre should be a synthesis of all the arts. A very useful formula! It allows one to respect the text, that inviolable basic element, and furthermore it provokes no conflict with the literary and the philological milieu. It must be stated, in parenthesis, that every playwright—even the ones we can only qualify as such out of sheer politeness—

feels himself obliged to defend the honour and the rights of Mickiewicz, Shakespeare, etc., because quite simply he considers himself their colleague. In this way Wagner's theory about "the theatre as the total art" establishes *la paix des braves* in the literary field.

This theory justifies the exploitation of the plastic elements of scenography in the performance, and ascribes the results to it. The same goes for the music, whether it be an original work or a montage. To this is added the accidental choice of one or more well known actors and from these elements, only casually coordinated, emerges a performance which satisfies the ambitions of the producer. He is enthroned on top of all the arts, although in reality he feeds off them all without himself being tied to the creative work which is carried out for him by others—if, indeed, anyone can be called creative in such circumstances.

Thus the number of definitions of theatre is practically unlimited. To escape from this vicious circle one must without doubt eliminate, not add. That is, one must ask oneself what is indispensable to theatre. Let's see.

Can the theatre exist without costumes and sets? Yes, it can.

Can it exist without music to accompany the plot? Yes.

Can it exist without lighting effects? Of course.

And without a text? Yes; the history of the theatre confirms this. In the evolution of the theatrical art the text was one of the last elements to be added. If we place some people on a stage with a scenario they themselves have put together and let them improvise their parts as in the Commedia dell'Arte, the performance will be equally good even if the words are not articulated but simply muttered.

But can the theatre exist without actors? I know of no example of this. One could mention the puppet-show. Even here, however, an actor is to be found behind the scenes, although of another kind.

Can the theatre exist without an audience? At least one spectator is needed to make it a performance. So we are left with the actor and the spectator. We can thus define the theatre as "what takes place between spectator and actor." All the other things are supplementary—perhaps necessary, but nevertheless supplementary. It is no mere coincidence that our own theatre laboratory has developed from a theatre rich in resources—in which the plastic arts, lighting and music, were constantly exploited—into the ascetic theatre we have become in recent years: an ascetic theatre in which the actors and audience are all that is left. All the other visual elements—e.g. plastic, etc.—are constructed by means of the actor's body, the acoustic and musical effects by his voice. This does not mean that we look down upon literature, but that we do not find in it the creative part of the theatre, even though great literary works can, no doubt, have a stimulating effect on this genesis. Since our theatre consists only of actors and audience, we make special demands on both parties. Even though we cannot educate the audience—not systematically, at least—we *can* educate the actor.

How, then, is the actor trained in your theatre, and what is his function in the performance?

The actor is a man who works in public with his body, offering it publicly. If this body restricts itself to demonstrating what it is— something that any average person can do—then it is not an obedient instrument capable of performing a spiritual act. If it is exploited for money and to win the favour of the audience, then the art of acting borders on prostitution. It is a fact that for many centuries the theatre has been associated with prostitution in one sense of the word or another. The words "actress" and "courtesan" were once synonymous. Today they are separated by a somewhat clearer line, not through any change in the actor's world but because society has changed. Today it is the difference between the respectable woman and the courtesan which has become blurred.

What strikes one when looking at the work of an actor as practised these days is the wretchedness of it: the bargaining over a body which is exploited by its protectors—director, producer—creating in return an atmosphere of intrigue and revolt.

Just as only a great sinner can become a saint according to the theologians (let us not forget the Revelation: "So then because thou art lukewarm, and neither cold nor hot, I will spue thee out of my mouth"), in the same way the actor's wretchedness can be transformed into a kind of holiness. The history of the theatre has numerous examples of this.

Don't get me wrong. I speak about "holiness" as an unbeliever. I mean a "secular holiness." If the actor, by setting himself a challenge publicly challenges others, and through excess, profanation and outrageous sacrilege reveals himself by casting off his everyday mask, he makes it possible for the spectator to undertake a similar process of self-penetration. If he does not exhibit his body, but annihilates it, burns it, frees it from every resistance to any psychic impulse, then he does not sell his body but sacrifices it. He repeats the atonement; he is close to holiness. If such acting is not to be something transient and fortuitous, a phenomenon which cannot be foreseen in time or space: if we want a theatre group whose daily bread is this kind of work—then we must follow a special method of research and training.

What is it like, in practice, to work with the "holy" actor?

There is a myth telling how an actor with a considerable fund of experience can build up what we might call his own "arsenal"—i. e. an accumulation of methods, artifices and tricks. From these he can pick out a certain number of combinations for each part and thus attain the expressiveness necessary for him to grip his audience. This "arsenal" or store may be nothing but a collection of clichés, in which case such a method is inseparable from the conception of the "courtesan actor."

The difference between the "courtesan actor" and the "holy actor" is the same as the difference between the skill of a courtesan and the attitude of giving and receiving which springs from true love: in other words, self-sacrifice. The essential thing in this second case is to be able to eliminate any disturbing elements in order to be able to overstep every conceivable limit. In the first case it is a question of the existence of the body; in the other, rather of its non-existence. The technique of the "holy actor" is an *inductive technique* (i.e. a technique of elimination), whereas that of the "courtesan actor" is a *deductive technique* (i.e. an accumulation of skills).

The actor who undertakes an act of self-penetration, who reveals himself and sacrifices the innermost part of himself—the most painful, that which is not intended for the eyes of the world—must be able to respond to the least impulse. He must be able to express, through sound and movement, those impulses which waver on the borderline between dream and reality. In short, he must be able to construct his own psycho-analytic language of sounds and gestures in the same way that a great poet creates his own language of words.

If we take into consideration for instance the problem of sound, the plasticity of the actor's respiratory and vocal apparatus must be infinitely more developed than that of the man in the street. Furthermore, this apparatus must be able to produce sound reflexes so quickly that thought—which would remove all spontaneity—has no time to intervene.

The actor should be able to decipher all the problems of his body which are accessible to him. He should know how to direct the air to those parts of the body where sound can be created and amplified by a sort of resonator. The average actor knows only the head resonator; that is, he uses his head as a resonator to amplify his voice, making it sound more "noble," more agreeable to the audience. He may even at times, fortuitously, make use of the chest resonator. But the actor who investigates closely the possibilities of his own organism discovers that the number of resonators is practically unlimited. He can exploit not only his head and chest, but also the back of his head (occiput), his nose, his teeth, his larynx, his belly, his spine, as well as a total resonator which actually comprises the whole body and many others, some of which are still unknown to us. He discovers that it is not enough to make use of abdominal respiration on stage. The various phases in his physical actions demand different kinds of respiration if he is to avoid difficulties with his breathing and resistance from his body. He discovers that the diction he learnt at drama school far too often provokes the closing of the larynx. He must acquire the ability to open his larynx consciously, and to check from the outside whether it is open or closed. If he does not solve these problems, his attention will be distracted by the difficulties he is bound to encounter and the process of self-penetration will necessarily fail. If the actor is conscious of his body, he cannot penetrate and reveal himself. The body must be freed from all resistance. It must virtually cease to exist. As for his voice and respiration, it is not enough that the actor learns to make use of several resonators, to open his larynx and to select a certain type of respiration. He must learn to perform all this unconsciously in the culminating phases of his acting and this, in its turn, is something which demands a new series of exercises. When he is working on his role he must learn not to think of adding technical elements (resonators, etc.), but should aim at eliminating the concrete obstacles he comes up against (e.g. resistance in his voice).

This is not merely splitting hairs. It is the difference which decides the degree of success. It means that the actor will never possess a permanently "closed" technique, for at each stage of his self-scrutiny, each challenge, each *excess*, each breaking down of hidden barriers he will encounter new technical problems on a higher level. He must then learn to overcome these too with the help of certain basic exercises.

This goes for everything: movement, the plasticity of the body, gesticulation, the construction of masks by means of the facial musculature and, in fact, for each detail of the actor's body.

But the decisive factor in this process is the actor's technique of psychic penetration. He must learn to use his role as if it were a surgeon's scalpel, to dissect himself. It is not a question of portraying himself under certain given circumstances, or of "living" a part; nor does it entail the distant sort of acting common to epic theatre and based on cold calculation. The important thing is to use the role as a trampoline, an instrument with which to study what is hidden behind our everyday mask—the innermost core of our personality—in order to sacrifice it, expose it.

This is an excess not only for the actor but also for the audience. The spectator understands, consciously or unconsciously, that such an act is an invitation to him to do the same thing, and this often arouses opposition or indignation, because our daily efforts are intended to hide the truth about ourselves not only from the world, but also from ourselves. We try to escape the truth about ourselves, whereas here we are invited to stop and take a closer look. We are afraid of being changed into pillars of salt if we turn around, like Lot's wife.

The performing of this act we are referring to—self-penetration, exposure—demands a mobilization of all the physical and spiritual forces of the actor who is in a state of idle readiness, a passive availability, which makes possible an active acting score.

One must resort to a metaphorical language to say that the decisive factor in this process is humility, a spiritual predisposition: not to *do* something, but to *refrain* from doing something, otherwise the excess becomes impudence instead of sacrifice. This means that the actor must act in a state of trance.

Trance, as I understand it, is the ability to concentrate in a particular theatrical way and can be attained with a minimum of goodwill.

If I were to express all this in one sentence I would say that it is all a question of giving oneself. One must give oneself totally, in one's deepest intimacy, with confidence, as when one gives oneself in love. Here lies the key. Self-penetration, trance, *excess*, the formal discipline itself—all this can be realized, provided one has given oneself fully, humbly and without defense. This act culminates in a climax. It brings relief. None of the exercises in the various fields of the actor's training must be exercises in skill. They should develop a system of allusions which lead to the elusive and indescribable process of self-donation.

All this may sound strange and bring to mind some form of "quackery." If we are to stick to scientific formulas, we can say that it is a particular use of suggestion, aiming at an *ideoplastic* realization. Personally, I must admit that we do not shrink from using these "quack" formulas. Anything that has an unusual or magical ring stimulates the imagination of both actor and producer.

I believe one must develop a special anatomy of the actor; for instance, find the body's various centres of concentration for different ways of acting, seeking the areas of the body which the actor sometimes feels to be his sources of energy. The lumbar region, the abdomen and the area around the solar plexus often function as such a source.

An essential factor in this process is the elaboration of a guiding rein for the form, the artificiality. The actor who accomplishes an act of self-penetration is setting out on a journey which is recorded through various sound and gesture reflexes, formulating a sort of invitation to the spectator. But these signs must be articulated. Expressiveness is always connected with certain contradictions and discrepancies. Undisciplined self-penetration is no liberation, but is perceived as a form of biological chaos.

How do you combine spontaneity and formal discipline?

The elaboration of artificiality is a question of ideograms—sounds and gestures —which evoke associations in the psyche of the audience. It is reminiscent of a sculptor's work on a block of stone: the conscious use of hammer and chisel. It consists, for instance, in the analysis of a hand's reflex during a psychic process and its successive development through shoulder, elbow, wrist and fingers in order to decide how each phase of this process can be expressed through a sign, an ideogram, which either instantly conveys the hidden motivations of the actor or polemicizes against them.

This elaboration of artificiality—of the form's guiding rein—is often based on a conscious searching of our organism for forms whose outlines we feel although their reality still escapes us. One assumes that these forms already exist, complete, within our organism. Here we touch on a type of acting which, as an art, is closer to sculpture than to painting. Painting involves the addition of colours, whereas the sculptor takes away what is concealing the form which, as it were, already exists within the block of stone, thus revealing it instead of building it up.

This search for artificiality in its turn requires a series of additional exercises, forming a miniature score for each part of the body. At any rate, the decisive principle remains the following: the more we become absorbed in what is hidden inside us, in the excess, in the exposure, in the self-penetration, the more rigid must be the external discipline; that is to say the form, the artificiality, the ideogram, the sign. Here lies the whole principle of expressiveness.

What do you expect from the spectator in this kind of theatre?

Our postulates are not new. We make the same demands on people as every real work of art makes, whether it be a painting, a sculpture, music, poetry or literature. We do not cater for the man who goes to the theatre to satisfy a social need for contact with culture: in other words, to have something to talk about to his friends and to be able to say that he has seen this or that play and that it was interesting. We are not there to satisfy his "cultural needs." This is cheating.

Nor do we cater for the man who goes to the theatre to relax after a hard day's work. Everyone has a right to relax after work and there are numerous forms of entertainment for this purpose, ranging from certain types of film to cabaret and music-hall, and many more on the same lines.

We are concerned with the spectator who has genuine spiritual needs and who really wishes, through confrontation with the performance, to analyse himself. We are concerned with the spectator who does not stop at an elementary stage of psychic integration, content with his own petty, geometrical, spiritual stability, knowing exactly what is good and what is evil, and never in doubt. For it was not to him that El Greco, Norwid, Thomas Mann and Dostoyevsky spoke, but to him who undergoes an endless process of self-development, whose unrest is not general but directed towards a search for the truth about himself and his mission in life.

Does this infer a theatre for the élite?

Yes, but for an élite which is not determined by the social background or financial situation of the spectator, nor even education. The worker who has never had any secondary education can undergo this creative process of self-search, whereas the university professor may be dead, permanently formed, moulded into the terrible rigidity of a corpse. This must be made clear from the very beginning. We are not concerned with just any audience, but a special one.

We cannot know whether the theatre is still necessary today since all social attractions, entertainments, form and colour effects have been taken over by film and television. Everybody repeats the same rhetorical question: is the theatre necessary? But we only ask it in order to be able to reply: yes, it is, because it is an art which is always young and always necessary. The sale of performances is organized on a grand scale. Yet no one organizes film and television audiences in the same way. If all theatres were closed down one day, a large percentage of the people would know nothing about it until weeks later, but if one were to eliminate cinemas and television, the very next day the whole population would be in an uproar. Many theatre people are conscious of this problem, but hit upon the wrong solution: since the cinema dominates theatre from a technical point of view, why not make the theatre more technical? They invent new stages, they put on performances with lightning-quick changes of scenery, complicated lighting and décor, etc., but can never attain the technical skill of film and television. The theatre must recognize its own limitations. If it cannot be richer than the cinema, then let it be poor. If it cannot be as lavish as television, let it be ascetic. If it cannot be a technical attraction, let it renounce all outward technique. Thus we are left with a "holy" actor in a poor theatre.

There is only one element of which film and television cannot rob the theatre: the closeness of the living organism. Because of this, each challenge from the actor, each of his magical acts (which the audience is incapable of reproducing) becomes something great, something extraordinary, something close to ecstasy. It is therefore necessary to abolish the distance between actor and audience by eliminating the stage, removing all frontiers. Let the most drastic scenes happen face to face with the spectator so that he is within arm's reach of the actor, can feel his breathing and smell the perspiration. This implies the necessity for a chamber theatre.

How can such a theatre express the unrest which one has a right to assume varies with the individual?

In order that the spectator may be stimulated into self-analysis when confronted with the actor, there must be some common ground already existing in both of them, something they can either dismiss in one gesture or jointly worship. Therefore the theatre must attack what might be called the collective complexes of society, the core of the collective subconscious or perhaps superconscious (it does not matter what we call it), the myths which are not an invention of the mind but are, so to speak, inherited through one's blood, religion, culture and climate.

I am thinking of things that are so elementary and so intimately associated that it would be difficult for us to submit them to a rational analysis. For instance, religious myths: the myth of Christ and Mary; biological myths: birth and death, love symbolism or, in a broader sense Eros and Thanatos; national myths which it would be difficult to break down into formulas, yet whose very presence we feel in our blood when we read Part III of Mickiewicz's "Forefathers' Eve," Slowacki's "Kordian" or the Ave Maria.

Once again, there is no question of a speculative search for certain elements to be assembled into a performance. If we start working on a theatre performance or a role by violating our innermost selves, searching for the things which can hurt us most deeply, but which at the same time give us a total feeling of purifying truth that finally brings peace, then we will inevitably end up with *representations collectives.* One has to be familiar with this concept so as not to lose the right track once one has found it. But it cannot be imposed on one in advance.

How does this function in a theatre performance? I do not intend to give examples here. I think there is sufficient explanation in the description of "Akropolis," "Dr. Faustus" or other performances. I only wish to draw attention to a special characteristic of these theatre performances which combine fascination and excessive negation, acceptance and rejection, an attack on that which is sacred *(representations collectives),* profanation and worship.

To spark off this particular process of provocation in the audience, one must break away from the trampoline represented by the text and which is already overloaded with a number of general associations. For this we need either a classical text to which, through a sort of profanation, we simultaneously restore its truth, or a modern text which might well be banal and stereotyped in its content, but nevertheless rooted in the psyche of society.

Is the "holy" actor not a dream? The road to holiness is not open to everyone. Only the chosen few can follow it.

As I said, one must not take the word "holy" in the religious sense. It is rather a metaphor defining a person who, through his art, climbs upon the stake and performs an act of self-sacrifice. Of course, you are right: it is an infinitely difficult task to assemble a troup of "holy" actors. It is very much easier to find a "holy" spectator—in my sense of the word—for he only comes to the theatre for a brief moment in order to square off an account with himself, and this is something that does not impose the hard routine of daily work.

Is holiness therefore an unreal postulate? I think it is just as well founded as that of movement at the speed of light. By this I mean that without ever attaining it, we can nevertheless move consciously and systematically in that direction, thus achieving practical results.

Acting is a particularly thankless art. It dies with the actor. Nothing survives him but the reviews which do not usually do him justice anyway, whether he is good or bad. So the only source of satisfaction left to him is the audience's reactions. In the poor theatre this does not mean flowers and interminable applause, but a special silence in which there is much fascination but also a lot of indignation, and even repugnance, which the spectator directs not at himself but at the theatre. It is difficult to reach a psychic level which enables one to endure such pressure.

I am sure that every actor belonging to such a theatre often dreams of overwhelming ovations, of hearing his name shouted out, of being covered with flowers or other such symbols of appreciation as is customary in the commercial theatre. The actor's work is also a thankless one because of the incessant supervision it is subject to. It is not like being creative in an office, seated before a table, but under the eye of the producer who, even in a theatre based on the art of the actor, must make persistent demands on him to a much greater extent than in the normal theatre, urging him on to ever increasing efforts that are painful to him.

This would be unbearable if such a producer did not possess a moral authority, if his postulates were not evident, and if an element of mutual confidence did not exist even beyond the barriers of consciousness. But even in this case, he is nevertheless a tyrant and the actor must direct against him certain unconscious mechanical reactions like a pupil does against his teacher, a patient against his doctor, or a soldier against his superiors.

The poor theatre does not offer the actor the possibility of overnight success. It defies the bourgeois concept of a standard of living. It proposes the substitution of material wealth by moral wealth as the principal aim in life. Yet who does not cherish a secret wish to rise to sudden affluence? This too may cause opposition and negative reactions, even if these are not clearly formulated. Work in such an ensemble can never be stable. It is nothing but a huge challenge and, further-more, it awakens such strong reactions of aversion that these often threaten the theatre's very existence. Who does not search for stability and security in one form or another? Who does not hope to live at least as well tomorrow as he does today? Even if one consciously accepts such a status, one unconsciously looks around for that unattainable refuge which reconciles fire with water and "holi-ness" with the life of the "courtesan."

However, the attraction of such a paradoxical situation is sufficiently strong to eliminate all the intrigues, slander and quarrels over roles which form part of everyday life in other theatres. But people will be people, and periods of depres-sion and suppressed grudges cannot be avoided.

It is nevertheless worth mentioning that the satisfaction which such work gives is great. The actor who, in this special process of discipline and self-sacrifice, self-penetration and moulding, is not afraid to go beyond all normally acceptable limits, attains a kind of inner harmony and peace of mind. He literally becomes much sounder in mind and body, and his way of life is more normal than that of an actor in the rich theatre.

This process of analysis is a sort of disintegration of the psychic structure. Is the actor not in danger here of overstepping the mark from the point of view of mental hygiene?

No, provided that he gives himself one hundred per cent to his work. It is work that is done half-heartedly, superficially, that is psychically painful and upsets the equilibrium. If we only engage ourselves superficially in this process of analysis and exposure—and this can produce ample aesthetical effects—that is, if we retain our daily mask of lies, then we witness a conflict between this mask and ourselves. But if this process is followed through to its extreme limit, we can in full consciousness put back our everyday mask, knowing now what purpose it serves and what it conceals beneath it. This is a confirmation not of the negative in us but of the positive, not of what is poorest but of what is richest. It also leads to a liberation from complexes in much the same way as psycho-analytic therapy.

The same also applies to the spectator. The member of an audience who accepts the actor's invitation and to a certain extent follows his example by activating himself in the same way, leaves the theatre in a state of greater inner harmony. But he who fights to keep his mask of lies intact at all costs, leaves the performance even more confused. I am convinced that on the whole, even in the latter case, the performance represents a form of social psycho-therapy, whereas for the actor it is only a therapy if he has given himself whole-heartedly to his task.

There are certain dangers. It is far less risky to be Mr. Smith all one's life than to be Van Gogh. But, fully conscious of our social responsibility, we could wish that there were more Van Goghs than Smiths, even though life is much simpler for the latter. Van Gogh is an example of an incomplete process of integration. His downfall is the expression of a development which was never fulfilled. If we take a look at great personalities like for example Thomas Mann, we do eventually find a certain form of harmony.

It seems to me that the producer has a very great responsibility in this self-analytic process of the actor. How does this interdependence manifest itself, and what might be the consequences of a wrong action on his part?

This is a vitally important point. In the light of what I have just said, this may sound rather strange.

The performance engages a sort of psychic conflict with the spectator. It is a challenge and an excess, but can only have any effect if based on human interest and, more than that, on a feeling of sympathy, a feeling of acceptance. In the same way, the producer can help the actor in this complex and agonizing process only if he is just as emotionally and warmly open to the actor as the actor is in regard to him. I do not believe in the possibility of achieving effects by means of cold calculation. A kind of warmth towards one's fellow men is essential—an understanding of the contradictions in man, and that he is a suffering creature but not one to be scorned.

This element of warm openness is technically tangible. It alone, if reciprocal, can enable the actor to undertake the most extreme efforts without any fear of being laughed at or humiliated. The type of work which creates such confidence makes words unnecessary during rehearsals. When at work, the beginnings of a sound or sometimes even a silence are enough to make oneself understood. What is born in the actor is engendered together, but in the end the result is far more a part of him than those results obtained at rehearsals in the "normal" theatre.

I think we are dealing here with an "art" of working which it is impossible to reduce to a formula and cannot simply be learnt. Just as any doctor does not necessarily make a good psychiatrist, not any producer can succeed in this form of theatre. The principle to apply as a piece of advice, and also a warning, is the following: "Primum non nocere" ("First, do not harm"). To express this in technical language: it is better to suggest by means of sound and gesture than to "act" in front of the actor or supply him with intellectual explanations; better to express oneself by means of a silence or a wink of the eye than by instructions, observing the stages in the psychological breakdown and collapse of the actor in order then to come to his aid. One must be strict, but like a father or older brother. The second principle is one common to all professions: if you make demands on your colleagues, you must make twice as many demands on yourself.

This implies that to work with the "holy" actor, there must be a producer who is twice as "holy": that is, a "super-saint" who, through his knowledge and intuition, breaks the bounds of the history of the theatre, and who is well acquainted with the latest results in sciences such as psychology, anthropology, myth interpretation and the history of religion.

All I have said about the wretchedness of the actor applies to the producer too. To develop the metaphor of the "courtesan actor," the equivalent among producers would be the "producer souteneur." And just as it is impossible to erase completely all traces of the "courtesan" in the "holy" actor, one can never completely eradicate the "souteneur" in the "holy" producer.

The producer's job demands a certain tactical *savoir faire*, namely in the art of leading. Generally speaking, this kind of power demoralizes. It entails the necessity of learning how to handle people. It demands a gift for diplomacy, a cold and inhuman talent for dealing with intrigues. These characteristics follow the producer like his shadow even in the poor theatre. What one might call the masochistic component in the actor is the negative variant of what is creative in the director in the form of a sadistic component. Here, as everywhere, the dark is inseparable from the light.

When I take sides against half-heartedness, mediocrity and the easy-come-easy-go attitude which takes everything for granted, it is simply because we must create things which are firmly orientated towards either light or darkness. But we must remember that around that which is luminous within us, there exists a shroud of darkness which we can penetrate but not annihilate.

According to what you have been saying, "holiness" in the theatre can be achieved by means of a particular psychic discipline and various physical exercises. In the theatre schools and in traditional as well as experimental theatres, there is no such trend, no consistent attempt to work out or elaborate anything similar. How can we go about preparing the way for and training "holy" actors and producers? To what extent is it possible to create "monastic" theatres as opposed to the day-to-day "parochial" theatre?

I do not think that the crisis in the theatre can be separated from certain other crisis processes in contemporary culture. One of its essential elements—namely, the disappearance of the sacred and of its ritual function in the theatre—is a result of the obvious and probably inevitable decline of religion. What we are talking about is the possibility of creating a secular *sacrum* in the theatre. The question is, can the current pace in the development of civilization make a reality of this postulate on a collective scale? I have no answer to this. One must contribute to its realization, for a secular consciousness in place of the religious one seems to be a psycho-social necessity for society. Such a transition ought to take place but that does not necessarily mean that it will. I believe that it is, in a way, an ethical rule, like saying that man must not act like a wolf towards his fellow men. But as we all know, these rules are not always applied.

In any case, I am sure that this renewal will not come from the dominating theatre. Yet, at the same time, there are and have been a few people in the official theatre who must be considered as secular saints: Stanislavski, for example. He maintained that the successive stages of awakening and renewal in the theatre had found their beginnings amongst amateurs and not in the circles of hardened, demoralized professionals. This was confirmed by Vakhtangov's experience; or to take an example from quite another culture, the Japanese Nō theatre which, owing to the technical ability it demands, might almost be described as a "super-profession," although its very structure makes it a semi-amateur theatre. From where can this renewal come? From people who are dissatisfied with conditions in the normal theatre, and who take it on themselves to create poor theatres with few actors, "chamber ensembles" which they might transform into institutes for the education of actors; or else from amateurs working on the boundaries of the professional theatre and who, on their own, achieve a technical standard which is far superior to that demanded by the prevailing theatre: in short, a few madmen who have nothing to lose and are not afraid of hard work.

It seems essential to me that an effort be made to organize secondary theatre schools. The actor begins to learn his profession too late, when he is already psychically formed and, worse still, morally moulded and immediately begins suffering from *arriviste* tendencies, characteristic of a great number of theatre school pupils.

Age is as important in the education of an actor as it is to a pianist or a dancer —that is, one should not be older than fourteen when beginning. If it were possible, I would suggest starting at an even earlier age with a four year technical course concentrating on practical exercises. At the same time, the pupil ought to receive an adequate humanistic education, aimed not at imparting an ample knowledge of literature, the history of the theatre and so on, but at awakening his sensibility and introducing him to the most stimulating phenomena in world culture.

The actor's secondary education should then be completed by four years' work as an apprentice actor with a laboratory ensemble during which time he would not only acquire a good deal of acting experience, but would also continue his studies in the fields of literature, painting, philosophy, etc., to a degree necessary in his profession and not in order to be able to shine in snobbish society. On completion of the four years' practical work in a theatre laboratory, the student actor should be awarded some sort of diploma. Thus, after eight years' work of this kind, the actor should be comparatively well equipped for what lies ahead. He would not escape the dangers that threaten every actor, but his capacities would be greater and his character more firmly moulded. The ideal solution would be to establish institutes for research which again would be subject to poverty and rigourous authority. The cost of running such an institute would be a half of the amount swallowed up by a state aided provincial theatre. Its staff should be composed of a small group of experts specializing in problems associated with the theatre: e. g. a psychoanalyst and a social anthropologist. There should be a troupe of actors from a normal theatre laboratory and a group of pedagogs from a secondary theatre school, plus a small publishing house that would print the practical methodical results which would then be exchanged with other similar centres and sent to interested persons doing research in neighbouring fields. It is absolutely essential that all research of this kind be supervised by one or more theatre critics who, from the outside—rather like the Devil's Advocate—analyse the theatre's weaknesses and any alarming elements in the finished performances, basing their judgements on aesthetical principles identical to those of the theatre itself. As you know, Ludwik Flaszen has this task in our theatre.

How can such a theatre reflect our time? I am thinking of the content and analysis of present-day problems.

I shall answer according to our theatre's experience. Even though we often use classical texts, ours is a contemporary theatre in that it confronts our very roots with our current behaviour and stereotypes, and in this way shows us our "today" in perspective with "yesterday," and our "yesterday" with "today." Even if this theatre uses an elementary language of signs and sounds—comprehensible beyond the semantic value of the word, even to a person who does not understand the language in which the play is performed—such a theatre must be a national one since it is based on introspection and on the whole of our social super-ego which has been moulded in a particular national climate, thus becoming an integral part of it.

If we really wish to delve deeply into the logic of our mind and behaviour and reach their hidden layers, their secret motor, then the whole system of signs built into the performance must appeal to our experience, to the reality which has surprised and shaped us, to this language of gestures, mumblings, sounds and intonations picked up in the street, at work, in cafés—in short, all human behaviour which has made an impression on us.

We are talking about profanation. What, in fact, is this but a kind of tactlessness based on the brutal confrontation between our declarations and our daily actions, between the experience of our forefathers which lives within us and our search for a comfortable way of life or our conception of a struggle for survival, between our individual complexes and those of society as a whole?

This implies that every classical performance is like looking at oneself in a mirror, at our ideas and traditions, and not merely the description of what men of past ages thought and felt.

Every performance built on a contemporary theme is an encounter between the superficial traits of the present day and its deep roots and hidden motives. The performance is national because it is a sincere and absolute search into our historical ego; it is realistic because it is an excess of truth; it is social because it is a challenge to the social being, the spectator.

—translated by Jörgen Andersen and Judy Barba

16

FROM RITUAL TO THEATRE AND BACK

Richard Schechner

I

The *kaiko* celebration of the Tsembaga of Highlands New Guinea is a year-long festival culminating in the *konj kaiko*—pig *kaiko*. *Kaiko* means dancing, and the chief entertainments of the celebrations are dances. During 1962 the Tsembaga entertained thirteen other local groups on fifteen occasions.[1] To make sure that the *kaiko* was successful young Tsembaga men were sent to neighboring areas to announce the shows—and to send back messages of delay should a visiting group be late: in that case the entertainments were postponed. The day of dancing begins with the dancers—all men—bathing and adorning themselves. Putting on costume takes hours. It is an exacting, precise, and delicate process. When dressed the dancers assemble on the flattened, stamped-down grounds where they dance both for their own pleasure and as rehearsal in advance of the arrival of their guests. The visitors announce their arrival by singing—they can be heard before they are seen. By this time many spectators have gathered, including both men and women from neighboring villages. These spectators come to watch, and to trade goods. Finally,

> the local dancers retire to a vantage point just above the dance ground, where their view of the visitors is unimpeded and where they continue singing. The visitors approach the gate silently, led by men carrying fight packages,[2] swinging their axes as they run back and forth in front of their procession in the peculiar crouched fighting prance. Just before they reach the gate they are met by one or two of those

Richard Schechner is professor of drama at New York University's School of the Arts. He is also co-director of The Performance Group, and author of *Theaters, Spaces, and Environments* (with Jerry Rojo and Brooks McNamara), *Public Domain,* and *Environmental Theater.*

locals who have invited them and who now escort them over the gate. Visiting women and children follow behind the dancers and join the other spectators on the sidelines. There is much embracing as the local women and children greet visiting kinfolk. The dancing procession charges to the center of the dance ground shouting the long, low battle cry and stamping their feet, magically treated before their arrival . . . to enable them to dance strongly. After they charge back and forth across the dance ground several times, repeating the stamping in several locations while the crowd cheers in admiration of their numbers, their style, and the richness of their finery, they begin to sing.[3]

The performance is a transformation of combat techniques into entertainment. All the basic moves and sounds—even the charge into the central space—are adaptations and direct lifts from battle. But the Tsembaga dance is a dance, and clearly so to everyone present at it. The dancing is not an isolated phenomenon —as theatre-going in America still is usually—but a behavior nested in supportive actions. The entry described takes place late in the afternoon, and just before dusk the dancing stops and the food which has been piled in the center of the dancing round (it might be said, literally, that the dancing is *about the food*, for the whole *kaiko* cycle is about acquiring enough pigs-for-meat to afford the festival) is distributed and eaten.

> The visitors are asked to stop dancing and gather around while a presentation speech is made by one of the men responsible for the invitation. As he slowly walks around and around the food that has been laid out in a number of piles, the speechmaker recounts the relations of the two groups: their mutual assistance in fighting, their exchange of women and wealth, their hospitality to each other in times of defeat. . . . When the speech of presentation is finished they gather their portions and distribute them to those men who came to help them dance, and to their women.[4]

After supper the dancing resumes and goes on all night. By dawn almost everyone has danced with everyone else: and this communality is a sign of a strong alliance.

With dawn the dancing around is converted into a market place. Ornaments, pigs, furs, axes, knives, shells, pigments, tobacco are all traded or sold (money has come into the Tsembagas' economy).

> The transactions that take place on the dance ground are completed on the spot; a man both gives and receives at the same time. . . . At the men's houses, however, a different kind of exchange takes place. Here men from other places give to their kinsmen or trading partners in the local group valuables for which they do not receive immediate return.[5]

This orchestrated indebtedness is at the heart of the *kaiko*. At the start of the celebration the hosts owe meat to the guests and the guests owe items of trade to the hosts. In the first part of the *kaiko* the hosts pay meat to the guests; in the second part of the *kaiko* the guests pay the hosts trade items. But neither payment ends in a balance. When the *kaiko* is over the guests owe the hosts meat, and the hosts owe the guests trade items. This symmetrical imbalance guarantees further *kaikos*—continued exchanges between groups. Often trade items are not given back directly, but traded back through third or fourth parties. After the public trading and the gift-giving, some dancing resumes which ends by mid-morning. Then everyone goes home.

The *kaiko* entertainments are a ritual display, not simply a doing but *a showing of a doing*. Furthermore, this showing is both actual (=the trading and giving of goods resulting in a new imbalance) and symbolic (=the reaffirmation of alliances made concrete in the debtor-creditor relationship). The entertainment itself is a vehicle for debtors and creditors to exchange places; it is also the occasion for a market; and it is fun. The *kaiko* depends on the accumulation of pigs and goods, and on a willingness to dress up and dance; neither by itself is enough. The dancing is a performance—and appreciated as such, with the audience serving as frequently acerbic critics—but it's also a way of facilitating trade, finding mates, cementing military alliances, and reaffirming tribal hierarchies.

> The Tsembaga say that "those who come to our *kaiko* will also come to our fights." This native interpretation of *kaiko* attendance is also given expression by an invited group. Preparations from departure to a *kaiko* at another place include ritual performances similar to those that precede a fight. Fight packages are applied to the heads and hearts of the dancers and *gir* to their feet so that they will dance strongly, just as, during warfare, they are applied so that they will fight strongly. . . . Dancing is like fighting. The visitors' procession is led by men carrying fight packages, and their entrance upon the dance ground of their hosts is martial. To join a group in dancing is the symbolic expression of willingness to join them in fighting.[6]

The *kaiko* dance display is a cultural version of territorial and status displays in animals; the rituals of the Tsembaga are ethological as well as sociological. They are also ecological: the *kaiko* is a means of organizing the Tsembagas' relationships to their neighbors, to their lands and goods, to their gardens and hunting ranges.

A *kaiko* culminates in the *konj kaiko*. The *kaiko* lasts a year, the *konj kaiko* a few days, usually two. *Kaiko* years are rare. During the fifty to sixty years ending in 1963 the Tsembaga staged four *kaikos*, with an average of twelve to fifteen years between festivals.[7] The whole cycle is tied to the war/peace rhythm which, in turn, is tied to the fortunes of the pig population. After the *konj kaiko*—whose major event is a mass slaughter of pigs and distribution of meat—a short peace is followed by war, which continues until another *kaiko* cycle begins. The cycle itself lasts for enough years to allow the raising of sufficient pigs to stage a *konj kaiko*. The *konj kaiko* of November 7 and 8, 1963, saw the slaughter of 96 pigs with a total live weight of 15,000 pounds, yielding around 7,500 pounds of meat; eventually about 3,000 people got shares of the kill.[8] What starts in dancing ends in eating; or, to put it in artistic-religious terms, what starts as theatre ends as communion. Perhaps not since classical Athenian festivals and medieval pageants have we in the West used performances as the pivots in systems involving economic, social, political, and religious transactions. With the re-advent of holism in contemporary society at least a discussion of such performances becomes practical. It is clear that the *kaiko* dances are not ornaments or pastimes or even "part of the means" of effecting the transactions among the Tsembaga. The dances both symbolize and participate in the process of exchange.

The dances are pivots in a system of transformations which change destructive behavior into constructive alliances. It is no accident that every move, chant, and costume of the *kaiko* dances are adapted from combat: a new use is found for this behavior. Quite unconsciously a positive feedback begins: the more splendid the displays of dancing, the stronger the alliances; the stronger the alliances, the more splendid the dancing. Between *kaikos*—but only between them—war is waged; during the cycles there is peace. The exact transformation of combat behavior into performance is at the heart of the *kaiko*. This transformation is identical in structure to that at the heart of Greek theatre (and from the Greeks down throughout all of Western theatre history). Namely, characterization and the presentation of real or possible events—the story, plot, or dramatic action, worked out among human figures (whether they be called men or gods)—is a transformation of real behavior into symbolic behavior. In fact, transformation is the heart of theatre, and there appear to be only two fundamental kinds of theatrical transformation: (1) the displacement of anti-social, injurious, disruptive behavior by ritualized gesture and display, and (2) the invention of characters who act out fictional events or real events fictionalized by virtue of their being acted out (as in documentary theatre or Roman gladiatorial games). These two kinds of transformation occur together, but in the mix usually one is dominant. Western theatre emphasizes characterization and the enactment of fictions; Melanesian, African, and Australian (aborigine) theatre emphasize the displacement of hostile behavior. Forms which balance the two tendencies—Nō, Kathakali, the Balinese Ketchak, medieval moralities, some contemporary avant-garde performances—offer, I think, the best models for the future of the theatre.

Much performing among communal peoples is, like the *kaiko*, part of the overall ecology of a society. The *Engwura* cycle of the Arunta of Australia, as described by Spencer and Gillen in the late nineteenth century,[9] is an elegant example of how a complicated series of performances expressed and participated in a people's ecology. The fact that the *Engwura* is no longer performed—that the Arunta, culturally speaking, have been exterminated—indicates the incompatibility of wholeness as I am describing it and Western society as it is presently constituted. Insofar as performing groups adapt techniques from the *kaiko* or *Engwura* they are bound to remain outside the "mainstream." But the chief function of the avant-garde is to propose models for change: to remain "in advance." The *Engwura* was an initiation cycle that spanned several years; the last phase consisted of performances staged sporadically over a three-to-four-month period. Each phase of the *Engwura* took place only when several conditions meshed: enough young men of a certain age gathered in one place to be initiated; enough older men willing to lead the ceremonies (particularly important in a non-literate culture); enough food to support celebration. Then the sacred implements and sacred grounds were prepared painstakingly and according to tradition. Finally, there had to be peace among neighboring tribes—but the announcement of a forthcoming *Engwura* was sometimes enough to guarantee a peace.

The daily rhythm recapitulated the monthly rhythm: performance spaces were cleared, implements repaired and laid out, body decorations applied, food cooked. Each performance day saw not one but several performances, with rest and preparations between each. Each performance lasted on an average ten minutes, and was characteristically a dance accompanied by drumming and chanting. Then the performers rested for about two hours; then preparations for the next performance began, and these preparations took about two hours.[10] The whole cycle recapitulates the life cycle of the Arunta male; and during his life he could expect to play roles co-existent with his status in society: initiate, participant, leader or onlooker. Thus on each day performers enacted condensed and concentrated versions of their lives; and the three-to-four-month culminating series of performances also replicated the life cycle. The whole cycle was, in fact, an important—perhaps the most important—set of events in an Arunta life.[11] Each phase of the cycle was a replication (either an extension or a concentration) of every other phase.

The subject matter of each brief dance-drama was life events of mythical Dreamtime beings who populated the world "in the beginning."[12] These mythic events were very important to the Arunta and constituted for them a history and, since each Dreamtime event was connected to specific places and landmarks, a geography.[13] The rituals are a concrete symbolization and reenactment of Dreamtime events, and to this extent the *Engwura* is familiar to us: it is not unlike our own drama except that we accept the reactualization of past events only as a convention. The Arunta, like the orthodox Catholic before the Eucharist, accepted the manifestation of Dreamtime events as actual.

The overall structure of the *Engwura* is analogic, while its interior structure is dramatic. The two structures are integrated because the Arunta believed concretely in the Dreamtime and experienced their own lives as divided between "ordinary" and "super-ordinary" realities. They experienced an interaction between these realities, and *Engwura* performances were the navel, or link, or point-of-time-and-place where the two realities meshed.

II

I saw an ecological ritual similar to the *konj kaiko* (but much less inclusive than the *Engwura*) in March 1972 at Kurumugl in the Eastern Highlands of New Guinea.[14] Surrounding the performance of the *kaiko* is no special self-consciousness—that is, the ritual functions without the Tsembaga being explicitly aware of its functions; and aside from commendatory or critical comments on the dancing no aesthetic judgments are passed. In other words there are neither performance theorists nor critics among the Tsembaga. At Kurumugl the people know what the ritual does and why it was established—to inhibit warfare among feuding groups. The ritual at Kurumugl is already travelling along the continuum toward theatre in the modern sense. Knowing what the ritual does is a very important step in the development of theatre from ritual.

It's my purpose to outline a process through which theatre develops from ritual; and also to suggest that in some circumstances ritual develops from theatre. I think this process ought to be documented from contemporary or near-contemporary sources because so often the jump from ritual to theatre is assumed, or attributed to ancient events the evidence for which is suspect.[15]

Unlike the *kaiko* dancing grounds, the "council grounds" (as they are called) at Kurumugl are near no regular village. The colonial Australian government set them up as a place where former enemies assemble to *sing-sing* (pidgin for drama-music-dance). The difference between the Tsembaga and the people at Kurumugl is that the *kaiko* brought together traditional allies while the Kurumugl *sing-sing* assembles traditional enemies. The performances at Kurumugl are always in danger of tipping over into actual combat, even though the performances are very much like those of the *konj kaiko:* dance movements adapted from combat, war chants, the arrival of a guest group at a dance ground piled high with freshly slaughtered, cooked pork. The celebration at Kurumugl that I saw took two days. The first consisted of arriving, setting up temporary house inside long rectangular huts, digging cooking ovens. All the people gathered—about 350—were of one tribal group. They awaited the arrival of their guests, a group comparable in size, but recently their enemies. The second day began with the slaughter of about two hundred pigs. These are clubbed on the snouts and heads. As each owner kills his animal he recites—sings—a speech telling how difficult it was to raise the pig, who it is promised to, what a fine animal it is, etc. These *pro forma recitatives* are applauded with laughs and roars, as they often contain jokes and obscene invective. The orations are accompanied by the death squeals of the pigs. Then the animals are gutted, butchered, and lowered in halves and quarters into earth ovens to cook. Their guts are hung in nets over the ovens and steamed. Their bladders are blown into balloons and given to the children. The sight and smell of so much meat and blood excites the people, including me. No special clothes are worn for the killing. The only ritual element I detected was the careful display of pig jawbones on a circular altar-like structure in the middle of the dance grounds. From each jaw flowers were hung.

As the cooking starts, the men retire to the huts to begin adorning themselves. From time to time a man emerges to try on a towering head-dress of cassowary and peacock feathers. The women cook and tend to the children. After about four hours the meat, still nearly raw, is taken from the ovens and displayed in long rows. Each family lays out its own meat—the women doing most of the work —like so much money in the bank: pork is wealth in the Highlands. As more and more men finish dressing they emerge from the huts to show off and admire each other in a grudging way—the adorning is very competitive. Some women also adorned themselves, dressing much like the men. I couldn't determine if this was traditional or an innovation. A man invited Joan MacIntosh[16] and me into his hut to watch him put on his makeup. He set out a mirror and tins of pigment (bought from a Japanese trading store) and then applied blue, red, and black to his torso, shoulders, arms, and face. He painted half his nose red and the other half blue. I asked him what the patterns meant. He said he chose them because he liked the way they looked. The Australian aborigines, by contrast, adorn their bodies with patterns each detail of which is linked to ancestral beings, sexual magic, or recent events. Aborigine body painting is map-making and myth-telling.

Our performer showed us his head-dress of four-foot-long feathers, and stepped outside to try it on. As he emerged from the hut his casual air dropped and he literally thrust his chest forward, gave a long whooping call, put on his head-dress, and displayed himself. He was costumed for a social not a dramatic role—that is, not to present a fictional character whose life was separable from his own, but to show himself in a special way: to display his strength, his power, his wealth, his authority. It is not easy to distinguish between these kinds of roles, except that in drama the script is already fixed in its details, the precise gestures of the role are rehearsed for a particular occasion (and other occasions, other "productions," might eventuate in different gestures), while "in life" the script is "replaced by an ongoing process, this process is set in motion by the objective demands of the role, and the subjective motives and goals of the actor."[17] An awareness that social and dramatic roles are indeed closely related to each other, and locating their points of convergence in the mise-en-scène rather than in the mind of the playwright, has been one of the major developments in contemporary theatre. This development has been helped by film and television—by film because it presents dramatic actions on location, as if in "real life," and by TV because all so-called news is staged. It is staged not only by the obvious editing of raw footage to suit TV format and the need to sell time (that is, to hold the viewer's attention), but also as it is actually made. Many guerrilla activities, terrorist raids, kidnappings, assassinations, and street demonstrations are theatricalized events performed by groups of people in order to catch the attention of larger masses of people by means of TV. This is the main way today in which powerless groups get a hearing. In response, the authorities stage their repressive raids, their assaults, and their reprisals: to show the world how the insurgents will be dealt with, to display the power of authority, and to terrorize the viewer. Thus an apparent two-person exchange between activist and authority is actually a three-person arrangement with the spectator supplying the vital link. Thus are we continually being educated to the histrionic structure of communication.[18]

The seeds of this histrionic sense are at Kurumugl. As these people are "technified" (already they have planes before cars, TV before newspapers) they will leap not into the twentieth century but beyond, going directly from pre-industrial tribalism to automation-age tribalism. The big difference between the two is that pre-industrial tribalism scatters power among a large number of local leaders, there being no way for people to maintain themselves in large masses; automation-age tribalism is a way of controlling megalopolitic masses. I mean by tribalism the shaping of social roles not through individual choice but by collective formation; the substitution of histrionic-ritualized events for ordinary events; the sacralization or increasingly closely codified definition of all experience; and the disappearance of solitude and one-to-one intimacy as we have developed it since the Renaissance. Automation-age tribalism is medievalism under the auspices of technology. Such tribalism is good for the theatre—if by good one means that most social situations will be governed by conventional, external gestures loaded with metaphoric/symbolic significances. Anomie and identity crisis are eliminated and in their places are fixed roles and rites of passage transporting persons not only from one status to another but from one identity to another. These transportations are achieved by means of performances. I call these kinds of performances "transformances" because the performances are the means of transformation from one status, identity, or situation to another.

When the performer at Kurumugl stepped outside his hut he joined a group of envious males whose costumes were, like his, peculiar amalgams of traditional and imported stuff: sunglasses and bones stuck through the septum; cigarette holders and home-made tobacco pipes; khaki shorts and grass skirts. But despite the breakdown in traditional costume an old pattern was being worked out—an ecological ritual where the pig meat was a "payback" (pidgin for fullfilling a ritual obligation) from the hosts to the guests. As among the Tsembaga every adult male at Kurumugl was in a debtor relationship to persons arriving in the afternoon of the second day. The nature of the payback is such that what is given back must exceed what is owed. (This is true even of war, where a perpetual imbalance in casualties must be maintained.) The payback ceremony involves an exchange of roles in which creditors become debtors and debtors become creditors. This insures that more ceremonies will follow when the new debtors accumulate enough pigs. Never is a balance struck, because a balance would threaten an end to the obligations, and this would lead to war. As long as the obligations are intact the social web transmits continuous waves of paybacks back and forth. The visitors approaching Kurumugl came not as friends but as invaders. The afternoon's performance was not a party but a ritual combat with the guests assaulting Kurumugl in a modified war dance, armed with fighting spears, and the campers at Kurumugl defending their ground and the immense pile of meat piled in the center of it. Instead of a secret raiding party there were dancers; instead of taking human victims, they took meat. And instead of doubt about the outcome everyone knew what was going to happen. Thus a ritualized social drama (as war in the Highlands often is) moves toward becoming an esthetic drama in which a script of actions is adhered to—the script being known in advance and carefully prepared for.

Again, differences between social and esthetic drama are not easy to specify.

Social drama has more variables, the outcome is in doubt—it is more like a game or sporting context. Esthetic drama is almost totally arranged in advance, and the participants can concentrate not on strategies of achieving their goals—at Kurumugl, to penetrate to where the meat was, or to defend the meat pile—but on displays; esthetic drama is less instrumental and more ornamental than social drama. Also, it can use symbolic time and place, and so become entirely fictionalized.

Early in the afternoon of the second day I heard from outside the camp the chanting and shouting of the invaders. The people in camp returned these shouts so that an antiphonal chorus arose. Then the men in camp—and a contingent of about twenty women who were fully armed—rushed to the edges of Kurumugl and the ritual combat began. Both sides were armed with bows and arrows, spears, sticks, and axes. They chanted in a rhythm common to the Highlands—a leader sings a phrase and is overlapped by the unison response of many followers. This call-and-response is in loud nasal tones, a progression of quarter and half notes. Such chants alternate with Ketchak-like staccato grunts-pants-shouts. From about one to five in the afternoon the two groups engaged in fierce ritual combat. Each cycle of singing and dancing climaxed when parties of warriors rushed forward from both sides, spears ready for throwing, and, at apparently the last second, did a rapid kick-from-the-knee step instead of throwing their weapons. The weapons became props in a performance of aggression displaced, if not into friendship, at least into a non-deadly confrontation.

The assaults of the invaders were repeated dozens of times; a lush and valuable peanut field was trampled to muck; each assault was met by determined counter-attack. But foot by foot the invaders penetrated to the heart of the campground—to the pile of meat and the altar of jaw bones and flowers. All the meat previously laid out in rows was now piled three feet deep—a hugh heap of legs, snouts, ribs, and flanks all tangled together. Three live white goats were tethered to a pole at the edge of the meat pile. Once the invaders reached the meat they merged with their hosts in one large, whooping, chanting, dancing doughnut of warriors. Around and around the meat they danced, for nearly an hour. I was pinned up against a tree, between the armed dancers and the meat. Then, suddenly, the dancing stopped and orators plunged into the meat, pulling a leg, or a flank, or a side of ribs, and shouted-sung-declaimed things like:

> This pig I give you in payment for the pig you gave my father three years ago! Your pig was scrawny, no fat on it at all, but my pig is huge, with lots of fat, much good meat—much better than the one my father got! And my whole family, especially my brothers, will remember that we are giving you today better than what we got, so that you owe us, and will help us if we need you beside us in a fight!

Sometimes the speechifying rises to song; sometimes insults are hurled back and forth. The fun in the orating, and the joking, stands on a very serious foundation: the participants do not forget that not so long ago they were blood enemies. After more than an hour of orating, the meat is distributed. Sleds are made to carry it shoulder high and whole families, with much singing, leave with their share of meat.

The performance at Kurumugl consists of displaying the meat, ritual combat, the merging of the two groups into one, orating, and carrying the meat away. Preparations for this performance are both immediate, the day before at the camp (and at the visitors' residence), and long-range: raising the pigs, acquiring costumes and ornaments. After the performance comes the clean-up, the travel home, the distribution of the meat, feasting, and stories about the *sing-sing*. By means of the performance the basic relationship—one might say the fundamental relationship—between the invading and the host groups is inverted.

ACTUALITY 1 ⟶ TRANSFORMANCE ⟶ ACTUALITY 2
Group A is debtor   Group B is debtor
     to Group B   to Group A

As in all rites of passage something has happened during the performance; *the performance both symbolizes and actualizes the change in status.* The dancing at Kurumugl is the process by which change happens and it is the only process (other than war) recognized by all the parties assembled at Kurumugl. Giving and taking the meat not only symbolizes the changed relationship between Group A and B, it is the change itself. This convergence of symbolic and actual event is missing from esthetic theatre. We have sought for it by trying to make the performer "responsible" or "visible" in and for his performance—either through psychodramatic techniques or other psychological means. This use of psychology is a reflection of our preoccupation with the individual. Where performances have been sociologically or politically motivated—such as happenings and guerrilla theatre—the authenticating techniques have included emphasis on the event in and for itself, the development of group consciousness, and appeals to the public at large. But a fundamental contradiction undermines these efforts. At Kurumugl enough actual wealth and people could be assembled in one place so that what was done in the performance focused actual economic, political, and social power. In our society only a charade of power is displayed at theatrical performances. When this is recognized, authenticating theatres preoccupy themselves with symbolic activities, feeling helpless in the face of the hollowness of the authenticating tasks they set up for themselves. So-called real events are revealed as metaphors. In a society as large and wealthy as ours only esthetic theatre is possible. Or authenticating theatres must seek a basis other than economics; or fully ally themselves with established authority. None of these options is as easy as it sounds.

At Kurumugl the change between Group A and B is not simply the occasion for a celebratory performance (as a birthday party celebrates but does not effect a change in age). The performance effects what it celebrates. It opens up enough time in the right place for the exchange to be made: it is liminal: a fluid mid-point between two fixed structures. Only for a brief time do the two groups merge into one dancing circle; during this liminal time/place *communitas* is possible—that levelling of all differences in an ecstasy that so often characterizes performing.[19] Then, and only then, the exchange takes place.

war parties	transformed into	dancing groups
human victims		pig meat
battle dress		costumes
combat		dancing
debtors		creditors
creditors		debtors
two groups		one group

The transformations above the line convert actualities into esthetic realities. Those below the line effect a change from one actuality into another. It is only because the transformations above the line happen that those below the line can take place in peace. All the transformations—esthetic as well as actual—are temporary: the meat will be eaten, the costumes doffed, the dance ended; the single group will divide again according to know divisions; today's debtors will be next year's creditors, etc. The celebration at Kurumugl managed a complicated and potentially dangerous exchange with a minimum of danger and a maximum of pleasure. The mode of achieving "real results"—paying debts, incurring new obligations—was performing; the dancing does not celebrate achieving results, it does not precede or follow the exchange, it is the means of making the transformations; the performance is effective.

The Tsembaga, Arunta, and Kurumugl performances are ecological rituals. Whatever enjoyment the participants take in the dancing, and however carefully they prepare themselves for dancing, the dances are danced to achieve results. In religious rituals results are achieved by appealing to a transcendent Other (who puts in an appearance either in person or by surrogate). In ecological rituals the other group, or the status to be achieved, or some other clearly human arrangement is the object of the performance. An ecological ritual with no results to show "below the line" would soon cease. The "above the line" transformations change aggressive actions into harmless and pleasure-giving performances (in the cases cited). One is struck by the analogy to certain biological adaptations among animals.[20]

In the New Guinea Highlands, at first under the pressure of the colonial police, later under its own momentum, warfare is transformed into dancing. As above-the-line activities grow in importance, entertainment as such takes over from efficacy as the reason for the performances. It is not only that creditors and debtors need to exchange roles, but also that people want to show off; it is not only to get results that the dances are staged, but also because people like dancing for its own sake. Efficacy and entertainment are opposed to each other, but they form a binary system, a continuum.

EFFICACY ⟷ ENTERTAINMENT	
(Ritual)	(Theatre)
results	fun
link to an absent Other	only for those here
abolishes time, symbolic time	emphasizes now
brings Other here	audience in the Other
performer possessed, in trance	performer knows what he's doing
audience participates	audience watches
audience believes	audience appreciates
criticism is forbidden	criticism is encouraged
collective creativity	individual creativity

The basic opposition is between efficacy and entertainment, not between ritual and theatre. Whether one calls a specific performance ritual or theatre depends on the degree to which the performance tends toward efficacy or entertainment. No performance is pure efficacy or pure entertainment. The matter is complicated because one can look at specific performances from several vantages; changing perspective changes classification. For example, a Broadway musical is entertainment if one concentrates on what happens onstage and in the house. But if the point of view expands—to include rehearsals, backstage life before, during, and after the show, the function of the roles in the careers of each performer, the money invested by backers, the arrival of the audience, their social status, how they paid for their tickets (as individuals, expense accounts, theatre parties, etc.) and how this indicates the use they're making of the performance (as entertainment, to advance their careers, to support a charity, etc.)—then the Broadway musical is more than entertainment; it reveals many ritual elements.

Recently, more performances have been emphasizing the rehearsal and backstage procedures. At first this was as simple as showing the lighting instruments and using a half-curtain, as Brecht did. But within the last fifteen years the process of mounting the performance, the workshops that lead up to the performance, the means by which an audience is brought into the space and led from the space and many other previously automatic procedures, have become the subjects of theatrical manipulations. These procedures have to do with the theatre-in-itself and they are, as regards the theatre, efficacious: that is, these procedures are what makes a theatre into a theatre regardless of themes, plot, or the usual "elements of drama." The attention paid to the procedures of making theatre are, I think, attempts at ritualizing performance, of finding in the theatre itself authenticating acts. In a period when authenticity is increasingly rare in public life the performer has been asked to surrender his traditional masks and be himself; or at least to show how the masks are put on and taken off. Instead of mirroring his times the performer is asked to remedy them. The professions taken as models for theatre are medicine and the church. No wonder shamanism is popular among theatre people: shamanism is that branch of doctoring that is religious, and that kind of religion that is full of ironies and tricks.[21]

At present efficacy is ascending to a dominant position over entertainment. It

208

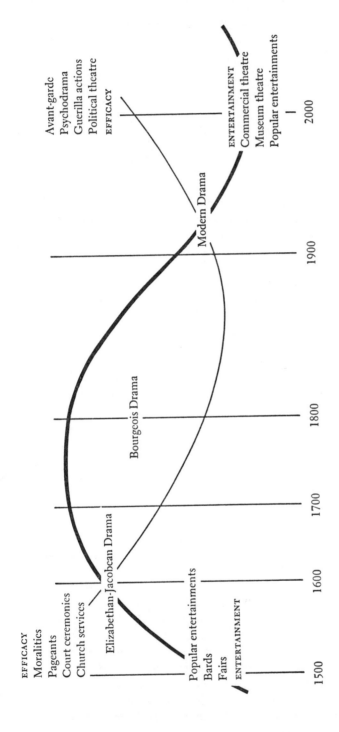

Fig. 16.1: Efficacy-Entertainment Braid
the fifteenth through the twenty-first centuries in English and American theatres

is my belief that theatre history can be given an overall shape as a development along a core which is a *braided structure* constantly inter-relating efficacy and entertainment. At each period in each culture one or the other is dominant—one is ascending while the other is descending. Naturally, these changes are part of changes in the overall social structure; yet performance is not a passive mirror of these social changes but a part of the complicated feedback process that brings about change. At all times a dialectical tension exists between efficacious and entertainment tendencies. For Western theatre, at least, I think it can be shown that when the braid is tight—that is, when efficacy and entertainment are both present in nearly equal degrees—theatre flourishes. During these brief historical moments the theatre answers needs that are both ritualistic and pleasure-giving. Fifth-century Athenian theatre, Elizabethan theatre, and possibly the theatre of the late nineteenth century and/or of our own times show the kind of convergence I'm talking about. When efficacy dominates, performances are universalistic, allegorical, ritualized, tied to a stable established order; this kind of theatre persists for a relatively long time. When entertainment dominates, performances are class-oriented, individualized, show business, constantly adjusted to suit the tastes of a fickle audience. The two most recent convergences—the rise of entertainment before the Elizabethan period and the rise of efficacy during the modern period—are necessarily opposites of each other. The model that I offer is of course a simplification. I present it as a help in conceptualizing my view of the progression of theatre history, which I think has its own logic and internal force. The late medieval period was dominated by efficacious performances: church services, court ceremonies, moralities, pageants. In the early Renaissance these began to decline and popular entertainments, always present, gained, finally becoming dominant in the form of the public theatres of the Elizabethan period. The private and court theatres developed alongside the public theatres. The private theatres were for the upper classes. Although some professionals worked in both public and private theatres, and some spectators attended both, these entertainments were fundamentally opposed to each other. The conflicts between the public and private theatres never worked themselves out because all the theatres were closed in 1642. When theatres reopened at the Restoration the Elizabethan public theatre was gone and all the theatres resembled the private theatres and masques, the property of the upper classes. During the eighteenth and nineteenth centuries this aristocratic theatre developed into the bourgeois theatre, as that class rose to displace the aristocracy. The dominant efficacious mode of the medieval centuries went underground to re-emerge in the guise of social and political drama during the last third of the nineteenth century. This new naturalistic theatre opposed the commercialism and pomposity of the boulevards and allied itself to scientific positivism.[22] It also spawned an avant-garde whose mission it was to reconstruct theatrical styles and techniques. The avant-garde identified itself both with Bohemianism—the outcasts of bourgeois society—and science, the source of power. Avant-garde artists used terms like "experimental" and "research" to characterize their work, which took place in "laboratories." Efficacy lies at the ideological heart of all aspects of this new theatre.

In the twentieth century the entertainment theatre, threatened with extinction, broke into two parts: an increasingly outmoded commercial theatre typified by Broadway and a subsidized community museum typified by the regional theatres. The recent FACT meeting at Princeton[23] was an attempt by commercial interests to ally themselves with the regional theatres. Although such an alliance is inevitable, it's most likely that the regional theatres will absorb the commercial theatres. Whatever the outcome, the entertainment theatres remain fundamentally opposed by the avant-garde—which has itself, by mid-twentieth century, expanded to include direct political action, psychotherapy, and other manifestly efficacious kinds of performances. It is my opinion that efficacious theatres are on the upswing and will dominate the theatrical world within the next twenty years.

III

Up to here I've said this: (1) in some social settings ritual performances are part of ecosystems and mediate political relations, group hierarchy, and economics; (2) in other settings ritual performances begin to take on qualities of show business; (3) there is a dialectical-dyadic continuum linking efficacy to entertainment—both are present in all performances, but in each performance one or the other is dominant; (4) in different societies, at different times, either efficacy or entertainment dominates, the two being in a braided relationship to each other.

O. B. Hardison quotes Honorius of Autun's twelfth-century view of the Mass as evidence that people at the time saw this ceremony as drama:

> It is known that those who recited tragedies in theatres presented the actions of opponents by gestures before the people. In the same way our tragic author [i.e., the celebrant] represents by his gestures in the theater of the Church before the Christian people the struggle of Christ and teaches to them the victory of his redemption. [Honorius then compares each movement of the Mass to an equivalent movement of tragic drama.] . . . When the sacrifice has been completed, peace and Communion are given by the celebrant to the people. . . . Then, by the *Ite, missa est,* they are ordered to return to their homes with rejoicing. They shout *Deo gratias* and return home rejoicing.[24]

What is extraordinary about Honorius' description is that it is a medieval view, not a backwards glance by a modernist. Honorius' Mass is more familiar to those who have attended avant-garde performances than to those whose experience is limited to orthodox theatre. The ninth-century Mass employed many avant-garde techniques: it was allegorical, it used audience participation, it treated time teleologically, it extended the scope of the performance from the church to the roadways to the homes. But for all this I still think it is fair to call this Mass a ritual rather than theatre. My opinion is founded on the almost totally efficacious nature of the Mass. As Hardison says, "The service . . . has a very important aesthetic dimension, but it is essentially not a matter of appreciation but of passionate affirmation."[25] The Mass was a closed circle which included only the congregation and the officiants; there was literally and figuratively no room for appreciators. The Mass was an obligatory action, entered into either joyfully and sullenly, through which members of the congregation signalled to each other and to the hierarchy their continued participation in the congregation. What I say of the ninth-century Mass, Rappaport has said of the Tsembaga:

> While the scope of the social unity is frequently not made explicit, it would seem that in some studies it is what Durkheim called a "church," that is, "a society whose members are united by the fact that they think in the same way in regard to the sacred world and its relations with the profane world, and by the fact that they translate these common ideas into common practices." . . . Such units, composed of aggregates of individuals who regard their collective well-being to be dependent upon a common body of ritual performances, might be called "congregations."[26]

Because of its all-inclusive hold on its congregation the Mass was not theatre in the classical or modern sense. Theatre comes into existence when a separation occurs between audience and performers. The paradigmatic theatrical situation is a group of performers soliciting an audience who may or may not respond by attending. The audience is free to attend or stay away—and if they stay away it is the theatre that suffers, not its would-be audience. In ritual, staying away means rejecting the congregation—or being rejected by it, as in excommunication, ostracism, or exile. If only a few stay away, it is those who are absent who suffer; if many stay away, the congregation is in danger of schism or extinction. To put it another way: ritual is an event upon which its participants depend; theatre is an event which depends on its participants. In no case is it cut-and-dry. But the evidence of the transformational steps by which theatre emerges from ritual—by which an efficacious event in which the participants depend on the perform-ance is transformed into an entertainment in which the entertainers depend on an audience—is not locked in ancient or medieval documents. The transforma-tion of ritual into theatre is occurring today.

Asaro is a village about seventy miles east of Kurumugl. There the famous dance of the Mudmen is performed as a tourist entertainment three times a week. It was not always so. The villagers originally performed only when they felt threatened by attack. Before dawn village men went to a local creek, rubbed their bodies with white mud (the color of death), and constructed grotesque masks of wood frames covered by mud and vegetation. Emerging from the creek at dawn, possessed by the spirits of the dead, the dancers moved in an eery, slow, crouching step. Sometimes they went to the village of their enemies and frightened them, thus preventing attack; sometimes they danced in their own village. The dances took less than ten minutes; preparations took most of the previous night. (This ratio of preparation to performance is not unusual; it is present even in modern Western theatre in the rehearsal-performance ratio.) The dance of the Mudmen was performed occasionally, when needed. After pacification by Australian authorities there was less need for the Mudmen. However, in the mid-sixties a photographer from the *National Geographic Magazine* paid the villagers to stage the dance for him. These photos became world famous—and it was not long before tourists demanded to see the Mudmen. (Even the name "Mudmen" is an invention for tourists; I don't know the original name of the ceremony.) Because Asaro is near the Mount Hagan-Goroka road it was easy to arrange for minibuses to bring spectators to the village. Tourists pay up to $20 each to see the short dances; of this sum the Asaroans get 10%. Because the ten-minute dance is not a long enough show by Western standards, the dancing has been augmented by a display of bow-and-arrow marksmanship, a photo session, and a "market." But Asaro is not (yet) a craft village, and the few necklaces and string bags I saw for sale were pathetic—the day I was there no one bought anything.

The people of Asaro don't know what their dance is any more. Surely it's not to frighten enemies—it attracts tourists. It has no relationship to the spirits of the dead who appear only before dawn, and the tourists come a little after midday. The social fabric of Asaro has been torn to shreds, but the changes required of the Mudmen dance are a result of the deeper disruptions of Highlands life and only in a minor way a cause of these disruptions. In fact, despite the exploitation of the village by the tourist agencies, the meager sums paid the Asaroans are needed desperately during a period when the barter economy has fallen apart. I expect future changes in the dance will make it longer, more visually complicated, possibly adding musical accompaniment; the craft skills of the villagers will improve, or they will import stuff to sell; their percentage of the take will rise. In short, the dance will approach those Western standards of entertainment represented by the tastes of the audience, and the benefits will rise accordingly. Presently, the Asaroans perform a traditional ritual emptied of its efficacy but not yet regarded as a theatrical entertainment.

Joan MacIntosh and I arrived before the tourists and stayed after they left. The villagers looked at us curiously—we were taking pictures of the tourists as well as of the dancers. After the other whites left, a man came up to us and in pidgin asked us to come with him. We walked four miles along a ridge until we got to Kenetisarobe. There we met Asewe Yamuruhu, the headman. He wanted us to go to Goroka and tell the tourists about his dancers; he wanted tourists to come and watch a show which, he assured us, was much better than the Mudmen. It began to rain very hard as we squatted in the entrance to a round hut—around us, in the rain, a few villagers watched. We agreed on a price—$4 a person—and a time, the next afternoon; not only would we see dances but we could tape-record songs too.

The next afternoon we arrived with two friends, paid our $16, and saw a dance consisting of very slow steps, as if the dancers were moving through deep mud, their fingers splayed, and their faces masked or tied into grotesque shapes. (Peter Thoady, headmaster of the Goroka Teacher's College, told us that the distortion of the faces probably was in imitation of yaws, a disfiguring disease common in the area.) The dancers moved in a half-crouch and occasionally shouted phrases and expletives. The Grassmen of Kenetisarobe were very like the Mudmen of Asaro. After the dancing we spent about an hour recording music, talking, and smoking.

The Kenetisarobe dance was adapted from ceremonial farces of the region. Asuwe staged them for us—he knew that Asaro was making money from its dance, and the Kenetisarobe show was modelled on the Asaro formula: slow dance, grotesque masks, plenty of opportunity for photographs, and a follow-up after the dance. What the people of Asaro did with a minimum of self-awareness, Asuwe did with a keen sense of theatre business. Examples of the same pattern abound. In Bali tourist versions of Barong and Ketchak are everywhere—along the Denpasar to Ubud road signs advertising these performances are as frequent as movie marquees in America. Signs, in English, often read: "Traditional Ketchak—Holy Monkey Dance Theatre—Tonight at 8," or "Barong—Each Wednesday at 8 on the Temple Steps." The Balinese, with characteristic sophistication, make separate tourist shows and keep authentic performances secret—and, more important, far from the main road. Tourists want to drive to their entertainments; they want a dependable schedule; and they want a way to leave conveniently if they choose to go early. Most authentic performances—of Ketchak and of other actual ritual performances—are accessible only on foot, through rather thick jungle, and only with the permission of the village giving the performance. During my two weeks in Bali I saw two such performances. We stumbled on a Ketchak while walking through the monkey forest near Ubud—we followed some women carrying offerings of food. Once we entered Tigal we stayed there for ten hours before the Ketchak began a little after 9:00 P.M. At Tenganan we saw the final two days of the annual Abuang. Some of the ceremony was public and about fifty tourists joined the villagers to enjoy the afternoon dancing. These people were asked to leave by 5:00 P.M. We were quietly told to remain in the town office. Then, after dark, we were taken to different compounds in the village for different aspects of the ceremony. We were also allowed to listen to special gamelan music played before dawn. We weren't allowed to photograph, and only a limited amount of tape recording was allowed. The daytime ceremonies definitely had the feel of an entertainment: outsiders came in, shops were open and doing a brisk business, the dances were carefully choreographed to the gamelan music. At night the operation was different: each aspect of the ceremony was privatized and done not with an eye to its prettiness but to its correctness; time gaps between elements were longer and more irregular; many discussions concerning how to do certain things were held, and this delayed the ceremonies. The subject matter of the Abuang—if I can use that phrase—is the presentation of all the unmarried females to all the unmarried males. The daytime dances showed everyone off; the nighttime ceremonies concerned actual betrothal.

Surely the tourist trade has influenced so-called "genuine" performances in Bali and elsewhere. I have no contempt for these changes. Changes in conventions, themes, methods, and styles occur because of opportunism, audience pressures, professionalism (itself often a new concept), and new technology. Tourism has been really important and worldwide only since the advent of cheap air-travel. Theatre historians will regard tourism as of as much importance to twentieth-century theatre as the exchange between England and the Continent was in the sixteenth and seventeenth centuries. Theatre people imitate popular imported modes, and the locals respond to the demands of rich visitors—or local audiences demand changes because they've absorbed the tastes of alien cultures. From one point of view these changes are corruptions—a clamor is raised to establish cultural zoos in which the original versions of age-old rituals can be preserved. But even traditional performances vary greatly from generation to generation— an oral tradition is flexible, able to absorb many personal variations within set parameters. And the cultural-zoo approach is itself the most pernicious aspect of tourism. I hate the genocide that has eradicated such cultures as that of the Australian aborigines. But I see nothing wrong with what's happening in Bali and New Guinea, where two systems of theatre exist. The relationship between these is not a simple division between tourist and authentic. More studies are needed on the exchange between what's left of traditional performances and emerging tourist shows. And at what moment does a tourist show become itself an authentic theatrical art?

Tourism is a two-way street: travellers bring back experiences, expectations, and, if the tourists are practitioners, techniques, scenes, and even entire forms. The birth ritual of *Dionysus in 69* was adapted from the Asmat of West Irian; several sequences in the Living Theatre's *Mysteries* and *Paradise Now* were taken from yoga and Indian theatre; Phillip Glass's music draws on gamelan and Indian raga; Imamu Baraka's writing is deeply influenced by African modes of story-telling and drama. The list could be extended, and to all the arts. Many innovators since World War II (a great war for travel) have been decisively influenced by work from cultures other than their own; this means, for Western artists, Asia, Africa, and Oceania. The impact of communal-collective forms on contemporary Western theatre is like that of classical forms on the Renaissance. The differences, however, are also important: in the Renaissance all that remained of classical culture were architectural ruins, old texts, and relics of the plastic arts. This material was frequently fragmented and corrupt. Also, Renaissance scholars looked with universal respect, even awe, at what they found of classical Greece and Rome. Today's cross-cultural feed is mainly in the area of performances; the shows have been seen intact; the originators of the performances are former colonial peoples, or peoples who were considered inferior by populations around the north Atlantic basin. In other words, it is logical that today's influences should be felt first in the avant-garde.

A very clear and provable Asian influence on contemporary Western theatre is seen in Grotowski's work, particularly its "poor theatre" phase, from around 1964 to around 1971. This period includes several versions of *Akropolis, The Constant Prince,* and the first versions of *Apocalypsis Cum Figuris.* The foundation of this work is the psychophysical/plastique exercises which Grotowski and Ryszard Cieslak taught in many of their workshops in Poland and abroad. Ever since I learned some of these exercises in 1967 I felt they were influenced not only by yoga, which Grotowski acknowledges, but by the south Indian dance-theatre form, Kathakali. In 1972, while visiting the Kathakali Kalamandalam in Kerala, I asked about Grotowski's visits to the school. No one remembered him, but Eugenio Barba was remembered, and in the school's visitors' book I found the following entry:

29 September 1963

The Secretary
Kalamandalam
Cheruthuruthy

Dear Sir:

I had not the occasion, last night at the performance, to thank you for all the kind help you have given me during my stay here. To you, and to the Superintendent, and to all the boys who were so willing to be of service, I would like to express my gratitude and sincerest thanks.

My visit to Kalamandalam has greatly helped me in my studies and the research material I have collected will surely be of the greatest assistance to those people working at the Theatre Laboratory in Poland.

Many thanks once again,

Yours sincerely,
Eugenio Barba [signed]

Barba brought Kathakali exercises to Grotowski in Poland—they form the core of the plastique and psychophysical exercises. When Barba founded his Odin Teatret he used these exercises—as modified by the Polish Lab—as the basis of his own work. Grotowski has visited India on several occasions, the first in 1956–57, when he also travelled to China and Japan.

Peter Brook's three-month trip in 1972–73 with a troupe of thirty through Algeria, Mali, Niger, Dahomey, and Nigeria is another version of the "trading partner" idea. Brook, even more consciously and fully than Grotowski-through-Barba, went to Africa to trade techniques, perform, observe performances. In Brook's words:

Once we sat in Agades in a small hut all afternoon, singing. We and the African group sang, and suddenly we found that we were hitting exactly the same language of sound. Well, we understood theirs and they understood ours, and something quite electrifying happened because, out of all sorts of different songs, one suddenly came upon this common area.

Another experience of that same sort occurred one night when we were camping in a forest. We thought there was no one around for miles, but as always, suddenly, children appeared from nowhere and beckoned. We were just sitting and doing some improvised song, and the children asked us to come down to their village, only a couple of miles away, because there was going to be some singing and dancing later in the night and everyone would be very pleased if we could come.

So we said "sure." We walked down through the forest, found this village, and found that, indeed, there was a ceremony going on. Somebody had just died and it was a funeral ceremony. We were made very welcome and we sat there, in total darkness under the trees, just seeing these moving shadows dancing and singing. And after a couple of hours they suddenly said to us: the boys say that this is what you do, too. Now you must sing for us.

So we had to improvise a song for them. And this was perhaps one of the best works of the entire journey. Because the song that was produced for the occasion was extraordinarily moving, right, and satisfying, and made a real coming together of the people and ourselves. It is impossible to say what produced it, because it was produced as much by the group that was working together in a certain way, with all the work that has gone into that, and as much by all the conditions of the moment that bore their influence: the place, the night, the feeling for the other people, so that we were actually making something for them in exchange for what they had offered us.[27]

Throughout Asia, MacIntosh and I found this same "exchange policy." We were invited to stay at Tenganan because the people knew we performed, and at the main public performance the chief insisted that I do a dance.[28] At Karamui in New Guinea—far from any road (we flew in)—we were shown funeral ceremonies (a villager, with much laughter, played the role of the corpse), but we were expected to sing songs in exchange. In the Sepik River village of Kamanabit the headman insisted that MacIntosh be awakened and brought to his house to sing even though she was exhausted from a day's travel; his demand came after I'd been listening to village women singing.

The kind of influence through observation and trading reflected in Barba's letter, Brook's trip, and my own experiences is different from Artaud's reaction to Balinese theatre. Artaud was influenced, but the Balinese didn't care; there was no exchange. In the more recent examples work was consciously traded, professionals sought to expand their knowledge.

Whatever the ritual functions of Kathakali within the context of Kerala village life, the Kalamandalam is a professional training school and its troupe performs for pay in India and overseas. Foreigners come to study at the Kalamandalam (while I was there about five Westerners were studying). This training does not eventuate in the establishment of Kathakali troupes outside India—rather the work is integrated into existing styles. It remains to be seen how the presence of outsiders at the Kalamandalam, and the frequent tours of the troupe, affect the work in Kerala. The situation with Brook is different. The African villagers were in the midst of a religious ritual (a funeral ceremony)—but they were also eager to share their entertainment (trading songs)—to use their ritual as an item of trade. That the exchange was mutually moving is no surprise—entertainment and ritual co-exist comfortably.

Touring ritual performances around the world—and thereby converting them into entertainments—is nothing new: the Romans were fond of importing exotic entertainments, the more authentic the better. Every colonial or conquering power has done the same. In 1972 at the Brooklyn Academy of Music the following show took place (I quote from the program):

> THE BROOKLYN ACADEMY OF MUSIC
> in association with
> Mel Howard Productions, Inc.
> and
> Ninon Tallon-Karlweis
> in cooperation with
> The Turkish Ministry of Tourism and Information
> Present
> THE WHIRLING DERVISHES OF TURKEY
> (THE PROGRAM IS A RELIGIOUS CEREMONY.
> YOU ARE KINDLY REQUESTED
> TO REFRAIN FROM APPLAUSE.)

The audience had to be told that what they paid money to see as an entertainment retained enough of its ritual basis to require a change in conventional theatrical behavior. The performance was simple and moving—I suppose a fairly accurate persentation of the dervish ritual. I know that several theatre groups in New York were influenced by it. Both Robert Wilson's Byrd Hoffman group and The Performance Group have used whirling.

In October 1973 the Shingon Buddhist monks came to the Brooklyn Academy of Music with "ceremonies, music, and epics of ancient Japan." The dervishes whirled on a stage facing the 2,000-seat opera house. The monks performed in a room designed for Brook's appearance after his African trip—a space 75' × 40', with a height of about 30'. The audience numbered around two hundred, seated on cushions scattered on the floor, and on bleachers. As at Asaro and Kenitsarobe the Buddhist rituals were not long enough to constitute an entertainment by Western standards. So the program was augmented by performances of Japanese contemporary music and a recitation of Japanese war tales from the twelfth to fourteenth centuries. Only after the intermission did the monks perform their temple service. The program described in detail what the monks were doing, what it meant, and how the ceremony is used in Japan. Thus the audience was treated as if it were attending Grand Opera, where the libretto is summarized, or a new kind of sport in which the rules, equipment, and structure are explained. It seemed to me that the monks, like the dervishes, were deeply into what they were doing. They were "in character"—and it was impossible to distinguish what they were doing from what Stanislavski required of actors. I was convinced: these dervishes were Dervishes, these monks were Monks. A defined interface between spectators and performers existed; on one side was authenticity, efficacy, and ritual, on the other side was entertainment and theatre.

Any ritual can be lifted from its original setting and performed as theatre—just as any everyday event can be.[29] This is possible because context, not fundamental structure, distinguishes ritual, entertainment, and ordinary life from each other. The differences among them arise from the agreement (conscious or unexpressed) between performers and spectators. Entertainment/theatre emerges from ritual out of a complex consisting of an audience separate from the performers, the development of professional performers and economic needs imposing a situation in which performances are made to please the audience rather than according to a fixed code or dogma. It is also possible for ritual to arise out of theatre by reversing the process just described. This move from theatre to ritual marks Grotowski's work and that of the Living Theatre. But the rituals created were unstable because they were not attached to actual social structures outside theatre. Also, the difference between ritual, theatre, and ordinary life depends on the degree spectators and performers attend to efficacy, pleasure, or routine; and how symbolic meaning and affect are infused and attached to performed events. In all entertainment there is some efficacy and in all ritual there is some theatre.[30]

IV

The entire binary "efficacy/ritual—entertainment/theatre" is performance: performance includes the impulse to be serious and to entertain; to collect meanings and to pass the time; to display symbolic behavior that actualizes "there and then" and to exist only "here and now"; to be oneself and to play at being others; to be in a trance and to be conscious; to get results and to fool around; to focus the action on and for a select group sharing a hermetic language, and to broadcast to the largest possible audiences of strangers who buy a ticket.

At this moment The Performance Group is working on Brecht's *Mother Courage*. Most of our rehearsals have been open—when weather permits, the big overhead front garage door of our theatre has been raised and people off the street, students, and friends have come in to watch us work. Every rehearsal has had from five to forty people watching. The rehearsals have a feeling of stop and go, with nothing special planned to accommodate the spectators. Yet their presence makes a deep difference: work on the play now includes a public social core; and the work is about showing-a-way-of-working. This theme will be worked into the formal performances. The space for *Courage*—designed by Jerry N. Rojo and James Clayburgh, collaborating with all the other members of the Group—expresses the interplay between Brecht's drama and the larger performance in which it takes place. A part of the room has been made into a Green Room wholly visible to the audience. When a performer is not in a scene he or she goes into the Green Room, gets some coffee, reads, relaxes. The rest of the theatre is divided into three main spaces: an empty cube 30′×30′×20′ (including an open pit 20′×8′×7′); a 20′×20′×20′ cube filled with irregular scaffolding, platforms, and ropes; galleries, walkways, and a bridge about eleven feet off the ground. The audience can move freely through the entire space, continually changing perspective and mood. It is possible to see everything from a single vantage, but only if one looks through other structures. Scene Nine takes place outside the theatre in Wooster Street, with the large garage door open. The door stays open for the final three scenes—in winter this means that the temperature in the theatre plunges.

Our production has one intermission, after Scene Five. During intermission supper is sold, and the performers mix with the audience. During supper the "Song of the Great Capitulation" (Scene Four) is sung, as in a cabaret, without insistence that people pay attention. When the drama resumes after supper I think it is experienced differently because of the hour of mingling, talking, and sharing of food and drink.[31] Another shift in the mode of experiencing the play comes when the performance moves outside, and the theatre takes on the feeling of the outside. *Mother Courage* is treated as a drama nested in a larger performance event. The ideas behind The Performance Group's production of *Courage* are common to ritual performances: to control or manipulate the whole world of the performance, not just present the drama at its center. In this way a theatrical event in SoHo, New York City, is nudged a little way from the entertainment end of the continuum towards efficacy. Without diminishing its theatricality, I hope to enhance its ritual aspects.

NOTES

1. In describing the *kaiko* I follow the account of Rappaport, 1968. Rappaport's study is a paradigm of how to examine ritual performances within an ecological context.

2. A fight package is a small bundle containing "the thorny leaves of the males of a rare, unidentified tree growing in the *kamunga,* called the 'fight tree,' and personal material belonging to the enemy, such as hair, fragments of leaves worn over the buttocks, and dirt scraped from the skin," Rappaport, 120. It is said that pressing the package to the heart and head will give a man courage and improve his chances of killing an enemy. Materials used in fight packages are acquired from neutrals who have relatives among the enemy; fight packages are items of trade. Their use in peaceful dancing shows the relationship between the dancing and combat; in many parts of Asia performance forms have arisen from martial arts.

3. Rappaport 1968:187.

4. Rappaport 1968:188.

5. Rappaport 1968:189.

6. Rappaport 1968:195–196.

7. Rappaport 1968:156.

8. Rappaport 1968:214.

9. Spencer and Gillen 1899. This study has the advantage over later ones that the tribes described were relatively intact, having just been contacted by the invading Europeans. In Australia contact meant extermination both demographically and culturally.

10. This rhythm of relatively long preparations followed by a brief performance, with a series of performances given on a single day, is common in Australia. See also Elkin and Catherine and Ronald Berndt, 1950, and Ronald and Catherine Berndt, 1964. Although we accept this rhythm in dance and music, it has not yet found acceptance in theatre. Still dominated by Aristotelian injunctions, we act as if a work has to be of a certain length to acquire seriousness.

11. In Oceania it is not unusual—or was not until the eradication of traditional ways

—for ritual performances to form the core of a person's life. Van Gennep's classic analysis of rituals as crisis moments preceded and followed by long periods of relative calm is not wholly descriptive of the situation in New Guinea and Australia. Although the performances are peak experiences, preparations for them continuing over months and years dominate the lives of the people. See Williams, 1940, and my "Actuals: A Look Into Performance Theory" (April–June 1971), 49–66. Also Turner, 1969 and 1974.

12. See Eliade's discussion of "reactualization" and its relation to the Dreamtime in *Rites and Symbols of Initiation* (New York, 1965).

13. An excellent recent account of the intimate association between events, landmarks, and body decorations is given by Gould, *Yiwara*, 1969, pp. 120–128. See also Róheim (1945; rpt. New York, 1969).

14. The Highlands consist of a central valley, and many spur valleys, surrounded by mountains rising to 15,000 feet. The whole area is about three hundred miles long and one hundred and fifty miles wide. It is sparsely populated, by less than three million; villages average four hundred inhabitants. Because of the terrain many local groups have little contact with each other —and there is much local warfare and feuding. There are about 500 languages, most of them mutually unintelligible, and the largest of them spoken by only 130,000 people. English and pidgin are the basic *linguae francae*. For more detailed information see *An Atlas of Papua and New Guinea* (Glasgow, 1970).

15. By now criticism of the Cambridge Anthropologists' thesis concerning the ritual origins and structure of Greek theatre is well known. See, for example, Dodds, 1951, and my "Approaches to Theory/Criticism" (Summer 1966), 20–28.

16. Joan MacIntosh, a performer with The Performance Group and my wife, was my partner on the trip to Asia in 1971–72

which forms the experiential background to this article.

17. Elizabeth Burns, 1972, p. 132. This way of looking at ordinary experience as theatre has roots, of course, in literature. But its systematic application has only recently begun. The key observations have been made by Erving Goffman, 1959, 1967, and 1971.

18. See Robert Brustein, "News Theatre," *The New York Times Magazine*, 16 June 1974, p. 7ff. According to Brustein news theatre is "any histrionic proceeding that results from a collaboration between newsworthy personalities, a vast public, and the visual or print media (television, films, book publishing, magazines and newspapers). News theater, in other words, is any event that confuses news with theater and theater with news." I think Brustein's description is accurate, but that he is wrong when he says that "news" and "theatre" should be kept distinct. Certainly there are areas of independence, but the two are inherently interdependent. Both are public, action-centered, and crisis dominated. Furthermore, as the means of news transmission abandons print and uses visual media they approximate the means of theatre. The problems stirred up are not solved by bemoaning the inevitable. Only in finding ways of controlling what's happening will a satisfactory process occur. Take one limited, but decisive, area—the ethics of news reporting. I refer to the ways in which reporting shapes people's responses to events. We all know that so-called "objective" reporting is anything but objective. But is it distorted simply through the evil designs of the news managers, or is there at work a deep structure which makes even attempts at objectivity impossible? Drama has long had an ethical purpose which is expressed not only overtly but in dramatic structure. News broadcasting uses the same structures but without consciousness of the ethics inherent in them. And it is axiomatic that an unconscious ethic will automatically rein-

force the *status quo;* or, as Brecht put it, to remain neutral is to support the stronger side. The need then is to make the structures of news reporting—especially its dramatic structures—more conscious; this will lead to greater control over what is being said. Whether these new powers will be used to advance the causes of the people or to repress them remains in doubt.

19. For extended discussions of the concepts of liminality and *communitas* see the writings of Victor Turner.

20. Konrad Lorenz, 1967, discusses at some length the development of "appeasement ceremonies" in animals. More technical descriptions are offered by I. Eibl-Eibesfeldt, *Ethology,* 1970. Lorenz's description of a special kind of ceremony is almost exactly what I saw in New Guinea, and what so many others have described. "Of all the various appeasement ceremonies, with their many different roots, the most important for our theme are those appeasing or greeting rites which have arisen from redirected aggression movements. They differ from all the already described appeasement ceremonies in that they do not put aggression under inhibition but divert it from certain members of the species and canalize it in the direction of others. This new orientation of aggressive behavior is one of the most ingenious inventions of evolution, but it is even more than that: wherever redirected rituals of appeasement are observed, the ceremony is bound to the individuality of the participating partners. The aggression of a particular individual is diverted from a second, equally particular individual, while its discharge against all other, anonymous members of the species is not inhibited. Thus discrimination between friend and stranger arises, and for the first time in the world personal bonds between individuals come into being" (pp. 131–2). Or, as the Tsembaga say, "those who come to our *kaiko* will also come to our fights." It is also important to note that the ceremonies Lor-

enz focused on were greeting ceremonies; the dances in the Highlands may correctly be called greeting dances.

21. See E. T. Kirby's interesting article, "The Shamanistic Origins of Popular Entertainments" (March 1974). Kirby sees shamanism as "the 'great unitarian artwork' that fragmented into a number of performance arts" (p. 6). Also see Kirby's "The Origin of Nō Drama," *ETJ,* 25 (October 1973), 269–284; and the chapter "Shaman," in my *Environmental Theater* (New York, 1973).

22. Of many documents available see especially Emile Zola's "Naturalism in Theatre" (1880) and Strindberg's "Naturalism in Theatre" (1888) both reprinted in Becker, 1963.

23. The First American Congress of Theatre met in Princeton June 2–6, 1974. It brought together more than 200 leaders of the American theatre—very heavily weighted towards producers, managers of regional theatres, and professional administrators. Also the conference was weighted toward New York, organized as it was by Alexander H. Cohen, the New York producer. Eleven panels discussed various problems confronting the theatre, but the real action was in the interaction among individuals and interest groups. It seems likely that a second Congress will be held, one which is less New York dominated. However, it does not appear as if theatre artists will be given any more prominence —that is, writers, directors, actors, and designers will still be under-represented in relationship to the overall number of delegates. The fundamental theme of the Congress—and future Congresses as well—is a growing recognition of a contradictory reality: theatre is marginal, economically speaking, but it seems also to have enduring roots in society. Means are therefore necessary to bring the disparate wings of the theatre together for a common rumination on basically economic issues. Whether politics can, or should, be kept out of these meet-

ings is another question. As for esthetics, forget it.

24. Hardison 1965:40.

25. Hardison 1965:77.

26. Rappaport 1968:1.

27. Peter Brook, September 1973, pp. 45–46. Brook's anecdote is a fine example of what I mean by "preparations" rather than rehearsals. Rehearsal is a way of setting an exact sequence of events. Preparations are a constant state of training so that when a situation arises one will be ready to "do something appropriate" to the moment. Preparations are what a good atheletic team does. Too often those interested in improvisation feel that it can arise spontaneously, out of the moment. Nothing is further from the truth. What arises spontaneously is the moment itself, the response is selected from a known repertory and joins with the moment to give the impression of total spontaneity. Most ritual performances among communal peoples are not rehearsed, they are prepared.

28. His invitation was based on my reputation on the island. Although I was there for only two weeks I used to play games with children in which I would imitate animals. I did one act that especially amused the children: making my hands into horns I would charge at them as if I were an enraged bull. On several occasions while riding a bus to a remote village some children would spot me and make the horn gesture. At Tenganan the dance I did at the public performance was a variation on the animal game. MacIntosh's singing was appreciated everywhere, and people would actually get very angry if she refused to sing. In New Guinea especially, almost anything—an object, a relationship, an event, a performance —is made into an item of trade; there are no neutral or valueless events.

29. The late sixties and early seventies saw a number of performances based on this premise. A family in Greenwich Village sold admission to their apartment where spectators watched them in their daily lives. Of course the Loud Family Epic on television carried this style of documentary drama to its logical end: the feedback from the weekly series actually affected the lives the Louds lived, and so we watched the family change under the impact of their knowledge that they were being watched. The theoretical foundations of this kind of art lie in Cage's assertion that theatre is actually an attitude on the part of the spectator—to set up a chair in the street and to watch what happens is to transform the street into a theatre. These ideas are still very much with us in Process Art.

30. The kind of classification I'm indicating for performance is one which is becoming increasingly used in the sciences, and is replacing older forms of classification where one class of events excludes another. "Classifications need not be hierarchic and the clusters may overlap (intersect). The whole idea of hierarchic, nonoverlapping (mutually exclusive) classifications which is so attractive to the human mind is currently undergoing reexamination. From studies in a variety of fields the representation of taxonomic structure as overlapping clusters or as ordinations appears far preferable." Sokal, 27 September 1974, p. 1121. One "locates" a performance by using the coordinates of efficacy and entertainment.

31. In *Commune* there was, one night, an interruption of more than three hours. During that time the spectators and the performers came to know each other in a way much more intimate and actual than is usual in a theatre. When the play resumed there was a feeling surrounding the performance that added power to it. The supper sequence in *Mother Courage* is an attempt at building-in the kind of relationship between performers and spectators that accidentally occurred that night at *Commune*. See Schechner, 1974, pp. 49–56.

BIBLIOGRAPHY

Adedeji, J. A. "The Origin of the Yocuba Masque Theatre: The Use of Ifa Divination Corpus as Historical Evidence." *African Notes*, Vol. 6, No. 1, Ibadan, 1970.

Alland, Alexander. "The Roots of Art." New York, 1975. Unpublished essay.

Altmann, Margaret. "A Study of Behavior in a Horse-Mule Group." *Sociometry*, Vol. 14, 1951.

Anisimov, A. F. "The Shaman's Tent of the Evenks." *Studies in Siberian Shamanism*. Toronto: University of Toronto Press, 1963.

An Atlas of Papua and New Guinea. Port Moresby: University Geography Department, 1970.

Bancroft, Hubert Howe. *The Native Races*, Vol. 1 of *The Works of Hubert Howe Bancroft*. 5 Volumes. San Francisco: History, 1886.

Bates, Daisy M. "Social Organization of Some Western Australian Tribes." *Report of the Fourteenth Meeting of the Australian Association for the Advancement of Science*, XIV, 1913.

Bateson, Gregory. *Steps to an Ecology of Mind*. New York: Chandler Publishing Company, 1972.

Beattie, John and John Middleton. *Spirit Mediumship and Society in Africa*. New York: Africana, 1969.

Beaujour, Michel. "The Game of Poetics." *Yale French Studies*. New Haven: Yale University Press, 40, 1968:58–67.

_____. *Le Jeu de Rabelais*. Paris: L'Herne, 1969.

Becker, George J., ed. *Documents of Modern Literary Realism*. Princeton, N. J.: Princeton University Press, 1963.

Bell, Daniel. "The Disjunction of Culture and Social Structure: Some Notes on the Meaning of Social Reality." *Daedalus* (Winter 1965):208–222.

Belo, Jane. "A Study of Customs Pertaining to Twins in Bali." *Tijdschrif voor Indische Taal-, Land, en Volken-Kunde*, 1935.

_____. *Trance in Bali*. New York: Columbia University Press: 1960.

Berndt, Ronald M. "The Concept of 'The Tribe' in the Western Desert of Australia." *Oceania*, XXX, No. 2, 1959.

Berndt, Ronald M. and Catherine H. Berndt. *The World of the First Australians.* Sydney: Ure Smith Ltd., 1964.

Birdwhistell, Ray. *Kinesics and Context.* New York: Ballantine Books, 1972.

Black, Max. *Models and Metaphors: Studies in Language and Philosophy.* Ithaca, N. Y.: Cornell University Press, 1962.

Blau, Harold. "Function and the False Faces." *Journal of American Folklore,* (October-December 1966).

Boas, Franz. *Kwakiutl Ethnography.* Chicago: University of Chicago Press, 1966.

––––––. *The Social Organization and the Secret Societies of the Kwakiutl Indians.* Washington: U. S. Government Printing Office, 1897.

Bourguignon, Erika. "World Distribution and Patterns of Possession States." *Trance and Possession States.* Edited by Raymond Prince. Montreal: R. M. Bucke Memorial Society, 1966.

Brook, Peter. "On Africa." *The Drama Review,* 17, September 1973.

Brown, John P. *The Darvishes, or Oriental Spiritualism.* Edited by H. A. Rose. London: Frank Cass, 1968 (1868).

Brustein, Robert. "New Theatre." *The New York Times Magazine* (June 16, 1974).

Bunge, Mario. *Intuition and Science.* Englewood Cliffs, N.J.: Prentice-Hall, 1962.

Burns, Elizabeth. *Theatricality: A Study of Convention in the Theatre and in Social Life.* New York: Harper & Row, 1973.

Buytendijk, Frederik J. *Het Spel van Menschen Dier als Openbaring van Levensdriften.* Amsterdam, 1932.

Caillois, Roger. *Man, Play, and Games.* Revised edition. Translated from the French by Meyer Barash. Glencoe, Ill.: The Free Press, 1968.

––––––. "Riddles and Images." *Yale French Studies.* New Haven: Yale University Press, 40, 1968: 148 58.

Carnap, Rudolf. *The Logical Syntax of Language.* New York: Harcourt Brace, 1937.

Carpenter, Carleton. "A Field Study of the Behavior and Social Relations of Howling Monkeys." *Comparative Psychology Monographs,* Number 10, 1934, pp. 1–168.

Colson, Elizabeth. "Spirit Possession Among the Tonga of Ambia." *Spirit Mediumship and Society in Africa.* Edited by John Beattie and John Middleton. New York: Africana, 1969.

Cooley, Charles H. *Human Nature and the Social Order.* New York: Charles Scribner's Sons, 1922.

Curtis, Edward S. *The North American Indian.* New York: Curtis, 1915; reprint ed. Johnson, 1970.

Dodds, E. R. *The Greeks and the Irrational.* Berkeley: University of California Press: 1951.

Douglas, Wilfred H. "An Introduction to the Western Desert Language." *Oceania Linguistic Monograph,* Number 4, 1964.

Drama Review, The. Volume 16, Number 3, 1972.

––––––. Volume 17, Number 2, 1973.

Du Chaillu, P. B. *Explorations and Adventures in Equatorial Africa.* London: J. Murray, 1861

Durkheim, Emile. *The Elementary Forms of the Religious Life.* New York: Collier Books, 1961.

D. W. M. "Oshogbo Celebrates Festival of Shango." *Nigeria* Magazine, Volume 4, Lagos, 1953.

Eibl-Eibesfeldt, I. *Ethology: The Biology of Behavior.* New York: Holt, Rinehart and Winston, 1970.

Eliade, Mircea. *Rites and Symbols of Initiation.* New York: Harper & Row, 1969.

Elkin, Adolphus Peter. "Kinship in South Australia." *Oceania,* X, Number 3, 1940.

Elkin, Adolphus Peter, Catherine Berndt and Ronald Berndt. *Art in Arnhem Land.* London: F. W. Cheshire, 1950.

Elliot, Alan J. A. *Chinese Spirit-Medium Cults in Singapore.* New York: Humanities Press, 1955.

Erikson, Erik H. *Childhood and Society.* Second Edition. New York: W. W. Norton, 1963.

Firth, Raymond. *Essays on Social Organization and Values.* London: Athlone, 1964.

———. *The Work of the Gods in Tikopia.* London: Athlone, 1967.

Freud, Sigmund. "The Moses of Michelangelo." *Collected Papers,* Vol. Four. New York: Basic Books, 1959, 257–87.

———. "The Relationship of the Poet to the Day-Dreamer." *Delusion and Dream.* Edited by Philip Rieff. Boston: Beacon Press, 1956 (1908).

Frobenius, Leo. *Kulturgeschichte Afrikas, Prolegomena zufeiner Historischen Gestaltlehre; Schicksalskundeim Sinne des Kulturwedens.* Leipzig, 1932.

Furst, Peter T. "The Olmec Were-Jaguar Motif in the Light of Ethnographic Reality." *Dunbarton Oaks Conference on the Olmec.* Edited by Elizabeth P. Benson. Washington, D. C.: Dunbarton Oaks Research Library and Collection, Trustees for Harvard University, 1968.

———. "The Roots and Continuities of Shamanism." *artscanada,* December 1973– January 1974, pp. 33–60.

Gardner, Howard. *The Shattered Mind.* New York: Alfred A. Knopf, 1975.

Garner, Richard Lynch. *Apes and Monkeys; Their Life and Language.* Boston: Ginn and Company, 1898.

Gelfand, Michael. *Shona Ritual: With Special Reference to the Chaminuka Cult.* Capetown, South Africa: Juta, 1959.

Giddings, R. W. *Yaqui Myths and Legends.* Tucson: University of Arizona Press, 1959.

Goffman, Erving. *Frame Analysis.* New York: Harper & Row, 1974.

———. *Interaction Ritual.* New York: Doubleday, 1967.

———. *Presentation of Self in Everyday Life.* New York: Doubleday, 1959.

———. *Relations in Public.* New York: Harper & Row, 1971.

Gould, Richard A. *Yiwara: Foragers of the Australian Desert.* New York: Charles Scribner's Sons, 1969.

Greenwood, Isaac J. *The Circus: Its Origin and Growth Prior to 1835.* New York: Dunlap Society, 1968.

Grotowski, Jerzy. *Towards a Poor Theatre.* New York: Simon and Schuster, 1968.

Guardini, Romano. *The Spirit of the Liturgy.* Freiburg: Ecclesia Orans I, 1922.

Gulliver, Philip. *Neighbours and Networks.* Berkeley: University of California Press, 1971.

Habenstein, Robert W. "The American Funeral Director." Unpublished Ph.D. Dissertation, University of Chicago, 1954.

Hale, Kenneth. "Language, Kinship and Ritual Among the Walbiri of Central Australia." *American Anthropological Association,* Washington, D. C., November 1967.

Hall, Edward T. *The Hidden Dimension.* New York: Doubleday, 1966.

Hallowell, Irving A. *The Role of Conjuring in Salteaux Society*. Philadelphia: University of Pennsylvania Press, 1942.

Halverson, John. "Dynamics of Exorcism: The Sinhalese Sanniyakuma." *History of Religions*. Vol. 10, Number 4, May 1971.

Hardison, O.B. *Christian Rite and Christian Drama in the Middle Ages*. Baltimore, Md.: The Johns Hopkins Press, 1965.

Harrison, Jane. *Themes: A Study of the Social Origin of Greek Religion*. Cambridge, England: Cambridge University Press, 1912.

Hawthorn, Audrey. *Art of the Kwakiutl Indians*. Seattle: University of Washington Press, 1967.

Hershenson, Maurice. *Journal of Comparative and Physiological Psychology*. Vol. 58, 1964.

Hershenson, Maurice, Harry Munsinger and William Kessen. *Science*, 1965.

Hess, W. *Das Zwischenhirn*. Basel: Schwabe, 1949.

Hilton, John. "Calculated Spontaneity." *Oxford Book of English Talk*. Oxford, England: Clarendon Press, 1953.

Hoffman, Walter James. "The Menomini Indians." *Fourteenth Annual Report of the Bureau of Ethnology*. Washington, D. C.: U. S. Government Printing Office, 1896.

Hopkins, Albert A. *Magic, Stage Illusion and Scientific Diversions*. New York: Benjamin Blom, 1967 (1897).

Huizinga, Johan. *Homo Ludens*. Boston: Beacon Press, 1955.

Huxley, Julian Sorell. "The Courtship Habits of the Great Crested Grebe (Podicepts cristatus); with an Addition to the Theory of Sexual Selection." *Proc. Zool. Soc.* Volume 35, London (1914), pp. 491–562.

International Encyclopedia of the Social Sciences. "Florian Znaniecki," by Robert Bierstedt. Edited by David L. Sills. New York: Macmillan and Free Press, 1968.

Jeffreys, M. D. W. "The Ekon Players." *Eastern Anthropologist*, 1951.

Jennings, John J. *Theatrical and Circus Life*. St. Louis: Sun, 1882.

Jensen, A. E. *Beschneidung und Reifezeremonien bei Naturvölkern*. Stuttgart, 1933.

Kerényi, Karl. *Vom Wesen des Festes*. Paideuma, Mitteilungen zur Kulturkunde I, Heft 2, Dez. 1938.

Kirby, E. T. "The Mask: Abstract Theatre, Primitive and Modern." *The Drama Review*, Volume 16, Number 3 (September 1972), pp. 5–21.

_____. "The Origins of Nō Drama." *Educational Theatre Journal*, 25 (October 1973).

_____. "The Shamanistic Origins of Popular Entertainments." *The Drama Review*, Volume 18, Number 1 (March 1974), pp. 5–15.

Kirby, Michael. *Happenings*. New York: E. P. Dutton, 1965.

Kleist, H. von "A Marionette Theatre." *The Theatre Arts Monthly*. Translated by D. M. McCollester. July, 1928.

Koch-Grünberg, Theodor. *Vom Roroima Zum Orinoco*. Vol. I. Berlin: D. Reimer, 1917–28.

Koestler, Arthur. *Act of Creation*. New York: Macmillan, 1964.

Korzybski, Alfred. *Science and Sanity*. New York: Science Press, 1941.

Kroeber, Alfred L. *The Nature of Culture*. Chicago: University of Chicago Press, 1952.

Kuhn, Thomas S. *The Structure of Scientific Revolutions.* Chicago: University of Chicago Press, 1962.

LaBarre, Weston. *The Ghost Dance: Origins of Religion.* New York: Dell, 1970.

Lantis, Margaret. *Alaskan Eskimo Ceremonialism.* Seattle: University of Washington Press, 1947.

Laughlin, Charles D., Jr., and Eugene G. D'Aquili. *Biogenetic Structuralism.* New York: Columbia University Press, 1974.

Leslie, Charles. "Review of the Ritual Process." *Science,* 168 (May 8, 1970): 702–704.

Lévi-Strauss, Claude. *The Savage Mind.* Chicago: University of Chicago Press, 1966.

————. *Structural Anthropology.* Includes "The Sorcerer and His Magic." Translated by Claire Jacobsen and Brooke Grundfest Shoepf. New York: Basic Books, 1963.

Lewis, I. M. *Ecstatic Religion: An Anthropological Study of Spirit Possession and Shamanism.* Baltimore, Md.: Penguin, 1971.

Loizos, Caroline. "Play Behaviour in Higher Primates: A Review." *Primate Ethology.* Edited by Desmond Morris. New York: Doubleday, 1969.

Lommel, Andreas. *Shamanism: The Beginnings of Art.* Translated by Michael Bullock. New York: McGraw-Hill, 1967a.

————. *The World of the Early Hunter.* London: Evelyn, Adams and Mackay, 1967b.

Lorenz, Konrad. *King Solomon's Ring.* New York: T. Y. Crowell, 1952.

————. *On Aggression.* Translated by Marjorie Kerr Wilson. New York: Harcourt Brace Jovanovich, 1967.

Lorenz, Konrad, Ray Birdwhistell, Margaret Mead, et al. "The Role of Aggression in Group Formation." *Transactions of the Fourth Conference on Group Processes.* New York: Josiah Macy, Jr., Foundation, October 1957.

Lyman, Stanford M., and Marvin B. Scott. *The Drama of Social Reality.* New York: Oxford University Press, 1975.

McNamara, Brooks, Jerry Rojo and Richard Schechner. *Theatre, Spaces, and Environments.* New York: Drama Book Specialists, 1975.

Malinowski, Bronislaw. *The Argonauts of the Western Pacific.* London: G. Routledge & Sons, 1922.

Marrett, R. R. *The Threshold of Religion,* 1912.

Meggitt, Merwyn J. *Desert People.* Sydney, Australia: Angus and Robertson,1962.

Michael, Henry N., ed. *Studies in Siberian Shamanism.* (Arctic Institute of North America, Anthropology of the North: Translations from Russian Sources, No. 4.) Toronto: University of Toronto Press, 1963.

Michelson, T. "Notes on Fox Mortuary Customs and Beliefs." *40th Annual Report, Bureau of American Ethnology (1918–19).* Washington, D.C., 1925.

Middleton, John, ed. *Magic, Witchcraft, and Curing.* Garden City, New York: Natural History, 1967.

Mikhailovskii, V.M. "Shamanism in Siberia and European Russia." *Journal of the Royal Anthropological Institute of Great Britain and Ireland,* Vol. 24, 1948.

Moore, Omar Kayam. "Autotelic Folk Models." Paper presented at the 1960 meeting of the American Sociological Association, New York.

Moore, Omar Kayam, and A. R. Anderson. "Some Puzzling Aspects of Social Interactions." *Metaphysics,* 15 (March 1962) pp. 409–433.

Morris, Desmond. *The Biology of Art.* New York: Alfred A. Knopf, 1962.

Nisbet, Robert A. *Social Change and History: Aspects of the Western Theory of Development.* London: Oxford University Press, 1969.

Obeyesekere, Gananath. "The Ritual Drama of the Sanni Demons: Collective Representations of Disease in Ceylon." *Comparative Studies in Society and History,* Vol. 11, Number 2, April 1969.

O'Neill, Eugene. "Memoranda on Masks." *The American Spectator,* November 1932.

Opie, Iona and Peter. *Children's Games in Street and Playground.* London: Oxford University Press, 1969.

Palthe, van Wulfften. "Over de Bezetenheid." *Geneeskundigtijdshrift Voor Nederlandsch Indie.* Alf. 36, Deel 80, 1940, pp. 2123–2153.

Park, Robert Ezra. *Race and Culture.* Glencoe, Ill.: The Free Press, 1950.

Parsons, Elsie Lewes, and Ralph L. Beals. "The Sacred Clowns of the Pueblo and Mayo-Yaqui Indians." *American Anthropologist,* Volume 36, Number 4 (October–December 1934).

Peacock, James L. "Society as Narrative." *Forms of Symbolic Action.* Edited by Robert F. Spencer. Seattle: University of Washington Press, 1969.

Pechuel-Loesche. *Volkskunde von Loango.* Stuttgart, 1907.

Pepper, Stephen C. *World Hypotheses.* Berkeley: University of California Press, 1942.

Pilsudskiy, B. "Na Neduezhyem Prazdnike Aynov Ostrova Sakhalina." ("At a Bear Festival of the Ainus of Sakhalin Island.") *Zhivaya Starina.* Numbers 1 and 2, 1914.

Pinelli, Babe. *Mr. Imp.* Told to Joe King. Philadelphia: Westminster Press, 1953.

Pirandello, Luigi. *Naked Masks: Five Plays.* Edited by Eric Bentley. New York: E. P. Dutton, 1952.

Plato. *Laws.* vii.

Prince, Raymond, ed. *Trance and Possession States.* Montreal: R. M. Bucke Memorial Society, 1966.

Radcliffe-Brown, Alfred R. *The Andaman Islanders.* Cambridge, England: Cambridge University Press, 1922.

――――. "The Social Organization of Australian Tribes." *Oceania,* Volume 1, Number 1. Melbourne: Macmillan, April 1930, pp. 34–63.

Rappaport, Roy A. *Pigs for the Ancestors.* New Haven, Conn.: Yale University Press, 1968.

Ray, Verne F. "The Country Behavior Pattern in American Indian Ceremonialism." *Southwestern Journal of Anthropology,* Volume 1, Number 1 (Spring 1945).

Read, K. E. "Leadership and Consensus in a New Guinea Society." *American Anthropologist,* Volume 61, Number 3, 1959.

Reichel-Dolmatoff, Gerardo. "Rock Paintings of the Vaupés: An Essay on Interpretation." *Folklore Americas.* Los Angeles: University of California Press, 1972. (Center for Folklore and Mythology). Volume XXVII, Number 2, pp. 107–13.

Richards, Audrey. *Land, Labour and Diet in Northern Rhodesia.* Oxford, England: Oxford University Press, 1939.

Roberts, J., and B. Sutton-Smith. "Child Training and Game Involvement." *Ethnology,* I, 1962:116–85.

Róheim, Géza. *The Eternal Ones of the Dream.* New York: International Universities Press, 1945.

Rose, Ronald. *Living Magic: The Realities Underlying the Psychiatrical Practices and Beliefs of Australian Aborigines.* New York: Rand McNally, 1956.

Ruesch, Jergen, and Gregory Bateson. *Communications: The Social Matrix of Psychiatry.* New York: W. W. Norton, 1951.

Sainer, Arthur, ed. *Radical Theatre Notebook.* New York: Avon Books, 1975.

Sartre, Jean-Paul. *Being and Nothingness.* Translated by Hazel E. Barnes. New York: Philosophical Library, 1956.

Schaller, George. *The Mountain Gorilla.* Chicago: University of Chicago Press, 1963.

———. "The Orangutan in Sarawak." *Zoologica,* Volume 46, Number 2, 1961, pp. 73–82.

Schechner, Richard. "Actuals: A Look Into Performance Theory." *Theatre Quarterly,* 1, April-June 1971.

———. "Approaches to Theory/Criticism." *Tulane Drama Review,* 10 (Summer 1966).

———. *Environmental Theater.* New York: Hawthorn Books, 1973.

———. "From Ritual to Theatre and Back." *The Educational Theatre* Journal, Volume 26, Number 4 (December 1974), pp. 455–80.

Schiller, P. "Figural Preferences in the Drawings of a Chimpanzee." Journal of Comparative and Physiological Psychology, 44, 1951: 101–11.

Slochower, Harry. *Mythopoesis: Mythic Patterns in the Literary Classics.* Detroit, Mich.: Wayne State University Press, 1970.

Smith, D. A. "Systematic Study of Chimpanzee Drawing." *Journal of Comparative and Physiological Psychology,* 82, 1973: 406–414.

Sokal, Richard R. "Classification: Purposes, Principles, Progress, Prospects." *Science,* 27 September 1974.

Speck, Frank G., and Leonard Brown. *Cherokee Dance and Drama.* Berkeley and Los Angeles: University of California Press, 1951.

Spencer, W. Baldwin. *The Arunta.* London: Macmillan, 1927.

———. *The Northern Tribes of Central Australia.* London: Macmillan, 1904.

Spencer, W. Baldwin, and F. G. Gillen. *The Native Tribes of Central Australia.* London: Macmillan, 1899.

Stanner, W. E. H. "On Aboriginal Religion." *Oceania Monograph.* No. 11, 1963.

Stott, R. Toole. *Circus and Allied Arts: A World Bibliography.* 4 Volumes. Derby, England: Harper and Sons, 1958, 1971.

Strehlow, T. G. H. *Aranda Traditions.* Melbourne, Australia: Melbourne University Press, 1947.

Strehly, Georges. *L'Acrobatie et les Acrobates.* Paris: Delagrave, 1903.

Suzuki, D. T. "An Interpretation of Zen Experience." *The Japanese Mind: Essentials of Japanese Philosophy and Culture.* Edited by Charles A. Moore. Honolulu: East-West Center Press, 1967.

Tinbergen, N. *Social Behavior in Animals with Special Reference to Vertebrates.* London: Methuen, 1953.

Tindale, Norman B. "Initiation Among the Pitjandjara Natives of the Mann and Tomkinson Ranges of South Australia." *Oceania,* Volume 1, Number 2, 1935.

Toulmin, Stephen. *The Philosophy of Science.* New York: Harper & Row, 1953.

Turner, Victor. "An Anthropological Approach to the Icelandic Saga." *The Translation of Culture: Essays to E. E. Evans-Pritchard.* Edited by T. Beidelman. London: Tavistock, 1971.

_____. *Dramas, Fields, and Metaphors.* Ithaca, N. Y.: Cornell University Press, 1975.

_____. *The Drums of Affliction.* Oxford, England: The Clarendon Press, 1968a.

_____. *The Forest of Symbols: Aspects of Ndembu Ritual.* Ithaca, N. Y.: Cornell University Press, 1967.

_____. "Introduction," *Forms of Symbolic Action.* Edited by R. Spencer. Seattle: University of Washington Press, 1970.

_____. "Mukanda: The Politics of a Non-Political Ritual." In *Local-Level Politics,* edited by M. Swartz. Chicago: Aldine, 1968b.

_____. *The Ritual Process.* Chicago: Aldine, 1969.

_____. *Schism and Continuity in an African Society.* Manchester, England: Manchester University Press, 1957.

_____, ed., with M. Swartz and A. Tuden. *Introduction to Political Anthropology.* Chicago: Aldine, 1966.

Van Gennep, Arnold. *The Rites of Passage.* Translated by Monika B. Vizedom and Gabrielle L. Caffee. Chicago: University of Chicago Press, 1960.

Van Lawick-Goodall, Jane. *In the Shadow of Man.* Boston: Houghton Mifflin, 1971.

Wavell, Stewart, Audrey Butt, and Nina Epton. *Trances.* London: Allen and Unwin, 1966.

Whitehead, Alfred North, and Bertrand Russell. *Principia Mathematica.* 3 Volumes, 2nd Edition, Cambridge, England: Cambridge University Press, 1910–13.

Whorf, Benjamin Lee. "Science and Linguistics." *Technology Review,* Vol. 44, 1940. pp. 229–48.

Williams, F.E. *The Drama of Orokolo.* Oxford, England: Oxford University Press, 1940.

Wilson, Edward O. *Sociobiology.* Cambridge, Mass.: Harvard University Press, 1975.

Winnicott, Donald W. "Transitional Objects and Transitional Phenomena: A Study of the First Not-Me Possession." *The Internal Journal of Psycho-Analysis,* Volume 34, Part 2, 1953.

Wirz, Paul. *Exorcism and the Art of Healing in Ceylon.* Leiden: Brill, 1954.

Wittgenstein, Ludwig. *Tractatus Logico-Philosophicus.* London: Harcourt Brace, 1922.

Yerkes, Robert Mearns. *The Mind of a Gorilla.* Worcester, Mass.: Clark University Press, 1926–28.

Znaniecki, F. *The Method of Sociology.* New York: Farrar and Rinehart, 1936.